David Garrick

DIRECTOR

KALMAN A. BURNIM

WITH A FOREWORD BY
GEO. WINCHESTER STONE, JR.

Southern Illinois University Press
Carbondale and Edwardsville

Feffer & Simons, Inc.
London and Amsterdam

Library of Congress Cataloging in Publication Data

Burnim, Kalman A.
  David Garrick, director.

  (Arcturus books, AB109)
  Bibliography: p.
  1. Garrick, David, 1717–1779. 2. London. Drury
Lane Theatre. 3. Shakespeare, William, 1564–1616—
Stage history.
[PN2598.G3B8   1973]   792′.028′0924   72–11834
ISBN 0–8093–0625–5 (pbk)

**ARCT
URUS
BOOKS** ®

Copyright © 1961 by University of Pittsburgh Press
All rights reserved
Reprinted by arrangement with University of Pittsburgh Press
Arcturus Books Edition April 1973
This edition printed by offset lithography
  in the United States of America

To Verna

ERRATA

Page xiv, line 2: *For* Garrick in the Green Room *read* Garrick at a salon in Italy — Alessandro Longhi

Page xiv, line 10: *For* Henry Woodward as Mercutio *read* Henry Woodward as The Fine Gentleman in *Lethe*

Page 139, line 27: *For* internment *read* interment

Page 143, line 31: *For* 1741–1747 *read* 1741–1776

Page 192, line 40: *For* Britian *read* Britain

ADDENDUM

Page 133: The print (plate 9) referred to as Woodward in the role of Mercutio is now identified as Woodward as The Fine Gentleman in *Lethe*

Foreword

BY

GEO. WINCHESTER STONE, JR.

A number of us who teach eighteenth-century drama have long tried to present the plays as plays—vibrant as they were in the first instance of their performance. Even in the classroom we have sought to look upon the plays not as books but as prompt books whose life lies not only in the text, but in its stage presentation whirling through the ages, and in the impact which it and its cumulative history may make upon us today. To do so allows us to bring to bear authors' intentions, the pressures of audience and actor, stage limitations, finances, and prevailing currents of ideas. Awareness of these factors broadens the aesthetic perspective and experience which drama seeks to achieve.

Materials have been in the making for a quarter of a century to aid us in this attempt at total recall. Dr. Kalman A. Burnim has long been studying the production techniques of Drury Lane Theatre under David Garrick, and has assembled a wealth of detail which illustrates Garrick's theory and practice in mounting his performances. Five of his chapters deal with problems of management—personnel, rehearsal, costume, scenery, lighting, and the welding of these into the stunning performances (and a few spectacular failures) which made the stage at Drury Lane the most interesting one in Europe from 1747 to 1776. Chapter V climaxes this section by assembling the fullest account yet to appear of production techniques in the mid-century.

Dr. Burnim's final chapters are devoted to five specific plays as produced by Garrick. Much has been written about them before. But here they derive novelty of treatment because of the focus he gives them of actual stage production. Scholars and teachers will welcome the instrument Dr. Burnim has provided to aid them in putting eighteenth-century plays back on the eighteenth-century stage.

Preface

—I assure You Sir, I am as delicate in my Care
of Yᵉ Performances, that are put into my hands,
as (I hope) I am punctual in keeping my Word
& doing Justice to Yᵉ Gentlemen who write 'Em—

David Garrick, in a letter to Sir
William Bunbury, July 28, 1752.

O F ALL THE CELEBRATED MEN who practiced the Art of Thespis
during the Age of Reason, both in England and on the Continent, David Garrick stood high above his contemporaries. Garrick
was surely more completely than any of them a man of the theatre in all its facets. As the most important theatrical figure of
Georgian Britain his fame, immediate and immense, spread
throughout Europe. He was hailed by his contemporaries as the
"English Roscius," and his interpretations of dramatic roles, especially Shakespearean, became the yardstick against which all co-
existent and future actors were measured.

Garrick's career on the stage spanned more than a third of a
century, during which time, in the words of Edmund Burke, "he
raised the character of his profession to the rank of a liberal art."
His fame as an electrifying actor, however, has always overshad-
owed the fact that as the manager of Drury Lane Theatre for
twenty-nine years he solely was responsible for almost all deci-
sions in theatrical matters.

Despite his almost mythical reputation in the annals of theatrical history and his special importance in introducing new production techniques, no single study has been devoted to his role
as a theatrical producer and stage director. Scholars have analyzed Garrick's treatment and alterations of Shakespearean and
non-Shakespearean texts. Others have focused upon his talents
as a poet and dramatist. Still others have illuminated his public,
his time, and the theatrical repertory. Considerable attention has
been given to chronicling the essential facts of his life and career.
But the substance of many of the biographies when it concerns
matters of theatrical production tends to be anecdotal. One fine

exception is Miss Carola Oman's recent biography, *Garrick,* the reading of which will serve as a nice point of departure for all interested in the career of this fascinating man of the theatre.

One of the early biographers, Arthur Murphy, wrote that in Garrick's time, "the theatre engrossed the minds of men to such a degree . . . that there existed in England a *fourth estate,* King, Lords, and Commons, and *Drury-Lane play-house.*" A revolution in the approach to theatre history of the past few decades now makes it possible, I believe, to bring up the lights once more on the stage of this *fourth estate.* This book hopes to illuminate Garrick as a director-producer—specifically his procedures of preparing and mounting a play.

The book conveniently divides into two parts. Part I treats Garrick's daily activities in the theatre, his approach to casting and directing, his training of actors. In addition, by a discussion of eighteenth-century staging practices and developments, especially as they were sophisticated and advanced by Garrick, the stage is set for the second part. In Part II several of Garrick's most significant productions are reconstructed. It is apparent immediately that Shakespeare's tragedies occupy the major share of Part II, perhaps striking an imbalance of emphasis. The reason is simple and honest. Although Shakespeare did not completely dominate the Drury Lane repertory, Garrick's avowed dedication to the Bard and his immense reputation as an interpreter of the great tragic roles naturally resulted in a considerable amount of contemporary comment, both public and private.

The available source materials, then, such as promptbooks, letters, diaries, and newspaper and periodical reviews, devote more space to the Shakespearean productions as a rule, and dictate the choice of plays to be reconstructed. The tragedies treated in Part II were among the most frequently played mainpieces in the repertory, and hence typify usual production procedures. These dramas have also reckoned greatly in the history of the theatre, and in them, as Professor Sprague has shown, is reflected much of the tradition of the English stage.

The choice of *The Provok'd Wife* as an example of comedy on Garrick's stage was determined by the availability of a rather fully annotated and important promptbook. Except for references to them in Part I which serve to illustrate certain facets of staging techniques, I have not included an extended discussion of pantomimes, processions, or spectaculars. The omission is arbitrary, and perhaps regrettable, but it seemed sensible that the book be limited by some boundaries. The reader may turn with profit to Dr. Ralph Allen's Yale dissertation on De Loutherbourg's career in London for a scholarly and comprehensive account of this important aspect of eighteenth-century theatrical production.

It has been remarked by a scholar of admirable industry, Mr. Charles Beecher Hogan, that the one melancholy fact constantly dangling before the theatre historian is "the familiar realization that most of the really important things that the theatre does and stands for are transient." The historian is prepared after the arduous labors of dedicated research to rattle off the facts of the theatre—the dates, the casts, and sometimes even the details of the production on the stage. Yet all too infrequently does such a catalog illuminate the effects of these details upon the minds and eyes of the spectators who sat in the theatres of yesterday. *Shadows* . . . Mr. Hogan calls them. It is humbly hoped that whatever the ultimate value of this book may be it will serve in part to dispel a number of these shadows.

The researcher of eighteenth-century theatrical history happily reaps the benefits sown by earlier distinguished scholars. During the course of my investigations I have become endebted to numerous people and institutions, and one of the final pleasures of the adventure is to acknowledge their assistance. I have tried to offer appropriate credit to all in the documentation of the book. Undoubtedly there may be unfortunate oversights, but these do not mean I am the less appreciative. Some people have been especially kind to me. They include Professors Arthur Colby Sprague of Bryn Mawr College, Dougald MacMillan of the University of North Carolina, Bernard Barrow of Brooklyn College, Frederick L. Bergmann of DePauw University, Ralph Allen of the University of Pittsburgh, W. M. Merchant of University College, Cardiff, Miss Sybil Rosenfeld, honorable secretary of the British Society for Theatre Research, and Dr. Harry W. Pedicord of Pittsburgh.

I am grateful for the cooperation and courtesies extended to me by the directors and staffs of the Sterling Library and the School of Drama Library at Yale University, the Harvard Theatre Collection, the Boston Public Library, the New York Public Library, the Library of Congress, and the University of Pittsburgh Library.

I am especially obligated to Dr. Louis B. Wright, director of the Folger Shakespeare Library, who made it possible for me to pass a happy and profitable time as a Fellow of that marvelous institution where a major portion of the research for this book was done, and to his most knowledgeable staff for their courtesy and patience.

To Dr. Jack Matthews of the University of Pittsburgh I am deeply grateful for material assistance and a stimulating environment, both of which hastened the completion of the revision. Dr. George M. Kahrl of Elmira College, presently engaged in editing Garrick's correspondence for the Harvard University Press, graciously allowed me to cull fascinating and significant items from his working manuscripts, and my effort has been made richer in content by his kindness. My dear friend and colleague, Dr. Marston Balch of Tufts University, has made many felicitous suggestions for revisions by which a number of sentences in the first half of this book were rescued from Cimmerian darkness.

The editors of *Shakespeare Quarterly, Shakespeare Newsletter, Theatre Notebook,* and *Yale Library Gazette* have kindly permitted the inclusion in more expanded form of materials which I originally published with them.

I am eager and pleased to express my appreciation to Dr. A. M. Nagler of Yale University, teacher and friend, who first suggested the need for this book, read the manuscript at several stages, and provided advice and inspiration throughout the work.

An immense debt is due Dr. George Winchester Stone, Jr., eminent Garrick authority, who placed at my convenience his vast file of notes and data which will soon form Part 4 of *The London Stage.* While the statistics and a number of facts included herein are the results of his endeavors, I must accept full responsibility for the inferences drawn from them. Dr. Stone's kindnesses, which include correspondence and conferences and the honor of a foreword to this book, exemplify his constant efforts as the Executive-Secretary of the Modern Language Association of America to encourage cooperation among scholars everywhere. For the courtesies shown by Dr. Stone's colleagues in *The London Stage* project, Professors Emmett L. Avery, Charles Beecher Hogan, Arthur Scouten, and William Van Lennep, and the publisher, the University of Southern Illinois Press, I am also most appreciative.

My wife, Verna Lesser Burnim, has contributed more to this book than anyone else. To her this book is dedicated, in loving gratitude for things too many and too obvious to enumerate.

Medford, Massachusetts, March, 1961   KALMAN A. BURNIM

Contents

Illustrations

Drury Lane Theatre, 1775.

A painting made of Garrick at a salon in Italy—Alessandro Longhi

I

Garrick's Rounds

S O PROTEAN A PERFORMER was David Garrick that he could put
his head between two folding doors and in the course of five
or six seconds alter his expression "successively from wild delight
to temperate pleasure, from this to tranquillity, from tranquillity
to surprise, from surprise to blank astonishment, from that to sorrow, from sorrow to the air of one overwhelmed, from that to
fright, from fright to horror, and thence . . . up again to the point
from which he started." [1] These drawing room exhibitions of versatility—in which he sometimes substituted a series of his famous
character portrayals in place of the pure pantomime—Garrick,
himself, termed his "busy rounds." It was indeed an appropriate
term, one analogous to Garrick's entire career. Such kaleidoscopic
virtuosity was the hallmark not only of his peculiar acting genius,
but of his managerial felicity as well.

Garrick was the very busiest of men. A compendium of his
manifold activities reveals a career of amazing industry. When
not attending to the daily duties of theatrical management, su-
pervising the rehearsals, casting a new play or revival, negotiating with dramatists, scenographers, and tradesmen, he was
engaged in writing special prologues, providing critical assistance
to Shakespearean editors, composing newspaper puffs, or sweep-
ing around the circles of the London gentleman and international
socialite. Conjointly, in an age which cultivated the art of the

letter, Garrick was surely one of the most assiduous and skillful of correspondents. "I frequently write Letters in a great hurry," Garrick once told Joseph Reed, "with the papers spread upon a Book, which is supported on my knee . . . and perhaps while I am scribbling, one is speaking to me on one side, and another on another, about matters that require an immediate answer—"[2] Meanwhile he salvaged time enough to write twenty-one plays and entertainments forming a corpus of dramatic literature which in its age must be ranked inferior in quality only to the works of Sheridan and Goldsmith.

In truth, Garrick was a man of many careers—supreme actor, expert dramatist, esteemed critic—excelling in each as few have ever done. But the career he worked at with the greatest effort was the one which in effect embraced all of them: above all, he was a theatrical director and producer.

I

After Garrick's now legendary debut as Richard the Third at Goodman's Fields Theatre on October 19, 1741, his ascension to prominence was meteoric. Creating eighteenth-century traffic jams in their eagerness to reach Henry Giffard's little outlaw theatre, the London spectators were immediately captivated by Garrick's exciting and revolutionary acting style, by which "he threw new light on elocution and action; he banished ranting, bombast, and grimace; and restored nature, ease, simplicity, and genuine humour."[3] Within two months of his debut the former Lichfield wine merchant, now only twenty-five years old, was proclaimed by William Pitt as "y[e] best Actor y[e] English Stage had produc'd."[4]

Although the new sensation brought much-needed financial succor to the floundering Goodman's Fields, the flush of success for Henry Giffard's house did not last the entire season. Charles Fleetwood and John Rich, patentees of Drury Lane and Covent Garden respectively, who night after night saw their theatres spurned in favor of the attraction at Goodman's Fields, brought official pressure to bear against the temporarily prosperous but illegal Giffard. The manager was intimidated, his theatre was closed by enforcement of the Licensing Act, and the following season (1742-43) Garrick found himself working for Fleetwood at Drury Lane.

In spite of having Garrick for a main attraction, Fleetwood could not overcome his personal propensity for failure. In the fall of 1744 he was obliged to indenture his interest in the patent to two bankers, Amber and Green. These two in turn recruited James Lacy, a former stage-manager at Covent Garden, to conduct the affairs of the theatre. Garrick was invited to take a share in the patent. On December 29, 1744, he wrote to his friend, the Reverend John Hoadly, "I have been very near buying ye Patent, Lease of ye House, Cloaths Scenes &c.— . . . what I shall do I have not yet resolved." [5] He refused the offer, finally, but remained as leading actor in the company. Subsequent difficulties with Lacy over his contract made Garrick regret his decision to remain a mere employee of Drury Lane. The main dispute centered in two contentions: Lacy refused to pay Garrick £250 in arrears, a debt originally due him from Fleetwood for which Lacy presumably had become obligated; and Lacy insisted on his prerogative to order Garrick to play any night the manager desired, an arrangement which Garrick insisted would injure his health. [6] The quarrel had its most violent eruption in the summer of 1745, after which Garrick forsook Drury Lane and his devoted London audience and embarked for a triumphal season in Dublin. The next season, 1746-47, he returned to London, but to Covent Garden Theatre, for the famous acting engagement with James Quin in which the old and new styles came to loggerheads.

Lacy realized that he desperately needed Garrick at Drury Lane if he hoped to avert financial disaster, so despite their former quarrels he again offered the actor half interest in the theatre. Garrick was now ready to accept. He raised the £8000 necessary to purchase his moiety, and on April 9, 1747, the agreement of partnership was signed by which Garrick and Lacy became "jointly and equally possessed" of an interest in the patent, the property lease, the furniture, scenes, costumes, and other accoutrements of the theatre. [7] A supplementary agreement, stipulating the division of duties and responsibilities of the partners, stated that "the settling or altering of the business of the Stage be left entirely to Mr. Garrick." [8] Lacy assumed the general maintenance of the theatre, its properties and "the economy of the household." Both were to concur on the hiring, discharging, and fixing of salaries of their employees, but Garrick seems to have done most of the negotiating. Either partner if ever dissatisfied could sell, first offering the other the option to buy.

A financial statement drawn up on April 11, 1747, details the incumbrances of Drury Lane which Garrick and Lacy assumed at the beginning of the partnership. [9] The total liabilities were £8808/14: of this amount £2447/14 represented salary arrears, a mortgage made up another £4700, £1100 was due tradesmen, £400 was coming to Lacy for money he had borrowed to keep the theatre going, and the balance consisted of miscellaneous debts. In addition to this total it was agreed to pay Fleetwood £4000 to relinquish his interest in the patent.

While it is difficult to equate present-day monetary values with those two centuries back, it is evident from the extant Drury Lane "Account Books," now at the Folger Shakespeare Library, that the operation of a major London theatre in the eighteenth century was an enterprise of high finance. Aside from the artistic responsibilities of theatrical management, the financial and operational details were immense and demanding. Drury Lane generally employed between seventy to one hundred performers (actors, singers, dancers, musicians, and supernumeraries). The staff of house servants fluctuated between forty and seventy-five in number: they included the scene painters, the scene shifters, the lampmen, the candlemen, the treasurer and his staff, the prompter and his pages and scribes, the billstickers, the coal men, the fruit men, the housekeeper and his staff, the numberers, the costumers, the dressers, and the various door and box keepers.[10] Traditionally the overhead had been high, the inventory unstable in value, and the consumers exceedingly fickle. No one had succeeded at Drury Lane since the triumvirate of Cibber, Wilks, and Booth had dissolved in 1732. The most recent incumbent, Charles Fleetwood, had also been the most woefully inadequate. Garrick and Lacy had bought Drury Lane at the time when its credit was nil and its prestige was at its lowest ebb in fifteen years.

In view of all this, the almost immediate financial prosperity of the new partnership is startling. Dr. Stone's analysis of the "Account Books" discloses that at the end of the first year of their management Garrick and Lacy realized a net profit of £6334 for the season. By the end of their third season (1749-50), they had their investment back. At the same time, each manager drew an additional £500 per year as salary. Garrick received another £500 per season as the leading actor, plus the profit of a clear benefit. It seems to have been the policy of the partners to divide the profits of each season (which averaged about £4850 a season for the eight years that the "Account Books" are available) and begin each campaign afresh.

But the new prosperity at Drury Lane was not only to be pecuniary.

The theatre was remodeled in the summer of 1747. The season opened under the new management on September 15 with Charles Macklin in *The Merchant of Venice*. Garrick did not play a role on opening night, but he delivered Samuel Johnson's inaugural prologue which deplored the recent miserable state of the theatre and announced that Drury Lane henceforth was dedicated to the rescue of nature and the revival of sense:

> To chase the charms of sound, the pomp of show,
> For useful mirth, and salutary woe,
> Bid scenic Virtue form the rising age,
> And Truth diffuse her radiance from the stage.

A new order in the affairs of the theatre was immediately apparent. On December 21, 1747, two months after the house opened under the new managers, Charles Wyndham—close friend to Garrick—wrote to Peter Garrick at Lichfield: "The affairs of the theatre go on extremely easy. everything is done with the greatest order, and regularity. and there is a most exact discipline observed, by all belonging to the house. Lacy and he agree very well; and every thing is done just as David pleases . . . there is a satisfaction and joy in all the folks at Drury Lane Theatre, that show they are under a good government, & in a thriving way. And I think every year must make it better." [11]

The association between Garrick and Lacy was to become distinguished by its remarkable harmony in artistic endeavors during the following twenty-seven years at Drury Lane.

But even if the co-managers had not possessed rather antipodal natures some minor incidents were inevitable in such a long relationship. In 1752 Lacy hired a celebrated equilibrist and rope dancer, Anthony Maddox. Garrick complained of this "defilement and abomination into the *house of William Shakespeare*" in a letter to friend Somerset Draper on August 17, 1752, and called Lacy a "mean mistaken creature," adding, "Oh, I am *sick, sick, sick* of *him!*" [12] Several weeks later Garrick wrote to his brother George that Lacy "ought to have a thorough Scouring before his inside will be tolerably clear from ye filth & Nastiness that he has been gathering from his youth upward till now—" [13]

Apparently the only really serious conflict in the partnership occurred upon Garrick's return in 1765 from his two-year Grand Tour. Lacy had meddled again in Garrick's province of the management, provoking a violent quarrel which was not reconciled until some twelve months later. In the fall of 1765 Joseph Reed heard that Garrick was determined to "have nothing to do with the theatre at the end of this season, Mr. Lacy will then have the sole management."[14] On November 9, 1765, the actor-manager wrote to his brother George, "my resolution is to draw my Neck as well as I can out of ye Collar, & sit quietly with my wife & books by my fireside."[15] The rift had gone sufficiently far enough for the drawing up of a contract of dissolution. Garrick's share of the patent was computed to be worth £27,500 at the time; but James Clutterbuck, Garrick's financial counsel, advised a reconciliation, since the financial structure of the partnership revealed the paradox that Lacy's share was worth more than Garrick's, simply because Garrick came with it, whereas a purchaser of Garrick's moiety would get only Lacy.[16] The partnership survived, but certain rumblings of dissatisfaction could be heard. In a letter to George on March 8, 1766, David expressed his repugnance for his partner's "maggot-breeding pericranium."[17] On December 16, 1767, *The Theatrical Monitor* stated it was well known that the Drury Lane patent had been for sale for some two years, and "that *Caesar* and *Pompey* had been in their hearts at continual variance for a long time." By January of 1769 all seemed peaceful again when *Town and Country Magazine* reported, "This association has generally subsisted with the utmost harmony, as both are equally satisfied with their authority and power, and are too sagacious to enter into any altercation by which their mutual interest would be greatly injured." This statement characterizes the nature of the partnership. Despite their sometime battles with each other, over the long term of the association, the partners managed and maintained, with unusual consonance, one of the most brilliant repertory theatres of all Europe.

II

Unquestionably the most formidable challenge Garrick had to face day in and day out was the selection and maintenance of the repertory, the very life-blood of the theatre. The determination of the theatrical bill was influenced by innumerable exigencies, each stirring a minor crisis at the time of its origin, each altering the best laid plans. But for the most part the theatrical season during the Garrick era conformed to a general pattern, and the stock piece, of course, was the principal fare.

The season at Drury Lane was launched in the middle of September, usually with proven favorites, requiring large casts, which served to effect the return of all the players from their summer activities and introduce new members of the company. For the first month or so the theatre was open three nights a week, usually Tuesday, Thursday, and Saturday, alternating with performances at Covent Garden. By the second week in October there were six performances weekly. By late November or early December, usually, there was the opening of a new play or the revival of a long-unproduced play. The months of January and February were the height of the season, marked by the presentation of several new plays and the reprise of the best stock productions the company had to offer. The benefits began in March—and "adieu to all Pleasures of the Theatre," Garrick once wrote his brother—with the actors again appearing in their favorite roles. The scheduling of the benefits caused many of Garrick's gray hairs. They usually began "fixing" in mid-February, with the highest paid actor privileged to the first choice of date and production. When those actors further down in the echelon of the theatre came to their choices, complications were inevitable, and chaos was probable. A grand ball, an opera, a rival theatre production, indeed almost any excuse could be found by them to deem the available nights undesirable. Once the actor received his own benefit night he was often reluctant to appear for another actor's, a practice which resulted in many personality clashes within the company. Finally, the season closed in late May or early June after some one hundred eighty nights of playing.[18]

"Y^e Manager of a Theatre," Garrick once wrote to James Ralph, "must be a very insufficient one who has not provided for the Winter's Entertainments before ye Opening of his Playhouse." [19] But so many contingencies were constantly arising that, at best, Garrick could seldom hope to maintain a tentative schedule planned even a month in advance. So frequent were the changes that on one occasion the press criticized the practice "of advertising one play in the morning bills, and presenting another at night." [20] Deviations were produced by last-minute royal desires or deaths, the uncertainty of the run of a new play (the regular run of a new mainpiece was normally nine nights, but many never made it), or the unaccountable caprice of a most outspoken and sometimes dangerous theatrical public. Frequently the threat of a spectacular production at Covent Garden was enough to create a quick shift in the plans of Drury Lane. When in 1754-55 Garrick learned that Rich was preparing *Coriolanus* "with infinite pomp and splendour," as Tate Wilkinson tells it, he rushed the same play into rehearsal at Drury Lane in his eagerness "to get

the start of the rival theatre . . . The very idea of a triumphal procession at Covent Garden, struck terror to the whole host of
Drury, however big they looked and strutted on common occasions." [21]

More often it was the real or feigned illness of a member of
the company which dictated the change in schedule. The memo-
randum diaries kept by Richard Cross and William Hopkins, successive prompters at Drury Lane during Garrick's management,
are replete with sidelight notices of such emergencies.[22] On December 4, 1773, *The Fair Quaker* was substituted for the advertised *Twelfth Night* because "Mrs. Abington sent word she was
hoarse & could not play." A week later on December 13, "The Bills
were posted for The School for Wives but Mr. King sent word
about Eleven o'clock that he was so ill he could not play & fresh
Bills were put up for Zara. Mrs. Barry being out of Town Miss
Young play'd Zara & was very well receiv'd." Again that season,
on March 24, it was necessary to substitute *The Alchemist* and
Note of Hand for *Phaedra and Hippolitus* and *The Wedding Ring*
when Mrs. Barry sent word in the morning she "was so ill she
could not play." When most pressed for time in a hectic day, Garrick frequently had to dash off letters of remonstrance or pacifica-
tion to his absent actresses. Sometimes order and regularity—that
exact discipline rightfully credited to Garrick's management—dis-
integrated in the matter of play scheduling because of temperamental stars. The plight of the manager, besieged by the daily
problems of production and administration, and faced with the
certain fact that tomorrow *some* play must be given, may be
witnessed in the frustrated tone of his letter to the actor William
Smith on November 1, 1775: "I shall not describe my distresses
and troubles, for many days last past, in fixing upon plays. I have
waited three and four hours at the playhouse before I could as-
certain a single play for the next day." [23]

In hopes of scheduling well in advance, in the summer Garrick sent his people a list of parts which he expected them to have
ready in the coming season. He tried to keep in mind the talents
and limitations—artistic and practical—of his performers and tech-
nicians. By the arrangement of his repertory, Garrick hoped to
preserve the energy of his company, but perhaps more important,
he designed to maintain the interest of his spectators.

III

In his study of eighteenth-century audiences, Dr. Harry Pedicord computes the theatre-going public at 11,874 weekly patrons.[24] Placing the population of London, including the liberties of London and Westminster, together with the Borough of Southwark and adjacent parts, at approximately 676,250 in 1750, Dr. Pedicord determines that about 1.7 per cent or 17 in every thousand attended the theatre during Garrick's management. Consequently Garrick's program had to be catholic and varied enough to draw the same people back to his house week after week. The audiences, moreover, entered the theatre anticipating a multi-course bill of fare.

An evening's bill included a full-length five-act mainpiece, a spectacular pantomime or three-act farce (sometimes both) as an afterpiece, and specialty masquerade dances, songs, or pageants as *entr'acte* diversions. An advertisement for December 23, 1758, typical of most, announced *Much Ado . . .* with a Masquerade Dance in Act II, and "a Pantomime Dance call'd The Prussian Camp," at the end of Act III, all to be followed by the pantomime of *Queen Mab*. The bill for January 25, 1763, included *The Two Gentlemen of Verona*, with a Serenade introduced into Act IV, and Garrick's farce, *The Farmer's Return from London*, at the end of the play; added to this was a Harlequinade *Fortunatus*, "to conclude with a Comic Dance call'd the Flemish Feast." [25]

Although it is commonly agreed that Garrick made the age "Shakespeare conscious," not always was the play the thing; the dances, pantomimes, spectacles, and other specialty numbers often held more appeal and excitement for the spectators than the mainpiece they accompanied. Mr. Arthur Scouten emphasizes the importance of this point for the statistician who attempts to arrive at reliable conclusions concerning the popularity of various plays during the period. In criticizing the method of Mr. Charles Beecher Hogan's *Shakespeare in the Theatre, 1701-1800* (Oxford, 1752), Mr. Scouten cautions that

> Seeing only the title of a Shakespearean play entered for a given night in Hogan's lists, the reader may be inclined to believe that this was what drew the audience. On the contrary, a full bill for that night might show that a new pantomime was the main attraction, a favorite stratagem, for example of David Garrick's . . . *The Beggar's Opera* may have made Rich gay, but according to the treasurer's account books it was the pantomime *Perseus and Andromeda* that made him rich.[26]

How successful Garrick was in meeting the heterogeneous demands of his audience may be judged by the prosperity of the management. Although Drury Lane was not always packed to its very roof, usually there was a good house. Garrick in a new or favorite role attracted mobs, many converging from afar, to the box, pit, and galleries. The experience of Sylas Neville was typical. On January 12, 1769, Neville made a brave effort to see a command performance of *Richard the Third,* and recorded in his diary: "In attempting to get into the Pit was forced into the two shilling gallery passages & after being squeezed abominably for an hour got into the street. Should not have received much pleasure if I had got in, as that calf headed son of a whore, George &c [King George III] was there." [27] Similarly, Dr. Thomas Campbell went to the theatre shortly after it opened at five o'clock (curtain usually was at six) on March 7, 1775, to see Garrick play Lusignan in *Zara,* but the place was already fully packed and he couldn't get a seat.[28] Among the many entries in the *Cross-Hopkins Diaries* which comment on the antics of audiences is a notice which suggests that those who managed to squeeze into the theatre were not always the most fortunate: in the holiday rush of December 26, 1757, "by the Crowd upon the upper Gallery Stairs two Women & a Man were kill'd."

The citizens that did manage to survive, however, were treated to a menu so devious and complex in its seasoning that it would have challenged the ingenuity and skill of any theatrical chef. The ingredients were rather overwhelming. During Garrick's career at Drury Lane the spectator was presented with 6,416 performances of 224 different mainpieces, and 5,820 performances of 209 different afterpieces. The 224 mainpieces numbered 81 tragedies, 116 comedies, and 27 miscellaneous-type productions (such as *Beggar's Opera, Cymon,* and the histories *Richard III* and *Henry VIII*).[29] Statistically at least, and undoubtedly actually, the most popular playwright was Shakespeare. The balance of the repertory of mainpieces consisted generally of the best and most popular plays the English theatre had offered from the time of Elizabeth to that present day.

When Garrick opened the theatre in September of 1747, Johnson's prologue had announced the purported high aim of rescuing Nature and reviving Sense. This dedication was reaffirmed in another prologue opening Drury Lane in 1750-51 when it was declared that

> Sacred to SHAKESPEARE was this spot design'd.
> To pierce the heart and humanize the mind.

By this time, however, Garrick had three years of managerial experience to his credit, and the prologue continued with a more practical philosophy:

> But if an empty House, the Actor's curse
> Shews us our Lear's, and Hamlet's lose their force;
> Unwilling we must change the nobler scene
> And in our turn present you Harlequin;
> Quit Poets and set Carpenters to work
> Shew gaudy scenes, or mount the vaulting Turk:
> For though we Actors, one and all, agree
> Boldly to struggle for our—vanity,
> If want comes on, Importance must retreat:
> Our first great ruling passion is—to eat.

Garrick satisfied the ruling passion with his afterpieces: 2,688 farce performances, 1,501 pantomime performances, and 881 various musical performances. He, himself, wrote two of the most popular farces, *Lethe* and *The Lying Valet;* the two most popular comedies, *A Peep Behind the Curtain* and *The Irish Widow;* the most popular musical pageant, *The Jubilee;* and the third most popular pantomime, *Harlequin's Invasion,* in which he introduced, contrary to tradition, a speaking Harlequin.[30] The prominence of his own afterpieces is all the more significant when it is realized that many of them were not written until the latter half of his career.

When one consults the figures of any single season, however, he can visualize the demands of such a repertory on a producer-director. Each season Drury Lane presented an average of 16 different tragedies, 30 different comedies, and 25 different afterpieces of one variety or another. And these are merely averages. More specifically, for example, for the season 1769-70, the *Cross-Hopkins Diaries* record 66 different plays and 23 different afterpieces in 195 nights of playing, or 22 more different productions than was average over the entire period. Of course, the rehearsal and production tasks were somewhat facilitated by the employment of highly competent stock actors with a wide range of parts and abilities, and by the use of stock scenery and costumes.

But the figures can be as misleading as they are revealing. It cannot be assumed that because a stock piece ranked high in frequency of appearances, that it always could be pulled out of the hat, so to speak, without any particular effort. For example, *The Fair Penitent* was played 85 times between 1741 and 1776. The average number of performances per year was less than 3, and these were seldom consecutive. In 1754-55 it was played November 6 and May 15; in 1755-56 on January 12 and April 3; in 1756-57 only on November 23.

To anyone with the slightest experience in the theatre it must be inconceivable that a play could be left for over a year, or in many cases with other plays in the repertory three or four years, and then suddenly appear on the stage without requiring some attention. Actors died or retired, scenery and costumes wore out, and certainly a number of refresher rehearsals were necessary. A letter by Garrick to Somerset Draper on August 17, 1752, provides some insight into the feverish routine: "I am working and studying here [at Londesbourgh] like a horse. I intend playing *Coriolanus* and the *Rehearsal* alternately, *All's Well* & *Merope* in the same manner; and then I shall present you with Don John *[The Chances]* and So [s]ia into the bargain." [31]

The season 1758-59 will serve to illustrate the relentless demands on Garrick's talents and time. The first of Garrick's major quarrels with Arthur Murphy erupted this season. This controversy concerned Murphy's *The Orphan of China*. The author had been unable to commit Garrick to a definite production date, and he accused the manager of nefarious and malevolent maneuvers to escape playing the piece as he had originally agreed. The persevering Murphy finally wheedled a promise from Garrick to open the play on February 25, 1759. Subsequently Garrick postponed the date to March 10, and then again to April 21, much to Murphy's chagrin. In the course of the quarrel neither man acted with credit, but whatever Garrick's personal reasons for protraction, a glance at his other activities at the time is instructive.[32]

In the month of January when his quarrel with Murphy was becoming most heated, Garrick presented 12 different full-length plays from the stock repertory (none of which played two nights consecutively) plus the afterpieces. He, himself, appeared in most of them. Of the 12 plays, three *(The London Merchant, The Miser,* and *The Conscious Lovers)* made their first appearance of the season. Another *(Aesop)* had opened under Garrick's management for the first time only a few days earlier, in December. In yet another *(The Busybody)*, only that season, on December 2, had Garrick undertaken the role of Marplot for the first time, replacing the invaluable Henry Woodward who had left the company to venture management in Dublin. In addition, he revived for the first recorded time since its supposed appearance in 1606 a splendid *Antony and Cleopatra*—complete with new habits, decorations, and scenery. During this hectic month of January the theatre was dark between January 21 and 28 because of the death of the Princess of Orange.

In February he offered 14 different stock plays with after-pieces and a new play, his own *The Guardian*. He presented 15 different stock pieces in March. In April, the month in which he finally mounted *The Orphan of China* in an elaborate production, he scheduled another 14 plays from stock. Fortunately the theatre was closed Holy Week (8-15) allowing him extra time to concentrate on Murphy's play. In fact, Garrick did not receive the complete script of *The Orphan of China* until January 23. On February 18 the play was still being cut and altered. In the middle of rehearsals Mrs. Cibber became ill and was replaced by Mrs. Yates (whom Murphy had been rehearsing secretly), and Garrick, deciding to play Zamti after much hesitation, took the part away from Mossop. Further confusion and pressures resulted from the deaths at the height of the season of one of Drury Lane's best scene painters, Mr. Oram, and two of its repertory stalwarts, Mrs. Macklin and Mr. Taswell.[33]

IV

The necessity to seek out fresh material for the stage constitutes an occupational hazard which constantly brings the theatrical producer in contact with numerous aspiring but inadequate dramatists, each convinced that his latest manuscript is his masterpiece. Garrick was beset by such gentlemen and ladies offering their plays for perusal. Consequently he was required to face the inevitable and eternal charge that he was suppressing good plays. Garrick's critics saw him as a petty tyrant, motivated by avarice and vanity, who was driving the stage to ruin.

Pamphlets and articles devoted to exposing his depravity in the choice of plays and his endeavors to suppress dramatic authors were not uncommon. Sometimes the attacks were mild, such as that of a critic who found the scarcity of new plays to be "very strong prejudices against him." [34] More frequently they were far-ragos of spleen and resentment, such as James Ralph's *Case of the Authors by Profession* (1758), a virulent reprisal by a rejected dramatist. In 1759 Oliver Goldsmith, whose best play Garrick failed to produce, complained that "no new play can be admitted upon our theatre unless the author chuses to wait some years, or to use the phrase in fashion, till it comes to be played in turn. . . . Yet getting a play on even in three or four years, is a privilege reserved only for the happy few who have the arts of courting the manager as well as the muse." [35]

Any post might bring Garrick several unsolicited play manuscripts or requests for permission to forward them. Obviously if he took the time to examine all with equal care, he would never have found time to produce any of them. Despite the criticisms of his detractors, the record shows that Garrick introduced approximately 85 new mainpieces and 150 new afterpieces during his management. As Dr. MacMillan suggests, they appear to be as good as the best the century could offer, and equal to the productions of most periods of comparable length in the English theatre.[36]

In order to cope with the many manuscripts, Garrick, like most managers, employed deputy readers who recommended promising material to him. Richard Cumberland was for a time one of his readers. Some plays of especial interest the manager read first himself. Garrick's correspondence with playwrights suggests that when he did read a submitted play he did so attentively and then gave a fair and candid opinion of it without equivocation. If he decided to accept the play, he generally scheduled it, as Goldsmith termed it, "to be played in turn"; if a definite commitment was impossible, he informed the author of his interest to play it at some future date. Garrick elucidated his policy to Mrs. Griffith in June, 1766: "We have six new performances in our hands, three of which are only farces; I am likewise to read a new comedy tomorrow. . . . Exclusive of this last piece, it will be impossible to perform yours this next winter; it shall come in its turn, and if it is received, you shall be acquainted with its situation upon our books, and with the names of those performances which, in justice, and by the custom of the theatres must precede it." [37]

Occasionally Garrick was intimidated by pressures, both royal and friendly, to accept inferior works. "I hate this traffick with friends," he once told George Colman, in resentment at Joshua Reynolds' soliciting for a nephew.[38] But in general he seems to have judged on the basis of actability of the play at his theatre. He wrote to Mrs. Benjamin Victor: "I can only judge with those materials for judging which I have—but if I am not entertain'd & interested in reading a play, I judge, and I think naturally enough, that it will not have the desir'd Effect upon an Audience & I might say for myself that hitherto I have been tolerably lucky enough in my guesses." [39]

His polite rejections were sometimes accompanied by a friendly but astute criticism of the play. His explanation of his refusal of one of Mrs. Sheridan's plays is typical (and at the same time imparts his views on comedy):

> that there were characters in the Play I allow'd but I thought they were not well employ'd: I felt the scenes languid for want of an interesting fable, & that Spirit of dialogue or Vis comica which was to be found in many Scenes of the Discovery . . . How could Mrs. Sheridan imagine that I wanted the passions to be interested? I should as soon expect to have my· laughter raised in a tragedy— I said indeed that the Comedy wanted interest, but of yᵉ *Passions*— I meant a Comic interest, resulting from yᵉ varying humours of the Characters thrown into spirited action & brought into interesting Situations, naturally arising from a well constructed fable or Plot— This, with a good Moral, deduc'd from yᵉ whole, is all I wish or look for in a COMEDY.[40]

To some novice dramatists he offered the most fundamental lessons in playwriting. "I presume a proper Skeleton of a Comedy should be drawn out into yᵉ 5 Acts," he advised Charles Jenner, "with a particular Account of the Scenes and their Subjects, with their Connection with yᵉ Whole . . . If Your inclination leads You to the Stage, the Study of the frame-work will be absolutely necessary, for without that Mechanical part all yᵉ Wit, humour &c Character, Which we know You are possess'd of, will be thrown away." [41]

In principle at least, Garrick seems to have attempted to adhere to the dedication of Johnson's 1747 prologue, and a common reason for rejecting a play was his considered opinion that it was not up to the standards he had set for Drury Lane. When he declined Victor's *Altamira* in 1766 he suggested that the play "will have better chance of succeeding at Covent Garden than with us, and that I am certain that 'Cleone' and 'Virginius,' 'The Double Mistake,' and many others would not have been well received at Drury-lane." The rejected author—who was also for a time Garrick's treasurer—agreed that audiences at Drury Lane were "inclined to severity," while at Covent Garden "pieces of little merit have been received with favour." [42] But the conflict between artistic standards and practical necessity has long been with us. Not always was the judgment of Drury's audiences "inclined to severity." Despite any loftier concept of theatrical art which Garrick harbored, he was obliged to bow frequently to the dictates of public taste. He explained his position to John Cleland, who questioned why the manager had rejected his *Titus Vespasion* and yet had subsequently produced several plays of infinitely inferior worth: "Why do you raise the ghosts of Boadicea [played December 1, 1753] and Barbarossa [December 17, 1754] to haunt me? If I had not performed the first, I should have been a very shallow politician; and if I had not received the last, I should have suffered as a manager, for no tragedy had more success" *(Private Correspondence,* I, 469-70). After the prematurely successful première of Joseph Reed's *Dido* (March 28, 1767), which Garrick had been pressured into producing after a long tiresome altercation with the author, the appalled manager wrote to his brother George, "And does 'Dido' please? Good God!—and will they come twice to see it? Good God! It is time to leave the stage, if such a performance can stand upon its legs. Good God!" *(Private Correspondence,* I, 252). His judgment was vindicated when *Dido* closed after the third performance, never to reappear during his management.

The fact that Garrick, himself, was responsible for some of the most absurd and extravagant bantlings of the drama did not make him any more popular with unfriendly critics and dramatists. When he produced *The Guardian*—not to be regarded as one of his bantlings—in 1759, he dared not reveal his identity as the author because he had so many enemies among the writers that he wished to avoid "the Torrent of abuse that their Malice" would pour upon him.[43] His "raree-shew" concoctions, such as *Harlequin's Invasion, Cymon, The Jubilee,* and *The Christmas Tale,* were allotted a substantial share of his budget, and consequently achieved unprecedented and most profitable runs. In reaction to them the critics, almost to a man, rose in righteous protest. They recalled the lofty purpose and ardor with which Garrick had launched his managerial career, and gave him credit for the accomplishment of a certain reformation in taste, stage morals, and judicious alterations; but they deplored, "What a change of Conduct! What an affront to Common Sense!"[44]

The idolator must seek indulgence for these insipid spectacles on the grounds that they can tell us much about eighteenth-century production procedures. As Elizabeth Stein has summarized, "Never at any time did Garrick disguise the real purpose of these plays. He presented them for what they were worth and, knowing their quality, he called upon his audiences and the critics to suspend judgment and accept in the spirit in which he offered them. He intended them as show pieces, and as such asked his audiences to receive them."[45] Dedicated though he may have been to loftier

artistic principles, Garrick was aware that no director could realize a "perfect stage" until he faced an informed and demanding
public. "When the taste of the public is right the Managers and
Actors must follow it or starve." [46] It must also be remembered
that the average Londoner—whose main dish was not necessarily
Shakespeare—was not released from his daily labors until well
after the 6:00 P.M. curtain-time at Drury Lane. By providing
spectacle and diversion for these latecomers at reduced prices
Garrick could frequently increase his evening's receipts significantly. Although Garrick resorted to these gilt gingerbread affairs
when the occasion demanded, perhaps it is all the more to his
credit that at the same time he could enthrall these same spectators with some of the finest and most exciting Shakespearean pres-
entations ever conceived.

V

Once Garrick decided upon a play he knew what to do with it.
And it is in the area of play-doctoring and altering, sometimes
even before the script was complete, that we begin to see the director at work. "It is very certain," wrote Thomas Davies, "that
no manager we ever heard of, was better qualified to serve an
author in the correcting, pruning, or enlarging of a dramatic piece,
than Mr. Garrick. His acute judgment and great experience had
rendered him a consummate judge of stage effect; and many
authors now living, men of greatest merit, will own their obligations to his taste and sagacity." [47] However, many dramatists less
aware of the discipline required by the stage, balked at his in-
trusions into their province. Familiar is the malediction of Horace
Walpole, who after the refusal of *The Mysterious Mother* in 1768
determined to expose himself no longer "to the impertinences of
that jackanapes Garrick, who lets nothing appear but his own
wretched stuff; or that of creatures still duller, who suffer him to
alter their pieces as he pleases." [48] Likewise Henry Crisp complained that Garrick would not allow his *Virginia* "to be acted in
its pristine state, but insisted on many alterations, greatly against
the author's judgment, and inclination, which however he was
necessitated to comply with, if he would ever have it brought on
the stage." [49]

    The spasmodic and stormy alliance between Garrick and
Arthur Murphy again may serve to exemplify the tensions between author and director which frequently resulted from Garrick's altering of plays. During the preparation of *The Way to*

Keep Him Murphy remarked acidly that he thought plays were brought into the green room for rehearsal, not for the purpose of treating the author "as if he were going to school" *(Private Correspondence,* I, 171). There may be some truth in Murphy's charge that Garrick insisted on revisions because the character of Sir Bashful was so much more attractive than Lovemore, the role Garrick was to play; however, the director's suggestions written in detail to the author indicate that the alterations were based on the most practical of theatrical considerations. Garrick criticized the overworking of the stage-letter device, and he found several scenes too long, some speeches too tawdry. "I think that the beginning of the third act," he continued, "between Mrs. Lovemore and me, had better be spared, for fear it should take from the last act; and there is another reason for rejecting it, and a much stronger one, which is that I shall never be able to change my dress from top to toe (as I must for Lord Etheridge) while the scene of the Ladies is acting. If I were to dress in a hurry I necessarily must to be ready, I shall be so blown that the following scene will suffer for it." [50]

Garrick's predictions were not infallible (he turned down *Douglas,* it will be recalled), but as he himself had stated, he had been "tolerably lucky enough" in his guesses. The fate of *Alzuma,* another of Murphy's plays, will attest to the consistency of his good judgment. Murphy had written *Alzuma* in 1762, but the political inferences and Garrick's coolness prompted every delaying tactic at the manager's disposal to prevent its production. After another quarrel with Garrick in 1773, Murphy gave the play to Colman at Covent Garden, who presented it on February 23. Although Murphy was obliged to submit to Colman's doctoring of the play, in the advertisement to the published version he praised the manager's treatment of the production, and pointedly added that for the first time in his life he felt no reason to be disgusted at the internal occurrences of a theatre. [51] The play, however, was coldly received, although not an outright failure. The *St. James's Chronicle* (February 25, 1773) stated that manager and actors "shewed an uncommon zeal to do Justice to this Piece; no Expence of Scenery or Dresses was spared," but the consensus of the other reviews indicates that the play was ill-staged and poorly acted. The drama itself was generally damned by faint praise. [52]

Garrick apparently knew what he was doing when he refused *Alzuma.* Murphy must have realized this when he received only

£270 for his benefits, a disappointing sum compared to the £600 and £800 he had taken at Drury Lane for *The Grecian Daughter* and *The Apprentice*, respectively.[53]

Similarly, Hugh Kelly—whose *False Delicacy* Garrick had doctored into a success in 1767—offered *The Man of Reason* to Covent Garden in 1775 after Garrick had pronounced it too faulty even for alteration. The play subsequently failed at the rival house, reputedly because of Woodward's misinterpretation of the leading role. In any event, as James Boaden so neatly noted, "Kelly then found to his sorrow, that the *man of reason* was at the other house" (*Private Correspondence*, II, 69).

The subject of Garrick's altering and adapting, important as it is, lies outside the mainstream of this particular book. Perhaps there is validity in William Whitehead's charge that as a Drury Lane author he was obliged to write "with a view to scenical effects only."[54] In a fine study of Garrick's non-Shakespearean alterations Dr. Frederick Bergmann makes clear that the manager altered for the requirements of his stage during the last half of the eighteenth century. Garrick restrained the language in the interest of good taste and decency, he removed archaisms, he rewrote for clarity, he shortened the playing time, and he tailored the plays for the physical requirements of his stage. One example among many is his production of *Everyman in his Humour,* where his telescoping of Jonson's scenes served not only to satisfy a pseudo-classical decorum but to reduce the number of settings and scene changes as well.[55] A singular feature of Garrick's alterations, and one which reflects his intention to avoid stagnancy in stage action, is the insertion of stage business into previously inanimate and passive scenes. His production of *The Alchemist* included a considerable amount of stage business which is not evident from the printed text. Furthermore, he often interrupted long speeches with interjections from unemployed characters in order to give the semblance of action. He took special pains to build up entrances—"Never let me see a hero step upon the stage without his trumpeters of some sort or another"—and to strengthen exits and scene endings.[56]

VI

It has been the intent of this chapter to illuminate in some degree the general nature of Garrick's busy rounds, before turning to the more specific matters of theatrical direction and production. Certainly the forming and maintaining of the repertory, the negotiations with authors, and the preparation of a script for the stage were all of vital concern to him, and to them he brought a profuse store of dramaturgical sagacity and a rare intuitive theatrical perception. The value of such faculties to Drury Lane may be suggested by Dr. Johnson's elliptic appraisal of Colman's *The Jealous Wife*, which Garrick had fashioned with his theatrical scissors and then nursed through to production. Johnson—"who always abused Garrick himself but when anybody else did so he fought for the Dog like a Tyger"—[57] allowed that *The Jealous Wife* "though not written with much genius, was yet so well adapted to the stage, and so well exhibited by the actors, that it was crowded for near twenty nights." [58]

II

Settling the Parts

IN THE VENTING OF SPLEEN, Joseph Reed condemned Garrick as "a Theatrical *Dictator* who *Caesar like* could bear no Equal."[1] Garrick was equated to Caesar again at a later date, but with inference quite different in tone to Reed's. In 1775 when the cognomen "Garrick" had become an English by-word, Captain Alexander Schomberg, the manager's acquaintance, wrote, "I can no more say Mr. Garrick than I could say General Caesar" *(Private Correspondence,* II, 63). How Caesar deployed his legions is now the business of this and the following chapter.

Thomas Davies, himself a dishonorably discharged legionary whom Garrick fired in 1763, relates that "Order, decency, and decorum, were the first objects which our young manager kept constantly in his eye at the commencement of his administration."[2] Garrick was a man so accomplished himself, and so dedicated in the labors for his profession, that his examples served to inspire the regularity which so distinguished his ministry at Drury Lane. John Bannister, who had the distinction of auditioning for a position in the company while Garrick shaved all the while, affirms that the manager could "assign the proper employment to all his employees, excite their useful efforts, restrain their exhuberances and, by his care and judgment give to their talents their most effective direction."[3]

Several months before his new managerial venture was officially launched Garrick wrote to his new treasurer William Pritchard: "I have a great stake, Mr. Pritchard, and must endeavour to secure my property and my friends to the best of my judgment. I shall engage the best company in England if I can, and think it the interest of the best actors to be together: I shall, to the best of my ability, do justice to all, and follow the bent of my judgment in my future management of the stage." [4] For the most part, Garrick succeeded in meeting these objectives.

Drury Lane opened that September with a troupe of seventy performers which, as Garrick intended, included the most eminent actors of the day. The twenty or so principal performers who were the nucleus of the company may possibly be regarded as one of the most illustrious aggregates of histrionic talent ever assembled on one stage. Spranger Barry, Garrick's only serious rival in tragedy, was at Drury Lane from 1749 to 1750, then after defecting to Covent Garden and trying his hand at management in Dublin, he returned to spend his last seven years with Garrick (1767-74). Henry Woodward, who supported all the comedies in which Garrick did not appear and was the important second actor in those in which the manager did play, played at Drury Lane during the first decade, 1748-58. Thomas King joined Garrick for two seasons 1748-50, then after an absence returned in 1759 to become a faithful and worthy assistant for seventeen years. Others like the elder John Palmer, John Moody, Richard Yates, and William Havard remained with Garrick for their entire careers on the London stage. Macklin and Foote appeared intermittently at Drury Lane, but never on a long-term contract basis.

Garrick was equally fortunate with his actresses, despite the infinitely greater heartache they caused. Hannah Pritchard and Kitty Clive continued with him from the beginning until their respective retirements in 1768 and 1769. Susannah Cibber was absent from Drury Lane from 1750 to 1753, but otherwise acted there until her death in 1766. It is unlikely that any company since has boasted of three such indisputably accomplished actresses. In their stead came Anne Barry, Mary Ann Yates, Elizabeth Pope, and Frances Abington, all acknowledged in their day as expert performers.

In distributing the parts to this company, according to Davies, Garrick "consulted the genius of the actors, and though he was not without those prejudices which no man can be entirely divested of, yet, in general the characters were very well suited to those who represented them." [5] In filling the roles of the standard

stock pieces, however, Garrick's managerial prerogative was frequently usurped by the very nature of the repertory system. The
actor returned to Drury Lane each season endowed with numerous specific roles or types of parts which were acknowledged by
tradition as his property. Innumerable plays could be cited, but
The Alchemist will serve to illustrate the stability of casts: between 1747 and 1776 Garrick played the role of Drugger every
performance of the play save three. Palmer spelled Face from 1755
to 1769, Packer was Lovewit from 1759 to 1776, and most of the
remaining roles were also the exclusive property of one or two
actors throughout the entire period. Occasionally other actors
would essay certain reserved roles, especially for benefits, but
the encroachment seldom became permanent. The audience,
therefore, knew Macklin as Shylock, Woodward as Falstaff, Mrs.
Pritchard as Lady Macbeth, and no manager—not even Garrick—
dared alter the arrangement except on very unusual occasions,
and then only at the hazard of his property. Once John Rich
proved intrepid enough to give out the bills for *King Lear* with
Miss Wilford as Cordelia, but came to regret it when George
Anne Bellamy, the retainer of the role at Covent Garden, had
her own handbills printed and distributed to the audience as it
entered the theatre, "telling them, that [as] I esteemed myself
the acknowledged child of their favour, I thought it my duty to
be ready in case I should, that evening, be honoured with their
preference." Upon poor Miss Wilford's first entrance the audience
created such a disturbance that the play was stopped and triumphant George Anne—ready dressed—made her appearance
"amidst a universal applause." [6]

The performers often continued to play their roles long
after they were physically and vocally suited to them. Mrs. Cibber
was still playing Ophelia and Juliet—incomparably—at forty-nine.
When Garrick retired in 1776 at the age of fifty-nine, he was still
unrivaled as Benedict and Hamlet. Of course, some critics of more
realistic bent ridiculed the practice:

> Wherefore, oh time, shouldst thou bring on decay,
> Nor let ripe women, girls for ever play?
>
> . . . . . .
>
> Why not? plump Davy, near fifty-six,
> Still perseveres to play his boyish tricks. [7]

In general the audiences seemed not to have noticed, or if they
did, cared less. Garrick himself was surely not insensible to the

improprieties. In his *A Peep Behind the Curtain* the Patentee, when confronted with the grievances of actresses quarreling over parts, tells his prompter, "There's not one of 'em but thinks herself young enough for any part; and not a young one but thinks herself capable of any part—but their betters quarrel about what they are not fit for. . . . What a campaign shall we make of it; all our subalterns will be general officers, and our generals will only fight when they please." Even the resolute demands of natural events failed to unloose an actress from her coveted role. In 1748-49 Mrs. Ward played Cordelia while obviously pregnant. Looking through the record of her performances that season one is hard put to determine when she took time out to give birth. And there is that delightful legend of the provincial actress who in the fifth act of *The Mourning Bride*—of all plays—became a joyful mother. But certainly the most startling notice in this vein is one in the *Cross-Hopkins Diaries* for September 11, 1748: "Miss Pit went to play in the Beg Opera for Mr. Usher at Richmond & was delivered of a fine Girl—N.B. She was Virgin." Evidently Garrick did draw the line somewhere. In 1762 when the pregnant Mrs. Palmer inquired why she hadn't been awarded the role of a 16-year-old in *The School for Lovers,* Garrick replied, "it would have been as improper in us to have given it to you, in your condition, as in you to accept it." The role went instead to 48-year-old Mrs. Cibber! (See *Private Correspondence,* I, 139).

It was usually during the summer months that Garrick notified his actors of the characters they were expected to play in the coming season. In addition to settling the schedule well in advance, the practice frequently was an effective means of cutting short salary disputes. If the actor wanted his roles reserved he was obliged to come to terms early. Performers who, like Miss Pope, in 1775, held out too long, were apt to find that Garrick had already distributed their accustomed roles to other people, and they consequently were out of a job. Sometimes the early settling of parts could work against Garrick's interest as well. In 1775 he lost an excellent prospect when Henderson decided to engage at Covent Garden because Reddish and Smith were already in possession of the roles at Drury Lane in which he hoped to distinguish himself.[8]

If the eighteenth-century performer was tenacious, temperamental, and unpredictable, he also had to be highly competent, extremely versatile, and amazingly retentive. In a season which averaged about 80 different plays, not including afterpieces, in

180 nights (and no long runs) most actors played over 50 nights in an amazing variety of roles. In 1773 William Smith sent to Garrick a list of 52 characters in which he could be ready at short notice, representing some 25,000 lines in all, and Smith was at the time preparing three more roles. When soliciting a position in 1766 Anne Reynolds forwarded a catalog of 32 parts in 26 plays in which she was prepared to appear. Similarly, Mrs. Henry King was on the mark at any time in 62 different roles. Garrick possessed 96 roles but his figure was not highest. Perhaps he was exaggerating somewhat, but in 1755 the redoubtable Theophilus Cibber listed 160 characters "in which for the course of many years, I have frequently been allow'd to entertain an indulgent Town." [9]

The length of time an actor required to work up a stock part for a night's performance varied of course with the size of the role and the interval which had elapsed since he last played the part. If a character had not been attempted for several years it is certain that a series of refresher rehearsals would be essential. Some of the urgency involved in relearning roles is reflected in Garrick's letter to his brother concerning his struggles over Oakly in *The Jealous Wife,* a role he was working up again for a command performance after not having played it for at least three years. "I am very much *flabbergasted,*" he wrote George Garrick, "that my good King will see me Oakly, & the deuce is in *you* for not sending me the Prompter's Book . . . that I must have as soon as possible. . . . I have forgot it all. . . . I have not play'd Oakly these three years. . . . I'd give 5 guineas to have the Prompter's Book now." [10]

The fact that the repertory actor was so facile diminished to some degree the problem of maintaining the schedule. Numerous notations in the *Cross-Hopkins Diaries* record last minute substitutions ostensibly as the result of illnesses. In one instance, at least, such replacement was required in the middle of a performance, when in *Jane Shore* on April 6, 1756, Mrs. Cibber was suddenly taken ill—"she came tho', & went thro' ye first Acts, & then Miss Noughton finish'd the Part." On October 2, 1759, for *The Conscious Lovers,* "Mrs Clive being ill—Mrs. Abington did Phillis." On many occasions the only illness preventing the appearance of a performer was a disease called "Box-book fever," which became rampant when the boxes were not well taken or a thin house was in prospect. It was believed in some circles that an epidemic of this malady among the heroines was what drove

Garrick from the stage long before he intended to retire. Especially susceptible to the illness was Mrs. Abington. Once the bill was changed because she claimed sickness, but she then appeared that evening in the audience. Her repeated abuses prompted the following note from the manager:

> I find by Hopkin's Young Man that you sent to me last Night about twelve, with all my Family in bed, to let me know you could not play today—I must desire you to change y^r mind—
>
> I hope when all ye rest have agreed to do their parts, that you will not be wanting this evening. I beg you for your own sake, my sake and ye credit of ye house; nay, I'll go farther, I will do anything I can for you in my power—do be in a good humour and meet me at ye house this morning . . .[11]

Although the wide range of talents within the company made it possible to cope with most emergencies, sometimes when all attempts at scaring up a substitute actor failed it was necessary to borrow someone from Covent Garden. On April 8, 1756, "Mrs. Cibber continuing ill, Miss Bellamy from Covent Garden did Sigismunda." On October 6, 1757, Mossop was scheduled for young Bevil in *The Conscious Lovers*, "but was taken ill & we borrow'd Mr Ross (who had but left us this Season) to play it." If an actor could not be borrowed then the last resort was to send a reader upon the boards with book in hand. Before a performance of *Cymbeline* on April 27, 1764, "Mr Havard sent word that his Wife dy'd and Mr Lee read his part."[12] The first time Mrs. Baddeley—a novice promoted into the Drury Lane company by her husband, the actor Robert Baddeley—ever appeared on any stage was as reader of Cordelia in 1764. Her biographer reports:

> During the representation of this piece a singular circumstance happened, (owing to her inexperience, having never seen the play, and being requested to read the part in the absence of an actress that was taken ill) that disturbed the performance much. When Edgar came in, as Mad Tom, his figure and manner gave her such an unexpected shock, that through real terror she screamed and fell down, motionless, and it was some time before she recovered. The audience, to an individual, sympathised with her, and she resumed her character, encouraged by the thunder of reiterated applause from every quarter of the house."[13]

But certainly the most delightful occurrence on this score was Reddish's failure to show for the title role in *Alonzo* on the seventh night of its run (March 9, 1773). In desperation, Frank Aicken consented to read the part, and his own role in the play was entirely cut out. An apology was offered to the audience that Reddish had not come, nor had he sent any word. "The play went on," relates Mr. Hopkins, "before the Play was finish'd Mʳ Reddish came to the house, when the Play was over Mʳ King and Mʳ Reddish went on the Stage. Mʳ King Apologis'd the Audience in behalf of Mʳ Reddish & told them that Mʳ R— was ready to make oath that he had entirely forgot that it was a play Night, & that it was by meer chance he came to the House at all—his looks were so truely pitiable, the audience had Compassion & excus'd him." Several days later Reddish published his affidavit confirming his forgetfulness and begging pardon. Evidently Reddish was one of the more eccentric members of the company. On April 1, 1775, Hopkins noted: "Matilda was advertis'd for this Night [*The Fair Penitent* was played] but Mʳ Reddish came Yesterday as Mad as a March Hare. Said he had all the Terrors of the Damn'd upon him, & that he had not had a Wink of Sleep all Night—Calld the great Gods & the dear Woman (Mʳˢ Canning) that lay by his Side to Witness the Truth of this Assertion & behav'd like a Man in Despair." A week later, April 6, Hopkins marked that Reddish was "still continuing a little Mad."

It must be allowed, however, that for all their personal and professional idiosyncrasies the leading performers in Garrick's company were generally intelligently employed in their stock roles. For the most part, they revealed themselves as artists of extreme versatility, self-sufficiency, and not least of all, talent.

II

In the casting of new plays or revivals where no tradition of playing had yet been established, Garrick was allowed more latitude.

The English stage tradition by which the author of a new play exercised the prerogative of distributing the parts has been pointed out by W. J. Lawrence.[14] Garrick himself, in a dispute with Mrs. Abington over a role in Murphy's *Know Your Mind* (1772) argued, "that I may hear no more of *this* or *that* part in Mr. Murphy's play, I now again tell you, that every author, since my management, distributed his parts as he thinks will be of most service to his interest, nor have I ever interfered, unless I perceive that they would propose something contrary to common sense" (*Private Correspondence*, II, 30). In light of many instances to the contrary, however, it seems that this bit of information, even from so authoritative a source, is an overstatement which was designed to extricate the manager as gracefully as possible from company squabbles. The *Private Correspondence* reveals that the director did consult the desires of the author—who frequently wrote his plays with specific performers in mind—and in some instances where the dramatist was not deficient in theatrical experience he allowed him to distribute the roles. Garrick's dealings with Aaron Hill, George Colman, and Arthur Murphy would attest to the generality that the casting of plays was usually a cooperative venture between director and author, very much as it is today.

Otherwise Garrick cast new plays according to his own desires and judgments. Throughout the years he seemed to be fairly successful in his assignments, and a number of plays owed their triumphs, in part, to his astuteness in casting. Davies found the cast of *Florizel and Perdita* to consist of "such portraits of nature as we must almost despair of seeing again in one piece." [15] The splendid casting of *The Clandestine Marriage*, in which even the most minor roles were taken by players who usually commanded leading parts, was mainly responsible for that play's success. *The Grecian Daughter* [16] and *Merope* [17] were distinguished by their judicious casting, as were the revivals of *Every Man in his Humour, Timon,* [18] and *Coriolanus.* [19] This is not to say that Garrick never erred. A reviewer of *Zenobia,* for example, discovered some impropriety in Barry's acting a youthful part while a young man of about twenty-one personated his father: "In old plays, where the parts are already cast, this may be allowable, where the actors have been long in possession of a character, and have in some measure out-lived it; but in new plays nothing is so sensibly felt as this inversion of scenical propriety." [20] The hierocracy of the theatrical order must have militated other similar solecisms.

One of the strangest and most flagrant bits of casting done by Garrick occurred in both revivals of *Epicoene,* in which he filled the title role with a woman. The first revival on October 26, 1752 ("Not Acted these Fifteen Years"), found Mrs. Pritchard as Epicoene, despite the fact that Garrick had supposedly selected his cast very carefully (there were only three actors in it unfamiliar with playing Jonson). The production was not greeted with enthusiasm, and after five performances was dropped from the repertory until it was revived again on January 13, 1776, in Colman's alteration. In this second revival Garrick was censured in many circles for again casting a female—this time none other than Sarah Siddons—in a role obviously designed for a male. Henry Bate pointed to "the coolness with which the audience received the discovery" as proof of the impropriety.[21] Dr. Hoadly expressed his opinion to Garrick that "a young smooth-face" man should definitely play the role, for "the force is entirely lost by its being acted by a woman" (*Private Correspondence*, II, 123-24). Garrick retracted and for the third performance the *Public Advertiser* (January 18, 1776) announced that "As many admirers of Ben Johnson have expressed a Desire to see the Silent Woman performed as the author originally intended it, Mr. Le Mash will perform the Part of Epicoene on Monday next." After the performance the same paper (January 24, 1776) observed that "the Performance of this Character by an Actor rather than an Actress . . . was received with particular Marks of Approbation, and the Comedy will be repeated (for the 5th Time) on Saturday."

Two reviews of the production which are entirely antiphonal in appreciation demonstrate the difficulty of properly evaluating the theatrical criticism of the day. The *Westminster Magazine* (January, 1776) rebuked all the actors except King and Parsons for acting indifferently:

> Bensley is the worst Old Man we ever saw. He presents the countenance of a sickly old Woman, and the uniform goggle of his eyes, by which he means to express infirmity and distress is the look of a man in anguish from the colic. Mr. Palmer, Mr. Brereton, and Mr. Davis, have a bloated vulgarity about them, which should ever deter the Manager from assigning them the parts of cavaliers or men of fashion. Baddeley, as usual, over-did his part; and Mr. Yates, as usual, was not very perfect in his.

Balanced against this epistle is the applause of Henry Bate in the *Morning Post and Daily Advertiser* (January 15, 1776):

> As to the performers they exerted every nerve; Mr. King did more than possibly could have been expected in *La Fool;* Mr. Parsons was very great in *Daw;* Mr. Bensley's *Morose* was capital [*Westminster Magazine:* "the worst Old Man we ever saw"]; now and then he forgot the surly old man, and sunk into the superannuated driveller. . . . Mr. Yates *Otter* and Mr. Baddeley's *Cutbeard* were all we could expect.—Mr. Palmer was admirable in the long unprofitable part of *True-wit*, and discovered great spirit and comic vivacity through every scene [*Westminster Magazine:* "bloated vulgarity"]: *Claremont* and *Dauphine*, altho' trifling parts, were well performed by Mess. Brereton, and Davis. The ladies in general played well. . . . Upon the whole the play had great justice done it in representation by the performers as well as the managers.

The fifth performance of *Epicoene* was the last one. On opening night Hopkins marked in the *Diary*, "received with some applause—but it does not seem to hit the present taste—A little hissing at the End."

Those critics less favorably inclined to Garrick carped incessantly about "the bad casts of parts," and those partial to the manager were in general agreement that usually the parts "were so well cast, that it is impossible to point out where the greatest excellence lay."[22] Somewhere between these antipodal assessments the truth will be found. For the early half of Garrick's management the more reliable critical writing would indicate that Drury Lane's casts were as strong and brilliant as any ever assembled, but as the final years drew on they became progressively less distinguished. This trend—if it really was a trend—does not necessarily reflect on Garrick's capabilities as a casting director; rather it suggests that as the actors of the giant race retired or died off Garrick found it increasingly difficult to replace them. He introduced many young actors of promising talent—Dexter, Holland, O'Brien, and Powell, to name a few—but they succeeded only moderately by comparison. The company of men, at least, at the end of Garrick's reign may be judged somewhat inferior to those on the board for the first fifteen years or so. By 1775 George Steevens, who was a close friend of Garrick with little cause to indulge in pervicacious criticism, could write privately to him of the "incomparable badness" of the acting in *Zara:* he had never witnessed "such a miserable pack of strollers," and asked Garrick if he had "no better stuff behind the scenes?" (*Private Correspondence,* II, 35). In the *Theatrical Review* for 1771-72, a corpus of criticism which appears relatively free from theatrical politics and personal bias, the critic (either John Potter or Hugh Kelly) was frequently moved to comment on the "present deplorable situation of our Theatres with respect to good Performers," yet when we examine his reviews of some forty-seven Drury Lane productions for that season it becomes evident that the charge is one which cannot be consistently applied.[23] In eleven plays the critic judges the casts in general either inadequate or inferior to previous repertory casts at Drury Lane. *The Conscious Lovers,* for example, is accorded luke-warm praise in the face of the present dearth of good actors. Several characters in it, we are informed, are grossly miscast: "*Sealand,* is a Character, into which, Mr. Aicken seems to be forced by Managerial Authority, without either his own consent, or the consent of Nature," and "there cannot really be a greater instance of Managerial Inattention, than the appointing Mr. *Waldon,* to the Part of *Daniel,* when it might be excellently played, either by Mr. *Weston,* or Mr. W. *Palmer"* (I, 142-44). In the review of *The Tempest* the critic finds it impossible to give an instance "where so many Performers have been placed in one Play, in Characters, in which their talents are so obviously inadequate" (I, 245-46). Balanced against these notices, however, are the same reviewer's evaluations of thirty-six plays in which the casts receive unqualified praise. Of *The Merchant of Venice* we read, "This Play is excellently performed here, with respect to the casting of the Parts" (I, 41-42), and of *The West Indian,* "With respect to the representation of this Piece, Mr. *Garrick* shewed great skill, in what is usually termed, casting the Parts. The excellence of the Performers, from the highest to the lowest in the first run of it, was such as deserved great praise; and except in one Character, they all retain their respective stations" (I, 9).[24]

The record of achievement at Drury Lane would seem to substantiate that within the confines of the tradition-bound system Garrick, for the most part, assigned the major parts in both repertory and new plays with some sagacity and care. But the casting of supporting and minor roles was not always executed with similar regard. In 1750 John Hill made the rather valid observation that managers were inclined to judge parts by their quantity, not their quality, with the result that smaller roles such as Montano in *Othello* usually went to a person "somewhat above the degree of a scene-shifter." Hill recommended that major actors could do great service in the so-called minor roles, and similarly some under-actors would on occasion do justice to specific major roles when better suited and possessed of more natural advantages than the incumbents. He advanced the rather modern theory that as much skill should be brought to the portrait of a soldier as to that of a monarch.[25] The *Theatrical Review,* among others, shared Hill's view that "many of our best Plays are greatly injured in the representation, by the distribution of the under Parts to Performers incapable of doing justice to them."[26]

Apparently in many plays with casts of moderate size Garrick was able to pay proper attention to the assigning of minor roles, but the strenuous nature of the repertory system did not often allow him the time, the personnel, or perhaps even the inclination to do so. The almost constant juggling in the air of some eighty different attractions each season denied him the luxury of time that most modern *régisseurs* enjoy. Moreover, however versatile his company may have been, it is not logical to assume that within the limit of its numbers he could find the appropriate actor for each of the literally thousands of roles which his repertory required. When the season 1749-50 opened, for example, the company consisted of forty men, twenty-one women, and fourteen dancers.[27] About twenty were performers of considerable talent and reputation who shared the main load of the major roles. Some were specialty artists employed for the singing and dancing of the afterpieces and *entr'acte* diversions. Others possessed a singular talent in one type of play or role. The balance were journeymen actors of varying degrees of competency whose presences were necessary to fill out the parts in the repertory. Sensible economics restricted the number of contracts possible (salaries represented over half of the theatre's expenditure) and when casting plays, mainstays or new, Garrick was obliged to draw from the company at hand. (Not until the latter part of the nineteenth century, when populations increased, theatres and actors became more plentiful, and repertories became more limited in their scope and numbers, making longer runs possible, could the director aspire to cast lesser roles with something approaching consistent competency.) The actor working for Garrick was required to be a jack-of-all-trades, and master of many. In his memoirs Edward Cape Everard disclosed what it meant to be an under-actor in Garrick's employ:

> The porter, or call-man used to come to my lodging of a morning, and knocking at my door, this little dialogue used to pass:—'Mr. Everard'. . . . At ten o'clock, if you please, to As You Like It . . . At eleven, in the Green Room, to the reading of the New Play . . . At twelve, to Much Ado about Nothing;—Mr. Garrick will be there . . . At one, in the practising room below, Mr. Grimaldi's dances in the Tempest . . . At two, on the stage, at Mr. Slingsby's dance, the Savage Hunters . . . At half-past two, Signor Dagueville's Double Festival . . . At three o'clock, Mr. Atkin's Sailor's Revels . . . At half-past three, Signor Galli's practice of . . .

and so it continued through the day and evening—rehearsals from ten to four, back at the theatre from five often till midnight.[28]

Frequently Garrick had to seek outside his theatre in the streets and alleys about Drury Lane for people to fill the low parts and supernumerary walk-ons. (The "Account Books" contain many entries of payments to such people.) A newspaper clipping in which it is hoped there is more fiction than truth advises that when Garrick first took over Drury Lane he discovered the need for a considerable army of low recruits; in the choice of these he apparently "paid attention to person and look, more than to genius," for they had little to say. One of his procurers of "actors" for these parts was a character named W. Stone, who once wrote the manager in 1748 to advise he had "a few Cupids you may have cheap, as they belong to a poor journeyman Shoemaker, who I drink with now and then." Garrick replied, "You are the best fellow in the world—bring the Cupids to the theatre to-morrow. If they are under six, and well made, you shall have a guinea apiece for them. . . . If you can get me two good Murderers, I will pay you handsomely, particularly the spouting fellow who keeps the apple-stand on Tower Hill; the cut in his face is just the thing. Pick me up an Alderman or two, for Richard, if you can, and I have no objection to treat with you for a comely Mayor." Another time when Garrick was in desperate straits for a Bishop of Winchester, Stone wrote, "Sir—The *Bishop of Winchester* is getting drunk at the Bear; and swears d—n his eyes if he'll play to-night." Garrick's response was as cryptic: "Stone—the *Bishop* may go to the Devil. I do not know a greater *rascal* except yourself." [29] The employment of extras as the murderers in *Macbeth* would give credence to the story that once when Garrick came to the door in the banquet scene and said, "There's blood upon thy face," one murderer was so startled by the intensity of the acting that he blurted out, "Is there by God!"

III

Garrick reputedly was "the most tenacious man alive" in his demands for order and regularity within his company.[30] But theatrical performers have always been an unpredictable and temperamental lot, and Garrick had his fair parcel of problems with them. Despite his constant efforts to keep the family happy and congenial, jealousies and rivalries were frequently upsetting the tranquillity of Drury Lane. He was ever feuding in the green-room with Mrs. Abington, Mrs. Yates, and Mrs. Palmer, and perhaps the antics of these actresses hastened his retirement. There is little reason, however, to suspect their deportment while on stage. However, irascible Kitty Clive was another matter. Garrick dreaded any altercation with her and generally deferred to her desires in order to avoid painful squabbles. Although a superb actress, especially in coquette roles, her stage discipline was not the best. Garrick frequently complained of her wandering eye which scanned the boxes for a familiar face instead of looking at him during the action of an important scene.

Garrick sometimes had to inveigle or chide his actors into accepting roles. Aaron Hill's *Merope,* a play in which no one was anxious to appear, is a case in point. Garrick took on Eumenes. After promising to accept the title role of Merope Mrs. Cibber decided against it, and Mrs. Pritchard was prevailed upon to play it. Barry turned down Polyphontes, obliging the director to settle for Havard.

The revival of *The Chances* in 1754-55 led to rather typical casting complications, resulting from a clash of company personalities. As one of the company's leading comic actresses, Mrs. Pritchard was most suitable for the Second Constantia; but the plot required that the Second Constantia be mistaken for the First Constantia—a role already awarded to the slender Miss Macklin—and unfortunately Mrs. Pritchard was growing obese. Then Mrs. Cibber, whose contract reputedly gave her the privilege of choosing any character she desired in a new play, demanded the Second Constantia from Pritchard although she was apparently unsuited to the comedy role. Garrick was caught in the middle. Finally he took the role from Pritchard and gave it to Cibber, perhaps as Davies suggests, because Garrick felt her immediate failure would convince her to resign it forthwith.[31] In any event, Mrs. Cibber opened in *The Chances* November 7 and continued until the ninth performance on November 28. On November 30, Cross marked in the *Diaries* that she had been taken ill and for the tenth performance on December 4 he entered, "Miss Haughton did 2^d Constantia—Mrs Cibber gave it up—some days ago."[32]

The celebrated and incomparable Mrs. Cibber, for whom Garrick seems always to have harbored a sincere affection, more often precipitated directorial dilemmas by reason of her ill health than by her temperament. George Anne Bellamy asserted that Mrs. Cibber's frequent indispositions were real, not feigned, but actual or not they usually arrived during the rehearsals of a new production or shortly after its opening night.[33] After Garrick had spent much of Holy Week in April 1756 rehearsing her in the cast of John Hill's new farce, *The Maiden Whim,* Mrs. Cibber sent him word she would be unable to perform. Garrick wrote Dr. Hawksworth that consequently "the holy week was very ill Employ'd by Me—we have got another person ready in ye Part & I shall certainly act it on Saturday."[34]

Mrs. Cibber's precarious health compelled another crisis during the preparation of Murphy's *The Orphan of China* in 1759. Murphy was understandably apprehensive over casting her in the leading role but Garrick was steadfast in the face of the author's admonition; moreover, the manager stubbornly refused to provide an understudy. As anticipated, the actress became ill on schedule, and in view of Garrick's previous attempts to put off the play there appears some reason to suggest that the malady may well have represented a collusion between actress and manager. Murphy meanwhile had provided for the emergency with his own collusion: he had been secretly rehearsing Mrs. Yates in the role for over a month. When it became apparent that a change in the cast was necessary Murphy insisted that Garrick listen to his protégée read the part, but lest the intrigue become all too obvious, Mrs. Yates was instructed to conceal her familiarity with the lines. Garrick listened, disapproved, but was prevailed upon to listen again. This time Mrs. Yates gave "such proofs of her superior intelligence, and perfect acquaintance with her part, that Mr. Garrick appeared to be quite transported with joy," and turning to Murphy with rapture declared, "This is the best thing that could happen; Mrs. Cibber's acting would be no novelty but Mrs. Yates will excite the general admiration." [35]

Although Murphy had been resourceful enough in coping with Mrs. Cibber at this time, nine years later he was undone by yet another actress during the strange events connected with the playing of his *Zenobia* in 1768. The result was an incident described by the dramatist as "without precedent in the annals of the theatre." Garrick had evidently taken great pains to give *Zenobia* first-rate scenery and actors, and the première on Saturday, February 27, 1768, was an obvious success. By March 10 the play had been performed five times when Mrs. Dancer (soon to become Mrs. Spranger Barry) reported too ill to play the title role on March 12. Yet when *False Delicacy* was substituted for that date she appeared in the character of Mrs. Harley, a role much less exacting than Zenobia. Why Mrs. Dancer should have been too ill to appear in one play yet not ill enough to stay out of another is a puzzle yet shrouded in mystery. *Zenobia* was offered once more on March 19, but then Barry's illness and the death of his son precluded any more performances that season. Naturally Murphy failed to understand why his play, which promised to have a prosperous run for the balance of the season, should be withdrawn at the whim of an actress. But, except for expressing the opinion that the manager should have insisted that

Mrs. Dancer perform Zenobia or give up Mrs. Harley, Murphy failed to implicate Garrick. Garrick himself was pointedly silent about the whole affair. Evidently Murphy felt that he had been victimized by the Barrys and not the manager, and he wrote Garrick that he believed he would have done him all justice "if it had been practicable." All in all, Murphy came off well financially despite the limited run, and his profits for the venture finally reached £467/6/6—a figure above average.[36]

However crucial most of the squabbles with artists may have looked at the moment, Garrick could usually restore harmony during the course of the season. The welfare of the theatre seldom seemed to be in imminent danger on this account. One breach, however, this one between the manager himself and several of his most necessary people, failed to heal in time and the situation at Drury Lane at the opening of the season 1750-1751 was serious. For some time things had not been well between Garrick and his three mainstays, Spranger Barry, Charles Macklin, and Mrs. Cibber. The three were envious of the manager's publicity, his success, and his wealth. Barry especially became disdainful of the manager's prerogatives and asked to be relieved of the inconvenience of playing on the very nights when his presence might be required elsewhere at some social function. Garrick humored him by allowing the actor his own choice of playing dates, but Barry still could not abide the fact that when the two alternated as Hamlet Garrick always drew the larger audience. Before the season opened Barry quit Garrick for Covent Garden. Macklin and Mrs. Cibber went with him. Each had been a leading attraction at Drury Lane, and their combined defections left the theatre in a rather tremulous competitive position. An intense competition ensued all season long, out of which grew the *Romeo and Juliet* war and *Queen Mab*, a fabulously successful pantomime at Drury Lane, among others. Ostensibly Drury Lane won the battle, and a famous print, *The Theatrical Steelyard of 1750*, shows Garrick tipping the scale decisively in his favor. In time Barry and Mrs. Cibber returned to Drury Lane—Macklin remained for the most part a free agent. Garrick once wrote that the "Actors of consequence who have left Me have all wished to return to me."[37]

IV

One more aspect of Garrick's procedures in casting plays remains for consideration. During his career Garrick had been frequently and severely attacked as a petty tyrant who was driving the stage to ruin through his efforts to suppress the works of dramatists who might compete with him for merit. In the main, this line of criticism generally resolved itself into scurrilous imputations which were motivated more by personal rancor than objective reasoning. Garrick could hardly expect to escape a similar assault on his integrity in the business of play casting. A typical tirade was that by David Williams (*A Letter to David Garrick*, pp. 41-42) which in 1770 attributed "a greater want of good actors than was ever known" to Garrick's vanity and avarice ("yet your avarice is a puny vice to your vanity"). Williams charged that Garrick had ridiculed and ground-under all challengers, that capital performers had had their reputations drudged away by ill usage. Williams went so far as to suggest that Garrick had brought about the premature death of the Irish actor Delane by magnifying his faults through mimicry. Another barb, this one aimed by William Shirley, scorned the "incessant Pamphleteering" employed to "deify him," lest "a Competitor in Merit would create a Competition in *Profit*." [38] Yet another libelous publication stated that Garrick "would never suffer a figure much taller than himself, or of a marking genius, to appear in capital parts." [39] In *Some Reflections on the Management of a Theatre* (1770), a bitter attack containing few details from someone with a grievance, he was called to account for wrapping up the merit of Mrs. Yates "in the Shade of Obscurity" after her success in *The Orphan of China*, "lest the Town should interest itself in her Favour, to have her Salary raised equal her Desart" (pp. 11-12).

The charge of avariciousness and stinginess had become a stock one against Garrick long before his death. It became matter for jesters and raconteurs as well as for savage detractors. The echoing legend, however, has by now been dispelled by his biographers, especially Percy Fitzgerald, whose swelling list of Garrick's charitable endeavors and generosities suggests, rather naively perhaps, that his life was one round of kindly duties and offices. [40]

There can be little doubt, however, of Garrick's vanity. By his constant concern for his reputation he exposed himself to ridicule and satire many times. However, it is a gross imputation to charge, as did Charles Dibdin, that "he had the fame, the honour, the interest of no human being in view but Garrick." [41] The fact of the matter is that David Garrick, the manager, was also the company's best actor. He was also the company's most versatile actor. Consequently he normally assigned himself the meatiest parts or, as with Drugger in *The Alchemist,* altered the script to fatten his role. Murphy complained that Garrick had insisted upon alterations to *The Way to Keep Him* because his own part was not strong enough. There is perhaps some parcel of truth in Davies' conjecture that Garrick had refused Dodsley's *Cleone*—which was very successful at Covent Garden—because he feared his role would have been sorely eclipsed by Mrs. Cibber's,[42] or in Mrs. Cibber's own allegation, related to Joseph Reed, that "Mr. Garrick never chooses to be equall'd if he can possibly help it; wherefore if you expect him to play *Oneas,* you must lower the parts of Dido, Nardal, and Archates, without such subordination I am afraid he will never receive your play." [43]

To insinuate that Garrick studiously designed to subordinate the talents of his company, however, is to prattle absurdly. The fact that he himself did not take on one new role in the thirty-eight mainpieces he produced after 1763 should be testimony enough to expose the inanity. He created his last role—Sir Anthony Branville in Mrs. Sheridan's *The Discovery*—on February 3, 1763. To cite the many individual triumphs achieved under his management by this giant race of actors and performers would appear to be unnecessary. Few garnered their laurels as mere supporting players to Roscius. The record as it stands in Dr. MacMillan's *Drury Lane Calendar* and in Dr. Hogan's *Shakespeare in the Theatre 1701-1800* manifests that many opportunities were presented to the actors to appear in even the roles which Garrick had immortalized for himself, but except in few instances, such as with Barry's Romeo or Woodward's Marplot, Roscius remained unapproachable. While there may have existed some inequality in opportunity at Drury Lane surely it must be acknowledged that the major inequality was in genius.

III

Plot and Practice

DAVID GARRICK HIMSELF was the director of almost all new plays and the general supervisor of the getting up of the repertory pieces. In these matters he had several capable assistants. One was his brother George, whose slavish devotion to David's every request soon became a standing joke with the actors but a source of infinite comfort to the manager. Charles Dibdin relates that "George was always in anxiety, lest his brother should have wanted him; and the first question he asked on his return was, 'Did David want me?' George Garrick died about three months after his brother, which circumstances being remarked in the Green-Room, and noticed as extraordinary, 'Extraordinary,' said old Bannister, 'not at all—David wanted him.' " [1] The other chief assistant was the prompter (Richard Cross until his death in 1759 and William Hopkins thereafter), who after Garrick himself must have been the theatre's busiest individual. The prompter's duties included the writing out of the parts, the obtaining of the licenses, the hearing of the line rehearsals, and the complete charge of the stage during the performances.

Others sometimes assisted in directing the chores at Drury Lane. Until his defection to Dublin in 1758, Henry Woodward was responsible for the preparation of all pantomimes and many other afterpieces. When illness incapacitated Garrick for weeks at a time, especially during the final decade of his management,

[39]

some of the slack was taken up by Thomas King, a leading comedian, who among other productions directed *Bon Ton* and the
very extravagant *Maid of the Oaks*.[2]

On certain occasions authors directed their own plays at
Drury Lane. In 1759 Macklin conducted the rehearsals of his own
Love-a-la-Mode, and in 1760 Thomas Sheridan directed his alteration of *The Earl of Essex.* Samuel Foote likewise prepared many
afterpieces of his own composition. Doubtless, other authors similarly employed themselves, but this practice was not common.
The testimonies of some of the major authors of the period point
rather to the opposite conclusion. Arthur Murphy's fair opinion of
Garrick could alter with the direction of the wind, but his preface
to *Zenobia* (1768) is typical of many dramatists' expressions of
gratitude for the manager's directing: "His politeness from the
moment he saw the play, his assiduity in preparing it for representation, the taste in which he decorated it, and the warmth of
his zeal for the honour of the piece, are circumstances that call
upon me for the strongest acknowledgements." Murphy, for one,
always actively participated in the preparation of his plays, a
circumstance which did not make the strained relations between
him and Garrick any easier. When the rehearsals for *The Grecian
Daughter* began about January 23, 1772, a date which coincided
with the opening of a new law term, barrister Murphy wrote to
Garrick, "Were the play to be got up at another playhouse, I
should think it absolutely necessary to attend rehearsals, but when
you are willing to undertake that trouble, the anxiety of an author may be natural, but it is superfluous."[3]

Although the dramatists did not as a rule direct their own
plays, they were usually found in the front of the house during rehearsals. In his farce *A Peep Behind the Curtain,* Garrick satirized
those dramatists more defective in technical knowledge who were
constantly intruding their inane thoughts and who brought in
chattering visitors. Some playwrights like Glib in Garrick's back-
stage farce no doubt proved themselves nuisances, but it seems
unlikely that the manager would have objected to the presence
of the dramatist of serious intent. For then, as now, the most ef-
fectual dramaturgy was forged at rehearsals.

II

It has been generally concluded by theatre historians that few
rehearsals were possible in the eighteenth-century repertory sys-

tem: the actors usually prepared their roles themselves, working out their own physical actions and interpretations; moving about very little, the performers supposedly relied upon conventional gestures and attitudes and a formalized cadence of utterance; rehearsals were necessary only to familiarize the cast with their general placements, entrances, and exits. In just about so many words as these the subject of rehearsals in the eighteenth-century English theatre has been often dismissed.[4]

The premise that a bare minimum of rehearsals was held for a new play, almost none for a stock piece, has been given support by the various annotations of William Powell—onetime prompter at Drury Lane at the end of the century— which appear on playbills now at the British Museum. From these manuscript markings it apparently becomes evident that during the final decade of the century stock plays as a rule were seldom rehearsed more than once before performance. Often only a few scenes were reworked rather than the entire play, and all too frequently many of the performers did not make themselves available for the rehearsal. *Measure for Measure,* for example, was revived after a nine-year interval with only two rehearsals. New plays were not much more fortunate. The first rehearsal for Cumberland's *The Jew* was held only two weeks prior to the opening on May 4, 1794; the play was then accorded four full rehearsals and six partial ones of smaller scenes, totalling some fifteen hours in all.

There are, of course, even earlier citations of abbreviated rehearsal schedules and paltry discipline. When Quin decided to venture *Lear,* he demanded no less than twenty-two rehearsals but—"being at that time [1730-31] young and dissipated, attended only two of them."[5] When George Anne Bellamy was preparing for her debut at Covent Garden in *The Orphan,* she was unable to persuade the principal actors to attend more than two rehearsals. She solved her dilemma by rounding the corner to see the play performed at Drury Lane the night before her appearance, a happy solution which made her "more acquainted with the *jeu de théatre* than twenty rehearsals could have done."[6] And by 1775, in a treatise dedicated to Garrick, the general charge was levied that rehearsals were "little better than a *theatrical muster* . . . for the night's review, without little more preparation than their [the actors'] base appearances."[7]

Bits of fragmentary evidence like a few markings on some playbills, a number of pleasant anecdotes of half-truths, together with the authority of a half-dozen or so contemporary denunciations of rehearsal techniques have all conspired to reflect a picture of general professional incompetency in the matters of play preparation during the century. It is a characterization which perhaps in truth will serve to delineate much of the theatrical activity of the period. It is also a characterization, however, which especially when applied to Drury Lane Theatre for the twenty-nine years of Garrick's management will be discovered to admit many qualifications and re-evaluations.[8]

Contemporary depositions are sufficient and reliable enough to conclude that for the most part rehearsals at Garrick's theatre were conducted in an orderly and purposeful fashion. Hugh Kelly, whose obligation to Garrick for the highly successful productions of *False Delicacy* and *The School for Wives* was considerable, stated that "in his method of conducting the business of the stage, he is unequalled."[9] We have already noted the various enconiums with which many authors acknowledged the assiduous efforts Garrick had extended in the mounting of their plays. To be sure, some of the testimonials prefaced to printed editions of plays must be discounted as fatuous platitudes, but there is evidence as well from sources which have no reason for such indulgences, or indeed which in their outright hostility inadvertently offer affidavits to Garrick's diligence. Joseph Reed's discontent with the slighting of the rehearsals of *Dido* would indicate that Garrick had behaved in a manner contrary to his usual procedure:

> When the play was in Rehearsal & we got it rough hew'd, I expected M[r] Garrick would have given his promis'd attendance, but he was so extremely remiss that some of the performers could not forbear complaining of the neglect. I only saw him at two rehearsals: he hardly staid half an hour at either. . . . As M[r] Garrick did not give his promis'd attendance at rehearsals it was no wonder that Dido was got up in so slovenly a manner. Poor Holland did his utmost, but as it was visible the manager was not overwarm in the Authors Interest, some of the performers were not altogether so asidious, nor so perfect as they would otherwise have been.[10]

In the government of his stage Garrick was a strict disciplinarian, if not an outright taskmaster. Although frequently obliged to endure the idiosyncrasies and temperamental tantrums of his principals, Garrick would accept little foolishness from his general performer. When young Tate Wilkinson reported in September 1757 for his initial commission at Drury Lane, Richard Cross the prompter assigned him to the role of torch-bearer in the last act of *Romeo and Juliet:* Wilkinson was manifestly piqued at the menial task—"On which, Mr. Garrick advanced, and before the company said aloud, 'This, Sir, is my command—if not complied with I shall take your coat off and do the business myself; and you, Sir, will immediately be dismissed my theatre'." [11] Even the charming yet vixenish Miss Bellamy, who along with Kitty Clive and Peg Woffington could be discovered on many occasions touring the boxes with their eyes, heedless to the business of the scene, warranted that "the most intense application was necessary for those who fought under his banners. As he was unremitting himself in his attention to business, he expected those he employed to be the same." [12]

Entries in the "Account Books" will corroborate Davies' statements that tardiness or absences from rehearsals were seldom tolerated, and actors who were habitually negligent in committing their lines to memory were "laid aside for some time" till they acquired the proper respect for their responsibilities. Forfeits and stoppages of small amounts appear frequently in the "Account Books" as fines against actors and musicians who absented themselves from rehearsals. The articles of agreement with performers also specify fines to be paid for not being book-perfect by dress rehearsal. Garrick seems to have demanded attendance of even his high-ranking performers who, having played their stock roles for years, supposedly were perfect in their lines and business. [13]

Habitual infractions of the regulations could provoke resolute action. Thomas Davies, who later and to his credit extolled Garrick's administration, was discharged from the company in 1763 for his failure to comply. Davies complained to Dr. Johnson that it had been Garrick's nasty temper at rehearsals which had finally prompted him—and many other actors before him—to quit the stage, but correspondence from the manager to his former employee would suggest otherwise:

> If you mean by the *warmth of temper* you have accused me of to Mr. Johnson, a certain anxiety for the business of the stage, your accusation was well founded; for I must confess, I have been often too much agitated by your want of that care and readiness in your parts, which I thought I had a right to resent, and which made your leaving us of such little consequence: this warmth of temper is certainly my weakness, but I could never find that any actors have left us on that account, nor do I remember that I have ever drove a single performer from the stage, always excepting him whose over-exquisite feelings have made my connections with him of small duration. [14]

Francis Aickin was similarly discharged after the season 1773-74 for flaunting Garrick's "rules and orders as a commanding officer." According to Aickin, his only offense had been to retort unthinkingly and abruptly to Garrick's reprimand for, of all things, wearing his hat behind the scenes "before a number of hair-dressers, tailors, and many other servants of the house." Garrick took violent exception to the insolence, and in a letter of August 24, 1774, which intimates that there was more to the affair, he dismissed both the issue and Aickin.[15] Almost exactly one year later Charles Dibden was fired for neglecting rehearsals.[16]

III

Specific information concerning the number of rehearsals Garrick allotted to a stock mainpiece is unfortunately tenuous and difficult to come by. The amount of time required to work up a stock play obviously depended upon the size of the roles, the degree of intricacy of the technical production, and the time which had elapsed since the last appearance on the bill. It is likely that a good parcel of plays could be readied for the evening's fare after only a brief morning review under the supervision of the prompter. Garrick once set little store in Mrs. Abington's requiring a whole day's notice to prepare for a role she was regularly playing. A glance through the *Drury Lane Calendar*, however, together with a realistic estimation of the many practical routine problems intrinsic to play production should make it clear that many stock plays which appeared but spasmodically, compared to those which took a regular turn in the repertory, would certainly require more than one or two rehearsals if they were to achieve the standard of excellence with which they were generally endowed. To cite but a few (with the time interval between the first and second runs): *Albumazar* (1747-1773), *All for Love* (1749-1765), *The Discovery* (1762-1775), *Epicoene* (1752-1775), *Medea* (1766-1774), *Neck or Nothing* (1766-1773), and *The Twin Rivals* (1758-1770). In each instance the second run was offered with almost entirely new casts, requiring Garrick—I presume—to treat them as new plays.

The possibility that occasionally even the most frequently presented stock pieces received more than a few rehearsals is implied by an undated letter from Garrick to an unidentified nobleman (perhaps Lord Holderness) concerning the pains he was taking to prepare *Macbeth* for a command performance: "I will order a Rehearsal of Macbeth immediately & will do myself the honour of waiting upon you Wednesday Morning to acquaint you when it can be ready: No Time shall be lost in getting the Play up." [17] That more than a few meager rehearsals were required for a command performance of *Every Man in his Humour* in 1759 is evident from Garrick's letter (on March 11) to Lord Holderness in which he expressed the fear that the performance "will disgrace Us, If I do not have a little more time for instruction." [18] The performance finally was given three weeks later on March 31, with completely different principals from those who had played it only ten months before. *Every Man in his Humour* presented a problem that was not encountered within the majority of repertory plays—"the language and Characters of Ben Jonson," Garrick told Lord Holderness, "are much more difficult than those of any other Writer, & I was three years before I durst venture to trust the Comedians with their Characters, when it was first reviv'd."

The number of instances when actors were found wanting in their lines on Drury Lane's stage would perhaps lend credence to the premise that a few skimpy hours at best were niggardly accorded to stock plays. The imposing of fines for negligence in line-learning did not, it seems, always achieve the intended effect. Particularly spotty performances were likely when a play was revived after an interval of anywhere from one to ten years, or when an actor was playing a role for the first time. When after seven years *Amphitrion* was played, on November 23, 1769, with near a new cast, *Lloyd's Evening Post* (November 24-27, 1769) reported that some of the players "had not their parts, which, in our opinion is a crying offence against the public." The reviewer blamed Garrick for the offense, finding it remarkable that he who never missed or transposed a word himself would fail to have a care for similar exactitude from his actors. On October 5, 1771, Mrs. Barry and Mrs. Morland appeared for the first time in the roles of Mrs. Beverly and Charlotte in *The Gamester* (last previous performance March 16, 1771) with the result that "so many instances of imperfection occured in the course of the Play, as lead us to conjecture, that they arose in some measure for want of a proper rehearsal." [19]

All things considered in the matter of rehearsals for stock plays, it is probably wise to tread a middle course and conclude that some mainpieces were seldom offered with more than a modicum of review, while others would seem to have demanded somewhat more rehearsal attention. We are, however, on infinitely surer ground when we turn to the preparation of plays entirely new to the theatre. Contrary to the general assumption which allots but few rehearsals even to new plays, we discover that Garrick frequently devoted from three to eight weeks (a period highly respectable by even present-day standards), and on one occasion at least a year, to their making ready. Evidence may be offered from a number of instances which yield specific information about rehearsal schedules.

On November 17, 1753, the *Gray's Inn Journal* announced that "A new Tragedy, entitled *Boadicea* is now in Rehearsal at the Theatre." *Boadicea* opened December 1, "with all the Advantages which the Exhibition could give it" (*Gray's Inn Journal,* December 8, 1753). *The Maid of the Oaks, Barbarossa, Virginia, Dido, Zenobia,* and *The School for Rakes* were all in rehearsal about four weeks prior to their appearances.[20] *The Grecian Daughter* commenced rehearsing about January 23, 1772, for its opening on February 26.[21] Hopkins entered in the *Diaries* for the opening night: "This Tragedy . . . is very carefully got up & well perform'd, & receiv'd uncommon applause." The reviewer in *Oxford Magazine* accorded the highest praise to the drama itself, and then added a qualification which suggests that on occasion Garrick continued to polish a production even after it opened: the critic noticed "a few trifling improprieties with respect to the conduct of the Piece; which, as they are too evident to escape notice . . . will undergo a critical and managerial Castigation, during the run of the piece: which has generally been the case with most modern productions of the Stage."

In the introduction to the printed text of *The Male Coquette* (produced March 24, 1757, and published the same year) Garrick stated that the short piece had been planned, written, and acted in less than a month. But there were also instances in which a play was rehearsed up to two months. Edward Gibbon's *Journal,* for example, records a pleasant breakfast with Garrick on the morning of November 26, 1762, and then a visit to Drury Lane to attend "a very private rehearsal in the Green-room" of Mallet's *Elvira,* which did not open until eight weeks later.[22] Garrick rehearsed *Timon* for two months.[23] Because of the chicane and delay involved in the preparation of *The Orphan of China* in 1759, perhaps that play cannot serve as a valid example, but the calendar of background events discloses that at the beginning of the turmoil Garrick was sure that if he had the complete script by January 25—some of the actors were already at work on the play— he would be able to stage it by the twenty-fifth of the following month.[24]

Garrick obviously regarded his first revival of *Every Man in his Humour* in 1751 as a *chef-d'oeuvre*, but perhaps his approach to that play while not necessarily typical may be regarded as somewhat indicative. That Garrick rehearsed the play frequently and conscientiously we gather from Davies.[25] Nearly a year in advance the *General Advertiser* announced the revival was preparing, and two months before the initial performance it was noted in the *Daily Advertiser and Literary Gazette* that the play had for "some time been in Rehearsal, and will be very shortly performed."[26] The importance of Garrick's direction in this play may be judged by the fact that even when Woodward and Shuter —his original Bobadil and Stephen—later played their roles at Covent Garden, Drury Lane's production still remained the superior. Even after abstracting Garrick's excellence as Kitely, *The Public Ledger* (November 12, 1771) proclaimed that on the whole Drury Lane's production was "more respectable than at the other House, the under Parts being well supported." *The London Chronicle* (October 23-25, 1766) observed that although some of the principal parts were now filled at Covent Garden by those actors who originally played them under Garrick, "yet the whole does not produce that agreeable effect it did at the time of its revival."

The examples just cited represent less than ten per cent of the new plays offered at Drury Lane during Garrick's management. For want of further information it cannot be truly determined if the rather respectable lengths of the rehearsal schedules allotted to them are indicative of the rule, or the exceptions to it. Nor can it be said with any certainty how many stage rehearsals a particular play received from the time it was first read in the greenroom till the first performance.

The only direct statement from Garrick himself concerning the number of rehearsals given a new play proves rather embarrassing to my contention, to be sure. When the manager was urging Mrs. Cibber out of her sickbed in December of 1759, to meet her commitment for the role of Mrs. Lovemore in Murphy's *The Way to Keep Him*, he wrote her that "The Comedy will require four or five regular Rehearsals at least, and tho *You* may be able to appear with two, Yet I am afraid the rest of the Dramatis Per-

sonae will be perplex'd and disjointed if they do not have the
advantage of your Character to Rehearse with them—"[27] Mrs.
Cibber never did play the role, and it will be recalled that the
prudent Murphy had been privately rehearsing his own candidate,
Mrs. Yates, who finally opened in the part. We do not, of course,
know what Garrick meant by "four or five regular Rehearsals."
Maybe he was referring to full run-throughs with entire cast assembled. Note, too, that this was the earlier and shorter three-act
version of the play. It was not until the next season that *The Way
to Keep Him* appeared in expanded five-act form on January 10,
1761.

It cannot be denied, certainly, that the preparation of a number of première productions was slighted. Some new plays—as
with the stock pieces—were played imperfectly on their opening
nights. Even when praising one production for the exactitude of
the cast, some critics were obliged to contrast the fine showing
with what they perceived to be the general state of affairs. *Town
and Country Magazine* (December, 1773), for example, in reviewing *The School for Wives* found "every performer more correct than is usual at a new play." In February, 1776, this same
periodical reported that *The Runaway* was acted with great
spirit by all the performers, "who were very correct for a first
representation."[28]

There is testimony enough, however, to conclude that rehearsals under Garrick's directorship were the rule, not the
exception. Edward Cape Everard's account of the routine of rehearsing which began at ten in the morning and took the actor
from one practice room to another until four in the afternoon
indicates that Drury Lane on most days was a beehive of activity.[29] Edward Gibbon marveled at the versatility of Mrs. Pritchard, whom he saw one morning rehearse "almost at the same
time, the part of a furious Queen [in *Elvira*] in the Green-room,
and that of a Coquette on the stage; and passed from one to the
other with utmost ease and happiness."[30] The coquette was obviously Millimant, which Mrs. Pritchard was rehearsing for that
evening's performance of *The Way of the World*. Mrs. Pritchard
had possessed the role for many years, yet had not at this time
played it in over a year. It would be interesting to know how
long she had been rehearsing for this particular performance.

Many contingencies determined the number of rehearsals any
new play might aspire to receive: the current pressures of the
season, the sudden changes in casting, or even Garrick's particular

concern or indifference for the piece. Frequently parts of a play were ready, but the company could not proceed because the whole script had not yet been completed. In Garrick's back-stage farce, *A Peep Behind the Curtain*, we discover the manager being advised by the author just after a full-scale dress rehearsal of an act that "the second act shall be ready for you next week." Garrick was not merely indulging in pleasant fiction in this little farce, as the exchange of correspondence over Jephson's *Braganza* will attest. *Braganza* arrived at Drury Lane from Dublin packet by packet, scene by scene. In January, about six weeks before the production of the play (on February 17, 1775), the author's wife wrote on his behalf to the manager, through the liaison of their mutual friend Edward Tighe:

> . . . the first act has been finished, since the second of this month. Unluckily there has not been a packet at this side, or you would by this time have received it. . . . He [Jephson] is advancing in the second act, according to the ideas which have been communicated by you from London, and several excellent hints from the judicious here. . . . He begs you will prepare Miss Younge in the fourth and fifth acts, as her part in them will be very little, if at all altered. If you can have interest with the rest of the performers and prevail upon them to get ready in the first, third, and fourth acts, he thinks it will be of use, and all the fifth as it stands in your copy from the entrance of the Duchess and Ines, as very little alterations are necessary to be made in them.—He hopes to have the second act finished in a few days, and put into your hands: the rest will, I hope, follow soon. . . .[31]

Garrick had required that the full text of *Braganza* be in his hands in time for him to allow three full weeks for the rehearsals. During the month of January (1775) he was also involved in the rehearsals of Francklin's *Matilda*. The balance of Jephson's play apparently arrived when promised, and after the launching of *Matilda* on January 21, Garrick could then turn on schedule to this new endeavor.

Perhaps the immediate success of so many Garrick-directed plays will attest to the probability that they were also respectably rehearsed. It seems evident, at least, that many productions were accorded more than the few sketchy practices by which the eighteenth-century English theatre is often so neatly characterized.

IV

The rehearsing of a new play usually commenced with Garrick reading the script to the cast in the greenroom. From the very outset he conveyed his concept of the characters and their interpretations by acting out all the roles with the appropriate facial expressions, vocal intonations, and feelings. "As no man more perfectly knew the various characters of the drama than himself," writes Davies, "his reading of a new or revived piece was a matter of instruction. He generally seasoned the dry part of the lecture with acute remarks, shrewd applications to the company present, or some gay jokes." [32]

Although Garrick respected the varied talents of his company, he seems to have fashioned each character to his own interpretation. During rehearsals he paced the actor through his role, often acting out the scenes for him—including the female roles—with convincing realism. Helfrich Peter Sturz, traveling in England in 1768, saw him at work during the preparation of Bickerstaffe's *The Padlock* and marvelled that his delicate health could endure the constant strain which he subjected it to as he turned from one actor and character to another, attempting to kindle a fire where often no spark existed. [33] Garrick once described his labors at "plot and practice" as a school for underlings where the teacher was required to transform parrots into scholars and orators. [34] Unlike most of his predecessors, however, he was convinced that only by "Rehearsals before ye Person you may think capable of instructing you" could the actor ever achieve a true proficiency in "the tones and actions." [35]

As the director took infinite pains to inform, he demanded according to Davies an implicit submission to his instruction. The supposition that most of his actors accepted his interpretations and readings is perhaps supported by the eminence Davies attaches to the one occasion when Woodward deliberately ignored Garrick's direction during the preparation of *Every Man in his Humour*. As was his custom Garrick had first read the play to the company and in the frequent rehearsals proceeded to mold the characters to his fashion. Although Woodward had always responded to his directions for playing Bobadil, one morning in the manager's absence he entertained the cast with the manner in which he claimed he really intended to play the role. Lurking somewhere unobserved during this revelry, Garrick finally stepped forward upon the stage and enthusiastically praised Woodward's conception even though it did not jibe with his own ideas. Some-what embarrassed, Woodward offered to continue rehearsing along the manager's plan, but Garrick would have none of it; he blessed the new interpretation with "you have actually clenched the matter—But why, my dear Harry, would you not communicate before?"[36] Even Woodward, notwithstanding he was one of the most imaginative actors of the day, profited much from Garrick's drill, and one of his most accomplished comedy characterizations, Marplot in Mrs. Centlivre's *Busie Body*, according to Garrick at least, had been "all beaten into him."[37]

At the beginning of his directing career, when his company was populated with actors who had already established substantial reputations in their own right, but were rather case-hardened in their manners and techniques, it is probable that whatever "beating in" of his own ideas Garrick could achieve must have been accomplished by the exertion of a great patience and effort. Indeed, from 1660 right through most of the period under consideration almost all discussion relative to acting centered upon the degree of excellence which an actor displayed in following the accepted traditions for portraying a particular character. The closer each succeeding actor approached imitating the preceding distinguished player of the part, the finer his performance was acclaimed. Especially prior to 1741, the year Garrick and Macklin finally asserted the actor's right to re-interpret a role according to his own peculiar genius, the tradition of fixed interpretation passed down from actor to actor naturally tended in most cases to reduce the art of acting to a matter of mere study, very often mere mimicry. Consequently even as late as 1771 the *Theatrical Review* (I, 4) could find praise for Jane Pope's characterization of Lucy in *The Beggar's Opera* "because she copied her inimitable predecessor, Mrs. Clive, so closely, that it is but just to observe that the merit of her playing amply compensated for her want of abilities as a Singer."

When Garrick took over Drury Lane one of his main artistic challenges was to convince the performers that a good voice, graceful manner of delivery, and easy treading of the stage were not the only qualifications essential to acting; nor was it enough to be the parrots of the poet's words without having any idea of their true meaning. Confiding in his private papers, Garrick lamented a breed of "automaton Players, who are literally such mere Machines that they require winding up almost every time before they act, to put them into motion and make them able to afford any pleasure to an audience." [38]

The new actors, however, who broke-in under his management were, for better or for worse, the products of their master's making. From the moment an applicant auditioned the shaping of the mold began. Garrick's custom was to hear the hopeful read or recite before him: he would then immediately correct him by rendering the bit himself. If the student improved by Garrick's instruction, on the next reading he was accepted. [39] It was Garrick's practice to have his more promising apprentices travel up to his Hampton villa during the summer months to receive instruction in the roles they were to play the coming season. When John Palmer joined Drury Lane, after sacrificing a more attractive contract with Beard at Covent Garden, he was relegated to attendants and messenger parts for the first season, but then made the pilgrimage to Hampton as often as possible to rehearse the roles "the little monarch had there in study." [40] Certainly one of the most profitable summer semesters held at Hampton was the one just prior to Garrick's departure for the Continent in 1763. The star pupil, William Powell—whom Garrick had discovered in a Wood Street spouting club—went on that season to become in Garrick's absence the rave of London. His string of rapid triumphs set him up in the town as the successor to Roscius himself. In the midst of all his prosperity Powell modestly wrote the itinerant manager to express his gratitude for "the foundation of all, [laid] by your kind care of me during the course of last summer" (*Private Correspondence*, I, 169). In Garrick's gracious yet temperate response will be found a lecture from a theatrical master by which any apprentice scholar might profit. He warned the young sensation that the hard work and sacrifice to his profession was now only beginning:

> You must, therefore, give to study, and an accurate consideration of your characters, those hours which young men too generally give to their friends and flatterers. . . . When the public has marked you a favourite, (and their favour must be purchased with sweat and labour) and you may choose what company you please, and none but the best can be of service to you. . . . Study hard, my friend, for seven years, and you may play the rest of your life. I would advise you to read at your leisure other books besides plays in which you are concerned. . . . But above all, never let your *Shakespeare* out of your hands, or your pocket; keep him about you as a charm. . . . One thing more, and then I finish my preaching: guard against *the splitting of the ears of the groundlings* . . . do not sacrifice your taste and

feelings to the applause of the multitude; a true genius will convert an audience to his manner, rather than be converted by to what is false and unnatural:—*be not too tame either*. [*Priv. Cor.*, I, 177-78]

Powell unfortunately did not live long enough to develop the full flow of his potential talent (he died 1769), so there is no telling how individualistic a style may have emerged from his own creativity. Many of Garrick's other students, lacking any special spark which might allow them to transcend imitation, remained mere shadows of their teacher. Garrick's method produced many excellent copyists but few artists. Charles Holland, who constantly endeavored "to conform his Gait, his Voice, and Look, to those of the much admired Manager," was generally dismissed as a happy but uninspired mimic "that meanly servile in his walks of parts . . . strives to shine by imitative arts." In his satirical ode which seized upon each Drury Lane actor and actress in turn, Nicolas Nipclose (p. 41) wondered that Garrick did not costume the performers with clothes of his own size—"they would most fit as well as his manner." The production of *Romeo and Juliet* will suggest how his interpretations manifested themselves in the characterizations of his actors. Among the many actors he had trained in Romeo was the younger Charles Fleetwood, son of the former patentee, whose performance on September 25, 1758, was "receiv'd with a great & deserv'd applause." The *London Chronicle* (October 3-5) pointed out that Fleetwood's moments of greatest excellence were those scenes wherein Garrick himself had appeared to greatest advantage: in the distraction scene at Friar Lawrence's cell "there was something astonishly wild and passionate"—and although Fleetwood failed to reach Garrick's heights in the last scene, he performed with extreme propriety, energy, and tenderness. In his performance of October 13, 1758, Fleetwood almost turned the final scene into real tragedy: "Mr. Fleetwood in ye fight with Paris . . . having a Sword by his Side instead of a Foil, run Mr. Austin (Paris) into his belly, he lay some time but at last call'd to be taken off—Surgeon was sent for— No harm, a small Wound, & he is recover'd" (*Cross-Hopkins Diaries*).

V

The degree to which Garrick pre-plotted the business and movements during rehearsals is not readily ascertained. The full nature of the Drury Lane promptbooks from Garrick's management (thirteen at the Folger Library, one in the Harvard Theatre Collection) will more appropriately be described in my subsequent discussions of the production techniques, the theatrical illustrations, and the individual plays. But it will not be premature to notice now that from the various stage directions for entrances, exits, and bits of business found in them, it is evident that Garrick gave thought to the matters of an easy and combined action by which the playing of a scene would be facilitated. The promptbooks are invaluable for reconstructing production procedures, but in the matter of specific stage action and position they are woefully secretive. We may learn from which side of the stage a character entered, where and when he exited, and with whom. Never, unfortunately, do the promptbooks in themselves disclose the arrangement of the characters on the stage during the playing of the scenes. None of them contains a single diagram. Since eighteenth-century promptbooks were never intended to be the fully annotated production books required by the modern theatre, it is also evident that many of the stage directions and pieces of business added in rehearsals and during the course of playing would never find their way to them.

The directions that are in the promptbooks, and in some of the especially complete printed editions of such plays as *The Alchemist, Every Man in his Humour, Bon Ton,* and *The Guardian,* will suggest that Garrick moved his productions along at a very brisk pace. In *The Alchemist,* for example, he adds five directional cues for entrances or exits where Jonson does not have them, which are designed to remove characters from the stage when they are no part of the present action.[42] *Bon Ton, Neck or Nothing,* and other farces achieve a rapidity through interjected bits of stage business. The multiple directions for entrances and exits in the promptbook of *The Provok'd Wife* (played in two hours and twenty-three minutes) give the impression of an exceptionally fast moving pace.[43] This rapid pace was facilitated, as we shall soon see, by a scenic production technique which by its relative simplicity and plasticity afforded easy transitions of location and supplied many places of access and egress for the playing area. Even after allowing for cutting, the fact that a play of such notorious length as *Hamlet* could be performed in about two and a half hours will testify to the fluidity of the action.

Surely Garrick never amalgamated the movements, gestures, and the attitudes of the stage pictures with the attention to the details of ensemble playing which directors now lavish upon their productions. On the other hand, neither did chaos exist. In a play like *Every Man in his Humour,* so eminently successful in Garrick's version which required at least 110 entrances and exits and the arrangement of up to seventeen speaking characters on the stage at one time, someone had, at least, to direct the traffic in an intelligent and effective manner.

Theatrical tradition and conditions in many instances dictated the manner in which much of the action was to be staged.[44] Also the lack of an effective means of illuminating the back regions of the stage during most of this period militated the playing of most of the action in the forward areas. Similarly, the absence of an act-curtain for most of the period dictated that the actors begin their movements toward the doors well in advance of their exits. The most skillful of all tag-line exits occurs in Cibber's *The Comical Lovers* where Act III ends with Florimel speaking:

> So have I seen in tragick scenes, a lover
> With dying eyes his parting pains discover,
> While the soft Nymph looks back to view him far
> And speaks her anguish with her Handkercher.
> Again they turn, still ogling as before,
> Till each gets backward to the distant Door;
> Then, when the last, last look their grief betrays,
> The act is ended, and the Musick plays.

As he read the lines both he and Celedon gradually retired to their respective proscenium doors and made their effective exits. Garrick himself, we are told, had devised a rather priggish way of "tripping off the stage with a bridled head and an affected alertness," which his actors copied.[45]

In the confines of the traditions, however, Garrick animated his plays with a considerable amount of action. Indeed, he was sometimes attacked for supplying his actors with stage tricks and gestures which were "often essential, but oftener used as a take in, to those who have more eyes than understanding."[46] In his direction, as well as in his own acting, there was reflected a "quick and amazing art of magnifying trifles, which is sometimes the force of trick: not always taste and nature."[47] The success of *The Wonder* and *Bon Ton* (which with its many hidings, discoveries, disguises, double-takes, and comedy groupings is almost all stage business) may be attributed to the animation that Garrick had provided. In innumerable instances the high points of the action, the very "moments" that the audience anticipated with delight and applauded with rapture, owed their excitement and attraction to Garrick's inventiveness, both as an actor and director. So much of *The Alchemist's* business never found its way into the printed version, but the famous scenes where Drugger dropped the urinal bottle and when, finding himself duped, he "stripped off his cloaths, rubbed his hands, clenched his fists, and threw himself into all the attitudes of a modern Broughtonian bruiser," certainly must have been admirably staged.[48]

Garrick's facility at creating dramatic contrast in his composition is best illustrated in Lichtenberg's description of the meeting between Archer and Scrub in *The Beaux' Stratagem:*

> Garrick wears a sky-blue livery, richly trimmed with sparkling silver, a dazzling beribboned hat with a red feather, displays a pair of calves gleaming with white silk, and a pair of quite incomparable buckles, and is, indeed, a charming fellow. And Weston, poor devil, oppressed by the burden of greasy tasks, which call him in ten different directions at once, forms an absolute contrast, in a miserable wig spoilt by the rain, a grey jacket, which had been cut perhaps thirty years ago to fit a better-filled paunch, red woollen stockings, and a green apron. . . . Garrick, sprightly, roguish, and handsome as an angel, his pretty little hat perched at a rakish angle over his bright face, walks on with firm and vigorous step, gaily and agreeably conscious of his fine calves and new suit . . . [Scrub] with dropped jaw and eyes fixed in a kind of adoration, he follows all of Garrick's movements . . . they sit down together. . . . This scene should be witnessed by any one who wishes to observe the irresistable power of contrast on the stage. . . . Garrick throws himself into a chair with his usual ease of demeanour, places his right arm on the back of Weston's chair, and leans toward him for a confidential talk; his magnificent livery is thrown back, and coat and man form one line of perfect beauty. Weston sits, as is fitting, in the middle of his chair, though rather far forward and with a hand on either knee, as motionless as a statue, with his roguish eyes fixed on Garrick. While Garrick sits there at his ease . . . Weston attempts, with back stiff as a poker, to draw himself up to the other's height, partly for the sake of decorum, and partly in order to steal a glance now and then, when Garrick is looking the other way, so as to improve on his imitation of the latter's manner. When Archer at last with an easy gesture crosses his legs, Scrub tries to do the same, in which he eventually succeeds, though not without some help from his hands, and with eyes all the time either gaping or making furtive comparisons. And when Archer begins to stroke his magnificent silken calves, Weston tries to do the same with his miserable red woollen ones, but, thinking better of it, slowly, pulls his green apron over them with an abjectness of demeanour, arousing pity in every breast. In this scene Weston almost excels Garrick by means of the foolish expression natural to him. . . . And this is, indeed, saying a great deal.[49]

Similarly, that electric moment, again described by Lichtenberg, which is quoted at length later in my discussion of *Hamlet*, when Garrick met the ghost on the ramparts of Drury Lane will attest that he was equally skillful in the matters of focus, timing, and dramatic emphasis.

VI

Madame Suzanne Necker, the French Mrs. Cibber, achieved a lifetime hope by traveling to London to witness Garrick's last rounds in June, 1776. She was not disappointed. "I will travel no more," she wrote Garrick later. "I have, in Mr Garrick's acting, studied the manners of all men, and I have made more discoveries about the human heart than if I had gone over the whole of Europe."[50] Garrick the actor was frame and flesh of Garrick the director. It was inevitable that many of his ideas and methods of acting would naturally be mirrored in the final effect of his productions.

In 1741 both Garrick and Charles Macklin rebelled against the worn-out formalism of the stage. Previous to this historic year the keyword for describing the school of acting represented by Cibber, Booth, and Quin was *exaggeration*. Striding across the boards in a tragic strut, they paid minute attention to the elaboration of characteristic gestures and traits. In an excess of gravity and solemnity better associated with religious worship they rolled out the declamations by a sing-song chant. Such a style in the hands of Booth or Quin seems frequently to have been grand, and even on occasion magnificent. In the hands of a less competent actor, such as Colley Cibber in tragedy, the result was often insipid. Garrick and Macklin together, although their individual approaches were different, sought to establish a foothold for a more realistic elocution and cadence. Macklin perhaps more nearly approached—in Shylock at least—what we now have come to understand as a natural manner of acting. Garrick's new "naturalistic" style retained much of the posing and posturing of the earlier actors; it was however infused with a vitality and spirit which took the town by storm. How the old and the new came to loggerheads—when Garrick "young and light and alive in every muscle," encountered Quin on the stage of Covent Garden in 1746—and how a whole century of tradition was swept over in the transition of a single scene, is now theatrical legend.[51]

The most outstanding feature of Garrick's acting which impressed both compatriot and foreigner alike was the protean quality of his characterizations and the astounding plasticity of his facial expressions. His exquisite feeling was likened to wax, ready to receive any impression. He had a face for each part, each of which he endowed with an acute sense of balance and modulation. "Do not think that this great actor was common, trivial and a caricaturist," cautioned Noverre; "a faithful worshipper of nature, he knew the value of selection, he preserved that sense of propriety which the stage requires even in the parts least susceptible of grace and charm." [52]

The true extent of the subjectivity of Garrick's approach to characterization is, of course, difficult to determine, despite many contemporary depositions that he entered fully into his roles. It is this facet of his acting that would be most apt to impinge upon the actors he was directing. In a letter to Sturz he pronounced that "the greatest strokes of genius have been unknown to the actor himself, till circumstances, and the warmth of the scene, has sprung the mine as it were, as much to his own surprise as that of the audience. Thus I make a great difference between a great genius and a good actor. The first will always realize the feelings of his character, and be transported beyond himself." Garrick thus judged Clairon not of the genius class because her heart had none of those "instantaneous feelings . . . that keen sensitivity that bursts at once from genius, and, like electrical fire, shoots through the veins, marrow, and bones and all of every spectator." [53]

Yet the studied grace of deportment, the deliberateness of his speech and action patterns (as they have been reported) make evident that Garrick was far from a completely introspective actor. To the contrary, many of his contemporaries argued that only by an artful suspension of all feelings could Garrick produce his most astonishing effects. Charles Dibdin vouched he never saw Garrick "either laugh or cry . . . spontaneously, involuntarily, and from the soul." Edward Cape Everard relates an episode which occurred after the first rehearsal of *Henry IV, Part 2*, in which as a child actor he was playing young Clarence. After the company assembled in the greenroom for the criticisms, Garrick praised Everard's delivery, but found fault with one line which he wanted read with more feeling. The young apprentice replied that he intended to do so "when I am dressed for the part, and the audience before me, and everyone seems to be in earnest." Whereupon the director exclaimed: "Then, you are no actor! If you cannot give a speech, or make love to a table, chair, or marble slab, as well as to the finest woman in the world, you are not, nor ever will be a great actor!" [55]

Unquestionably Garrick's most significant contributions to the development of a "natural" style were his rendering of lines in a more conversational tone than was traditional and the elimination of the excessive mannerisms of movement and gesture. One of his unfailing rules, he claimed, was never to engage a performer "who should be marked with that blackest of all Sins of Nature—Affectation." [56] One time, however, he became obligated to employ Jane Cibber, grandchild and protégée of old Colley who had trained her in a manner of acting which was fast losing its appeal. Of the novice's debut as Alicia in *Jane Shore,* the manager wrote: "the Young Lady may have Genius for ought I know, but if she has, it is so eclips'd by the Manner of Speaking ye Laureat has taught her, that I am affraid it will not do—We differ greatly in our Notions of Acting (in Tragedy I mean) & If he is right I am & shall ever be in ye wrong road." [57] He was on the right road however. Cross entered into the *Diaries,* October 19, 1750, "Miss Jane Cibber play'd Alicia—quite in ould Style, not lik'd at all, tho not Hiss'd—given out again & great [ly] hiss'd & so not done."

Garrick was striving to direct his performers in his more realistic style, and he believed he had for the most part made progress in stripping his players of pretention. "I don't know how it is," he wrote brother Peter after seeing a miserable pack of strollers at Lichfield, "but, the Strollers are a hundred years behind—we in Town are Endeavouring to bring the Sock & Buskin down to Nature, but *they* still keep to their strutting, Bouncing, and Mouthing, that with whiskers on, they put me in mind of ye late Czar of Russia who was both an Ideot & a Madman." [58]

One technique by which Garrick achieved many of his most startling effects was the breaking up of speeches with pauses, followed by sudden starts and shiftings in tone. His peculiar excellence in breaks and half lines was almost universally acknowledged—"no man ever did, nor possibly ever will, speak . . . broken sentences, and make transitions with such penetrating effect." [59] In the speaking of soliloquies especially, Garrick taught that "the great art is to give variety & which only can be obtain'd by a strict regard to ye pauses—the running the different parts of a Monologue together, will necessarily give a Monotony & take away ye Spirit, & Sense of ye Author." [60] In some circles, however, the famous Garrick pause became matter for mild ridicule and often very severe abuse. The criticism ranged all the way from the pleasant anecdote of the Italian bass player in Drury Lane's orchestra who having fallen asleep during a performance stretched wide his jaws and yawned loudly in the midst of one of Garrick's solemn pauses, to the biting scurrility of William Shirley who branded the "false pauses, stammerings, hesitations and repetitions" as clap-trap designed "to extort applause from the injudicious."[61]

In movement and gesture, as well as in speech, Garrick employed the devices of contrasting tone, speed, and vigor. His detractors complained of studied tricks and overfondness for extravagant attitudes, his scene-stealing, his affected agitations, his over-agonized death scenes, and

> His frequent turning round about,
> His handkerchief forever in and out,
> His hat still moulded to a thousand forms,
> His pocket clapping when his passion storms,[62]

But even so dedicated a muckraker as William Shirley was obliged to acknowledge that "in serious playing, his strength is very great . . . surprise, impatience, interruption, are circumstances he always manifests high excellences in exhibiting. His sudden transitions, in particular, he has the happy art of making extremely swift. . . . He falls from fury into tears with a breath; and is pure and entire in both sensations."[63] This ability to create pictures of startling contrast in movement and composition became most manifest in the staging of his productions. The most astute analysis of Garrick's general movement patterns comes from the German traveler Georg Christoph Lichtenberg:

> There is in Mr. Garrick's whole figure, movements, and propriety of demeanour something which I have met with rarely in the few Frenchmen I have seen and never, except in this instance, among the large number of Englishmen with whom I am acquainted. . . . For example, when he turns to some one with a bow, it is not merely that the head, the shoulders, the feet and arms, are engaged in this exercise, but that each member helps with great propriety to produce the demeanour most pleasing and appropriate to the occasion. . . . With him there is no rampaging, gliding, or slouching, and where other players in the movements of their arms and legs allow themselves six inches or more in scope in every direction farther than the canons of beauty would permit, he hits the mark with admirable certainty and firmness. It is therefore refreshing to see his manner of walking, shrugging his shoulders, putting his hands into his pockets, putting on his hat, now pulling it down over his eyes and then pushing it sideways off his forehead, all this with so slight a movement of his limbs as though each were his right

hand. It gives one a sense of freedom and well-being to observe the strength and certainty of his movements and what complete command he has over the muscles of his body . . .[64]

If any director was ever qualified to instruct his actors by example certainly Garrick was. Charles Macklin, who styled himself a teacher of actors, charged that Garrick's art consisted of pushing and pulling the actor about the stage,[65] but despite Macklin's pettiness the century as a whole freely acclaimed Garrick as a magnificent genius. Even Samuel Johnson, critic so reluctant to praise, grudgingly joined the chorus, proclaiming, "He was the only actor I ever saw, whom I could call a master both in tragedy and comedy. . . . A true conception of character and natural expression of it were his distinguished excellences." [66]

The eloquent but sincere tribute paid to his directing by Kitty Clive upon his retirement perhaps best expresses the significance of the contribution the manager had made to his actors during rehearsals:

> . . . I have seen you, with your magical hammer in your hand, *endeavouring* to beat your ideas into the heads of creatures who had none of their own—I have seen you, with your lamblike patience, endeavouring to make them comprehend you; and I have seen you when that could not be done—I have seen your lamb turned into a lion: by this your great labour and pains the public was entertained; *they* thought they all acted very fine,—they did not see you pull the wires.
>
> There are people *now* on the stage to whom you gave their consequence; they think themselves very great; now let them go on in their new parts without your lead-strings, and they will soon convince the world what your genius is; I have always said this to every body, even when your horses and mine were in their highest prancing.[67]

IV

New Dress'd and Fine Scenes

THE THEATRE commonly referred to as the second Drury Lane, which Garrick came by in 1747, had retained its essential form and features since its erection in 1674. The original plan by Christopher Wren indicates that the auditorium was an ellipse. The pit with its fixed and backless benches sloped upward from the front of the stage to meet the first of two galleries of boxes which encircled the house. A third gallery faced the stage but did not extend around the sides of the house until late in the Garrick period. No figures are available for the original seating capacity of the theatre, but most estimates would place it as less than a thousand.[1]

The original stage area seems to have been approximately thirty-two feet deep. Seventeen feet of this depth consisted of the apron which projected forward in a semioval shape to the benches of the pit. The other fifteen feet, designated as the scenic area, were behind the proscenium arch. The entire stage sloped slightly upward from front to back. Flanking the apron on either side and set into the proscenium arch were the ever-important proscenium doors, originally two on either side, through which the performers made most of their entrances and exits. Above these doors were stage boxes, which when not utilized for balcony and window scenes served as spectator boxes.

About 1700 Christopher Rich, to increase the seating capacity, shortened the apron about four feet and converted the forward stage doors into boxes. Although Colley Cibber lamented the resultant loss of intimacy—the actors "are kept so much more backward from the main audience, than they used to be"—[2] the theatre was still small enough in Garrick's day so that "the moving brow and penetrating eye of that matchless actor came home to the spectators . . . nothing was lost." [3]

According to an indenture on a mortgage drawn up in 1753, the lot of land which contained the auditorium and stage measured 112 feet by 58 feet—truly not very commodious in comparison to many continental theatres in which the stages alone were nearly this size.[4] The indenture does not indicate how much of the area was occupied by auditorium and stage respectively, but the stage probably remained during the Garrick period at about the depth of 28 feet to which Rich had altered it, simply because it could not be extended back beyond the confines of the east wall of the building. The width of the stage, if we allow for the greenroom and some smaller rooms off to the sides, was perhaps in the vicinity of 45 feet. We do not know the dimensions of the proscenium opening.

Drury Lane had been refurbished from time to time in the earlier part of the century, and in the summer before it opened under Garrick-Lacy management it was again to be found in the midst of alterations and mortar.[5] The precise nature of the work is not known, but it seems to have been chiefly concerned with the redecoration of the front of the house. In 1753 the theatre was again "painted, gilded, and decorated with new Scenes, &c" (*Public Advertiser,* September 1, 1753).

The first major alteration to the theatre occurred in 1762 when Garrick finally resolved to drive the spectators from their seats on the stage. At the very outset of his management, indeed on the very first playbill for *The Merchant of Venice,* September 15, 1747, he had announced that no one would be admitted behind the scenes. The bills throughout the following years continued with the same notice. The exception, however, had been for benefit performances at which bleacher-like scaffoldings were erected on the sides and rear of the stage. And the battle of Bosworth Field was often fought "in a less space than that which is commonly allotted to a cock-match." [6] Some idea of the characteristic chaos of benefit performances which found two audiences in the theatre, one in front of the stage and the other on it, may be gathered from Cross's entry of December 2, 1749: so mobbed was it behind the scenes that "yᵉ farce was stop'd for half an hour" while Cross drew lines with chalk to divide players from spectators, and then "yᵉ farce *[The Chaplet]* went on with great Applause.—" What could happen on these evenings when actor could scarcely be distinguished from patron was unpredictable. On one occasion the stands "broke Down, but luckily nobody was hurt" (*Diaries*, December 6, 1750); yet another time "as yᵉ Curtain was rising for yᵉ farce a Gentleman's sword was taken out of yᵉ Scabbard & carry'd up with yᵉ Curtain and there Hung to yᵉ Terror of those under it (least it shou'd fall) & yᵉ Mirth of yᵉ Rest of yᵉ Audience"—the performance was delayed while a scene man fetched it down (*Diaries*, March 14, 1748). In order to eliminate the physical dangers and the obvious artistic improprieties, and at the same time compensate his performers for what would be a loss of benefit revenue, Garrick greatly increased the capacity of the house itself and drove the audience from the stage forever. On November 6, 1762, after the alterations, Davy wrote to brother Peter, "our theatre is most amazingly improved, &c. I really think it the first Playhouse in Europe." [7]

The final and most major alteration to Drury Lane was done in the summer of 1775, just prior to Garrick's last season, when according to *Oxford Magazine* (September 1775) the building was converted by the Adam brothers from "an old barn into the most splendid and complete theatre in Europe." The old side boxes were replaced by larger ones, supported by light elegant pillars, the ceiling was raised twelve feet, new passages were installed to the upper and lower boxes, and a more spacious entrance was effected from the Bridges Street front. All this work made the house much more comfortable and admission to all locations more easily accessible. *Town and Country Magazine* (September 1775) offers a detailed description of the new alterations and decorations which validates in detail the extant Adam's engraving of the theatre (see frontispiece):

> Drury-Lane house opened on the 23rd of September, when the improvements that theatre had undergone greatly charmed every spectator, who testified their approbation by repeated plaudits. The front in Bridges-street being visible to every passenger, a description of it is needless, but we must observe, that it is the opinion of some of the best judges in architecture, that there reign in it at once simplicity and elegance which do honour to Mess. Adams.
>
> The interior alterations consist of new side boxes, both upper and under, which are far more spacious and commodious than the former. The pillars, which support the upper boxes and gallery, are

leste and brilliant, being inlaid with plate glass on a crimson and green ground, and which produce a most splendid and agreeable effect. They are also ornamented with some well fancied paintings, with variegated borders. The boxes are lined with crimson spotted paper, which added to the light festoon curtain, affords great relief. New gilt chandeliers are placed in front. The ceiling is heightened twelve feet, whereby the voice of the performers is greatly improved. The stage doors have also received great improvements, and manifest a peculiar taste in the regulator. Such extraordinary and unexpected improvements, failed not to excite the approbation of all present; nevertheless, some hypercritics were of opinion, that such a blaze of ornament, in the audience part of the theatre, would diminish the effect of the stage decorations, which would appear gloomy, unless heightened at a considerable expence.

[The theatre was opened with an "overture" called *The Dramatic Candidates.*] . . . Upon the curtain drawing up (which by the bye is judiciously constructed without a slit) a clap of thunder precedes the entrance of Mercury, who compares the new painting of the theatre to the arts of *a fille de joye,* who tickles her face afresh to tickle your fancy.

An unidentified clipping at the Folger Library states that "the improvements and various decorations inside and out . . . are estimated at near 4,000 guineas." The "Account Books" for that year do not contain any discernible entries for the work.

The various capacities of the theatre during the Garrick period have been closely estimated by Dr. Harry Pedicord: about 1,268 after the alterations of 1747; and about 2,206 after 1762. The alterations by Adam in 1775 were probably more a consideration of luxurious appointments than a desire to increase the capacity by any measurable degree.[8]

II

In the same manner that the eighteenth-century theatrical repertory reveals the use of stock plays as its basic ingredient, so it also suggests as a general rule the employment of stock scenic pieces. The well-known "Covent Garden Inventory" (1743) and the less-known but equally illuminating inventory of the Crowe Street Theatre in Dublin, drawn up in 1776, leave little doubt that scenic pieces were used time and time again, not only for the same stock play, but for many different plays whose setting requirements were similar.[9] Tate Wilkinson in 1790 fondly recalled that one scene "used from 1747 to this day in the Fop's Fortune &c. which has wings and flat, of Spanish figures at full length, and two folding doors in the middle:—I never see those wings slide on but I feel as if seeing my very old acquaintance unexpectedly."[10] The general scenic situation at about mid-century is obvious from a contemporary pamphlet, *The Case of the Stage in Ireland:*

> The stage should be furnished with a competent number of painted scenes sufficient to answer the purposes of all the plays in the stock, in which there is no great variety, being easily reduced to the following classes. 1st, Temples. 2dly, Tombs. 3dly, City walls and gates. 4thly, Outsides of palaces. 5thly, Insides of palaces. 6thly, Streets. 7thly, Chambers. 8thly, Prisons. 9thly, Gardens. And 10thly, Rural prospects of groves, forests, desarts, &c. All these should be done by a master, if such can be procured; otherwise, they should be as simple and unaffected as possible, to avoid offending a judicious eye. If, for some particular purpose, any other scene is necessary, it can be got up occasionally.[11]

Several of the Garrick promptbooks at the Folger Library confirm the case for stock scenery. The annotations for scene-changes in the promptbook of *The Chances* (revived on November 7, 1754 and played 32 times thereafter) call for Drury Lane's *Town, Wood,* and *Chamber.* The crossing out of "Town" in the promptbook and the new annotation, "Fr[ench?] Town," indicates that at some time during this play's history the stock town was discarded for a newer one. At this same time Garrick furnished the play with a "New Hall." The "Ch[imney] Ch[amber]" called for in *The Chances* is probably the same one which did service in *The Provok'd Wife* and played such a prominent role in *Bon Ton.* *The Provok'd Wife* required the stock *Street* and *Wood,* and one notation in the promptbook which reads "Pal[ace]" for Brute's living room makes us think that John Hill had some cause to suggest that "the scenery should always represent at least the place where the action represented is said to be perform'd, than it should be left at random at this point."[12]

In the production of legitimate drama, at least, there existed a general sloppiness and indifference which resulted from the use of stock scenery and the employment of a rather uninspired technical staff. James Boaden, writing in 1825, relates his impressions of "the miserable pairs of flats that used to clap together on even the stage trodden by Mr. Garrick; architecture without selection or propriety; a hall, a castle, or a chamber; or a cut of wood of which all the verdure seemed to have been washed away." [13] A letter signed "Dramaticus" in *Gentleman's Magazine* for May 1789—printed with the explanation that it was written "thirty years before" and hence describes conditions *circa* 1759—criticizes the "want of due order and regulation in the lower department of scene-shifters . . . by whose frequent inattention we are often presented with dull clouds hanging in a lady's dressing room or overcasting an antichamber." And even as late as 1775 when the scenic art had already asserted itself at Drury Lane under De Loutherbourg, we could find that "the parting scene between Jaffier and Belvidera was exhibited in Yorkshire, amidst serpentine walks and flowing cascades," and what was supposed to be a rural village of Mansfield was actually represented by a "fine Venetian city." [14]

At least several reasons may be suggested for the apparent apathy—except in pantomime and opera which were seldom less than splendid affairs—in the matters of scenic production and propriety during the earlier part, at least, of Garrick's career. Compared to the Continent, perhaps because the English court supported neither opera nor theatre, London seems to have had a dearth of scenographic artists. With the possible exception of John De Voto, [15] who may have done some work for Garrick in the forties, the English theatre could boast of no scenic artist who approached Servandoni, Juvarra, Righini, or the Bibienas. Indeed, after Jones and Webb nothing very distinguished in the way of scenic art happened in the London theatre until the arrival of Philippe Jacques De Loutherbourg, an Alsatian, at Garrick's theatre in 1772-1773. The scenery apparently was usually designed and executed by competent but uninspired journeymen about whom we know so little. In *A Compleat Treatise on Perspective* published in 1775, Thomas Malton observed that by this date the scenographers had not yet developed any real skill in the basics of perspective.

> It is the least qualification of a scene painter to be excellent in landscape, in which a small knowledge of perspective is prerequisite; but in order to execute designs in architecture with correctness, and a just proportion of the several parts, requires a thorough knowledge of perspective. It is somewhat surprising, that all who are concerned . . . in scene painting, do not make perspective their immediate study; being the basis . . . of their profession; yet . . . several artists employed in it, are not totally ignorant of it, in theory, but they are almost wholly unacquainted with its rules, which, to me, is unaccountable. [16]

Malton's statement, of course, does not encompass all scenographers: there were undoubtedly some more skilled than those "totally ignorant." I hasten to add, lest the impression be given that the scenic art was a lost cause at this time in London, that it did maintain its position as an important department of theatre art. However, in the eighteenth century we must remember to distinguish "legitimate" drama from pantomime and opera. The scenery of a pantomime or an opera was a special thing, points out Richard Southern, which had its own merit along with the other rich adornments of singing, jesting, and dancing. The scenery of a play for the most part was mere background—as Dr. Southern says, "the unnotable handmaiden of a plot, a screen for the poet's play to act against." [17] The essential attitude toward the function of scenery in the *drama* is expressed in John Hill's *The Actor* (p. 254): "Something is necessary in this [scenery], but too much is faulty . . . because we would not have them engross the attention which is more due to the player." The attitude persisted until the last decades of the century. Boaden tells us that when Mrs. Siddons appeared on the stage as Lady Macbeth, the appropriateness of the picture of the castle behind her mattered little: "It is to the terror of her eye, it is to the vehement and commanding sweep of her action—it is to the perfection of her voice that I am captive." [18] Little wonder, then, in an age which boasted of a giant race of actors that the scenographer and his wares were kept in the background for so long.

As with the matter of rehearsals at Garrick's theatre, however, there is yet much to be recorded from hitherto unnoted sources. The traditional impression of the status of scenic art at Drury Lane is also subject to re-evaluation and qualification. For, as it was with rehearsals and acting technique, under Garrick's management the visual aspects and the technical skill of the theatre experienced many advances.

The scenographic art began its slow but surely steady rise to prominence under Garrick even in the mounting of regular drama. Although as late as 1769 the *Theatrical Monitor* (December 19) castigated the manager of Drury Lane for the sums lavished upon "simple *Cymon*" at the continued neglect of dramatic pieces, it is quite evident that by this time Garrick had considerably improved the visual qualities of his mainpieces. In a pamphlet occasioned by the advanced-price riots at Drury Lane, in January 1763, the argument was set forth that if Garrick had not expended so much money on scenery the higher admission charges would be unnecessary. The pamphleteer contrasted the new splendor to the age of Cibber when "few scenes were required . . . and those poorly executed, compared with the excellent paintings now produced, where *one single* flat or front shall be fairly worth their whole stock." [19]

Throughout the entire period Drury Lane bills carry notices that both stock and new plays were "new decorated," but more often than not the reference was to a single new scene or a procession, pageant, or new ballet which had been added for the benefit of the galleries. Such was the case with the revival of *Coriolanus* (1754-55) in which Garrick was obliged to provide a triumphal entry in competition to the one preparing at Covent Garden. With a fair percentage of productions, however, there is no question that entirely brand new scenery was especially provided to suit the scenic ascriptions supplied by the dramatist.

The first drama under his direction for which Garrick seems to have provided new scenery was *Mahomet and Irene* (February 6, 1748), the early and undistinguished effort of his former schoolmaster, Samuel Johnson. Despite the superb costumes and exotic settings—one, a Turkish garden, was considered a triumph of scenic skill—the play achieved but moderate success, running the conventional nine nights. (Garrick apparently prolonged the run in deference to his attachment to the then struggling author).

Aaron Hill's letter, dated July 11, 1749, expressing his concern over the scenes for *Merope*—"the chief difficulty will be found your *painter's*"—makes evident that a new setting was provided for at least the final scene of this play—a setting incidentally which we shall discover in a subsequent discussion to be most fascinating in its implications. [20]

The practice of providing new scenery for new plays did not really become vogue until the later part of the 1750's when we begin to observe that, contrary to the general belief that any old combination of wings and shutters would do for an eighteenth-century premiere, most new plays were mounted with more than common comeliness and attention. On January 3, 1759, after five months of preparation Garrick produced a splendid *Antony and Cleopatra*. Cross entered in the *Diary* on opening night: "This play tho' all new Dress'd & had fine Scenes did not seem to give ye Audience any great Pleasure or Draw any Applause." Garrick never recouped his expenses on the production which lasted only six performances, but some observers appreciated the endeavor, and one made the curious comment that "upon the whole, we think this play is now better suited for the stage than the closet, as scenery, dresses, and parade strike the eye, and divert one's attention from the poet." [21] In the same year *The Orphan of China* was brought on with infinite splendor, possibly employing what remained of the magnificent scenery from the ill-fated *Les Fêtes Chinoises*.[22] By 1759 Chinese motifs in settings had become quite popular, especially in opera. Even before the appearance of *The Orphan of China*, William Shirley and his friends were already "horribly weary of *Chinese* rails, architecture and ornaments" (*The Herald*, March 2, 1758).

But a trend developing in the painting of fresh scenes more important than Chinese motifs was one that is probably best described as romantic-realistic. In Murphy's *Desert Island*, the next play to be accorded new settings at Drury Lane (January 24, 1760), a variety of romantic scenery was introduced beginning with that of the first act which represented "a vale in the Desart Island, surrounded by rocks, caverns, grottos, flowering shrubs, exotic trees, and plants growing wild."

Only two weeks later followed *The Way to Keep Him* (February 5, 1760)—"With New Scenes, Cloaths and other Decorations." [23] Two seasons later *Cymbeline* (November 28, 1761) was done up in fine fashion with expensive scenes which—especially the second act bedchamber of Imogene—were "really executed in a taste that does no little honour to the abilities of the artist, and the judgment of the manager." [24]

While Garrick was touring the Continent in the years 1763-65 Lacy kept up the trend toward new and better scenery with "a grand and elegant" mounting for *The Rival Queens* (March 20, 1764).[25] When Garrick returned to London much impressed by some of the achievements of scenographic splendor which he had viewed in Paris, a new impetus was given to Drury Lane's scenic activities. From the season 1765-66 until his retirement in 1775-76, we shall find the statistics rather enlightening, if not truly startling in the face of the previous general conclusions concerning scenery at Drury Lane. During this period Garrick introduced thirty-seven new mainpieces to London audiences. Of these, at least nineteen, more than half, were mounted with spanking new settings especially designed and executed for them. Included in these nineteen were *Cymon, King Arthur, A Christmas Tale*, and *The Maid of the Oaks*, all avowed "raree-shew" extravaganzas, to be sure, but the remaining fifteen were regular dramatic fare.

The first was *Zenobia* (February 27, 1768) whose decorations were described by *Court Miscellany* (March 1768) as "magnificent and new," followed by *Zingis* (December 17, 1768)—"remarkable for giving a glaring picture of Indian manners."[26] In the same season Drury Lane audiences were treated to "remarkably striking"[27] scenes, dresses, and decorations in *The Fatal Discovery* (February 23, 1769), even though the editors of *Biographia Dramatica* discovered an absurd impropriety in allotting a Grecian palace to the monarch of a rock.[28]

By 1770 scenery had indeed assumed an eminence which it had never previously enjoyed at Drury Lane, and we find Garrick asking George Steevens for advice on new fields to conquer:

> Have you ever thought of any Play unreviv'd in Shakespear, that could credit to us well decorated & carefully got up?—What think you of Rich.ᵈ 2ᵈ? . . . An.ʸ & Cleopatra I reviv'd some years ago, when I & Mʳˢ Yates were younger—it gain'd ground Every time it was play'd, but I grew tir'd, & gave it up,—the part was laborious—I should be glad to Employ our Painter upon some capital *Creditable* Performance.[29]

Richard II never materialized, but perhaps the play finally decided upon was Cumberland's abortive *Timon* (December 4, 1771) which when it appeared was announced by the *Theatrical Review* (I, 253-54) to have

> new Scenes . . . well executed, and the Dresses . . . pleasingly imagined; nor is the Illumination in *Timon's* Hall inconsistent with that ostentatious *Athenian's* extravagance and love of splendour. The truth and perfection of Theatrical Representations, in a great measure, depends on proper Decorations; otherwise all that the Player can inculcate will prove ineffectual. In this particular, even envy must allow, Mr. *Garrick* has generally discovered great judgment; and, we recollect few instances of his erring with respect to this point; which is more than we can say of any other Manager within our Knowledge.—Scenery and Decorations are very important auxiliaries, to the keeping up the illusion, and carrying on an appearance of reality in Theatrical Representations. But, it requires great knowledge to introduce them properly; because they should never engross that attention in an Audience, which is primarily due to the Player.

Curiously, like *Antony and Cleopatra,* this production of *Timon* was also a failure despite its fine scenery and unusual effects.

The settings of Murphy's *Grecian Daughter* (February 26, 1772) as puffed by the press indeed gave the author sufficient cause to admit that on this occasion he had not been *"fobbed off*

with a touched-up palm-tree" (*Private Correspondence*, I, 460).
"The Representation of the city of Syracuse, with the view of the
sea, and the Temple Scene, with the mausoleum in particular,
are extremely well executed," reported *Oxford Magazine* (March
1772), "and do credit to the Theatre, and honour to the Artists
who designed and painted them."

It is unnecessary to multiply instances: the record of new-
decorated plays at Drury Lane continues with telling consistency. It includes *'Tis Well 'tis no Worse, The Fashionable
Lover, Alonzo, The Choleric Man,* and *The Runaway.*[30] *The Duel,
Sethona, Electra, Braganza,* and *Matilda* all had new scenery
as well.[31]

It is evident that Garrick had effected important advances
in enhancing the significance of scenery to regular dramatic fare.
But it cannot be denied that the spectaculars and pantomimes
still demanded most of the energy and attention of the Drury
Lane scene painters. Even prior to the arrival of Philippe Jacques
De Loutherbourg for the season 1772-73, Garrick had to a certain
extent competed successfully with the spectacles of Covent Garden. In the Christmas Holidays of 1750, Garrick made good his
announced intention to give his audiences Harlequin, if Shake-
peare failed to please, with an elaborate staging of Woodward's
Queen Mab, using additional "Scenes brought from Sadler's
Wells" (*Cross-Hopkins Diaries,* December 26, 1750). The tremendous success of *Queen Mab* lured audiences back to the
sacred temple of Shakespeare. Similarly the production of *Arcadia,
or the Shepherd's Wedding* (October 26, 1761), occasioned by
the recent royal nuptials, was all new, "finely painted and in very
elegant taste"—a performance that spoke strongly in favor of "the
Imagination of that Creative Genius, which is forever exercising
itself for the Entertainment of the Publick."[32] The elegance of
Arcadia perhaps explains why Garrick had been so reluctant to
provide his version of *The Coronation* in the same month with
new costumes and decorations. His ill-timed parsimony (in contrast to Rich's profusion of fine clothes, velvet, silk, satin, and
equally splendid scenes) left nothing to support his *Coronation*
but "gilt copper and old rags."[33]

Another typical Christmas pudding, complete with spectacular effects and transformations, was Garrick's *Cymon* (January 2,
1767). Although termed by the *Theatrical Monitor* (October 24,
1767) as "the stupidity of all stupid things," from the textual directions it is certainly clear that at this time Drury Lane was

as fully equipped for spectacle as the Haymarket or Covent Garden. One of the more ambitious effects required that a tower be enveloped in flames before sinking into the ground. Perhaps it was for *Cymon,* then, that Garrick had sought information from Monnet concerning the torches used in the Paris production of *Castor and Pollux.* The Parisian manager forwarded a model of the special torch made by Boquet with the explanation that there hadn't been time

> to have it painted red, as it should be. To the torch I have joined a little packet of the powder with which it is already filled, and which is called here licopodium; you will easily get it at London. To moisten the wick you need the strongest and best spirits of wine you can procure. You will take care, if you want the torch to act properly, not to fill it more than halfway; that is, up to the cross I have made on the tin.[34]

In an autograph notebook (Harvard Theatre Collection) Garrick made several notations to himself about the scenic requirements of *Cymon:*

	Cymon's Scenes	Act 1st
1ˢ sc:	Palace 2ᵈ Groove. changes to	
2 S:	Garden magnificent wᵗʰ change	
3ᵈ S:	Country.	
		Act 2ᵈ
Scene 1ˢᵗ	Landscape curtain	
2ᵈ	Country Scene wᵗʰ bank forrsᵗ	
3ᵈ	Palace (Uganda's)	
4th	Country—	
		Act 3ᵈ
Scene 1ˢᵗ	[notations end here]	

Other spectacles followed in quick order: *The Jubilee, The Institution of the Garter,* and *Alfred,* were but a few. In all these, however, scant attention appears to have been paid to uniting in harmony the roles of the author, musician, performer, scene painter, and machinist. They were professedly pageantry for pageantry's sake.

In 1771, Garrick's Parisian friend Monnet sent him a most valuable gift in the person of Philippe Jacques De Loutherbourg, an artist of reputation in Europe who had done some work at the Paris Opera under Boucher and Boquet. Garrick was immediately impressed with the Alsatian's exciting ideas and decided that here was the man who could coordinate even the more extraordinary scenic efforts with the *mise-en-scene* which the manager had been striving to create in his regular dramatic offerings. De Loutherbourg worked part-time at Drury Lane in the season 1772-73, probably first bringing his talents to *The Pigmy Revels,* a pantomime afterpiece produced December 26, 1772. For the next season, 1773-74, Garrick accepted the designer's proposals that he be given complete command "of all that which concerns the Effects, the necessary mechanism, with the decoration of the scenery in harmony with the costumes and the Subjects of the dramas." De Loutherbourg designed scenes for at least thirteen productions at Drury Lane for Garrick, and realized a distinguished record. He devoted his talents mainly to pantomime and ballet spectacles, but made several excursions into the legitimate drama, which included Francklin's *Electra* and *Matilda,* and Jephson's *Braganza,* all three in the season 1774-75.

De Loutherbourg is commonly acknowledged as the most important and influential designer of the English eighteenth-century theatre. He not only improved the quality of stage spectacle but stimulated the practice, already begun by Garrick, of bolstering plays with new scenes and decorations. By refining the technical use of ramps, levels, set-pieces, and profile-wings—all items which had been seen on the English stage prior to De Loutherbourg— and especially by his skillful employment of colored lights, he advanced along the path to a romantic and more realistic treatment of stage space. Although he did not introduce transparencies to the English stage, his experiments with them led to startling effects. As a result of this new spirit of freedom in his stage designs many aspects of the rigid system of stage mounting which had persisted for over a century were discarded and the way was readied for the coming of the pictorial art of the next century.[35]

One facet of the trend toward spectacular production techniques and the mounting of regular dramatic fare with new and appropriate scenery, of which De Loutherbourg was both the culmination and the pioneer, is brought to light in the Drury Lane "Account Books." Here the figures speak more eloquently perhaps than any contemporary accounts of scenographic achievement.

In the first and third season of his management Garrick spent £ 290 and £ 213 respectively for scenes and machines (exclusive of wardrobe and lighting, to be considered in turn). No records are again available until 1766-67, the second season after Garrick's return from the Continent, when the figure is £ 652. There is another lacuna in the record until 1771-72 when £ 1073 were expended on decorations. The following season the expenditure soars to £1365, and then in 1773-74—oddly enough the year in which De Loutherbourg arrived in earnest—drops slightly to £1227. The final two seasons, however, reflect a substantial increase—£1594 and £1674 respectively.[36]

The same growth may be seen in salaries for scenographic personnel. Most of Garrick's scenographers we know only by name: Serres, Royer, Greenwood. Robert Carver, a Dublin landscape painter, had been invited to London by Garrick as resident painter, but he left with Barry in 1750 for Covent Garden. The first scenographer whose name appears in the "Account Books" is Oram, who in 1747-48 was paid at least £130 for his services. Oram remained at Drury Lane until his death in 1758. John French was chief painter from 1767 to 1773: in the season 1766-67, for example, he received £213 of the total £320 outlay to scenographic personnel. The itemized accounts for 1773-74 disclose that De Loutherbourg received £335 of the £659 total expenditure for designers and painters (an additional £203 went to carpenters).[37] By the time Garrick retired, he was paying almost six times as much money for scenery and scenographic salaries as at the outset of his management.

III

Garrick gave sharp attention to matters of costume right from the beginning. The bills of innumerable productions, both new and stock, announce "the Characters New Dress'd," and although the costumes were not always appropriate they were almost sure to be sumptuous and attractive. Shabby dress and tarnished lace could still be found on Garrick's actors, but the rather disgusting costuming conditions which had prevailed over the first half of the century were constantly being improved.[38] The *Public Advertiser* (October 9, 1766) could still complain of "a mean dirty Senate," the members of which looked like pickpockets, in Drury Lane's production of *Venice Preserv'd* on October 6, 1766; to the contrary, however, most critics found fault not with the meanness of dress but with its inappropriate extravagance. Rather than "suiting the dress to the character, with the most minute exactness to complete the deception of the scene," each actor strove to obtain the richest suit in the wardrobe without consideration of the nature of his role.[39] In her appearance in *Jane Shore* on October 13, 1775, for example, Mrs. Yates "disguised the former part of her character in a kind of dress calculated only for an Italian Princess." [40]

For the most part Garrick and his colleagues were playing the tragic heroes in contemporary eighteenth-century dress, regardless of the setting or time of the action in the play, but there too inroads were being paved. Roman plays, at least, were presented with something akin to appropriate dress, even if the same costumes appeared in every play of that period. In the summer of 1757 Dr. Young requested the loan of Drury Lane's Roman "Shapes" for a private theatrical, and Garrick's reply of August 3 is illuminating:

> Our Roman Shapes at Drury Lane are so very bad, that we are now making new ones for ye Revival of Anthony & Cleopatra, & our false trimming will not be put upon 'Em till a little time before they are wanted, as it is apt to tarnish with lying by. I cannot therefore accommodate you wth Drapes & indeed if we had any . . . how could we let you have 'Em in ye Month of Sep^{br}?—for we after ye 15th S make use of those kind of Drapes in Every Roman & Greek Play. [41]

Although stage costuming during Garrick's management—indeed during the entire century—was characterized by casualness and a lack of realistic propriety, perhaps one possible reason which has not been taken into full account may be offered for the persistence of bad practices. The theatrically astute Lichtenberg caught the implications in his comments on Garrick's wearing of a French suit in *Hamlet*. Regarding Garrick as "an extremely ingenious man," who was able to gauge to a nicety the taste of his audiences, Lichtenberg advanced the thought, with some logic, that certainly the manager with "a whole house full of ancient costumes" was not unaware of the anachronism, especially when every London Macaroni realized it. He decided that Garrick used the French suit for theatrical effect which might never have been achieved with more cumbersome and awkward historical uniforms and cloaks. "Our French coats have long ago been advanced to the dignity of a tunic, and their creases to the importance of play of features; while all wrestling, writhing, fencing, and falling in an unfamiliar dress we can, indeed, understand, but do not feel sensibly." When Garrick drew his sword on Horatio, he "had partly turned his back on the audience, and I perceived that his exertions had produced that well-known diagonal crease from the shoulder to the opposite hip. . . ." We should not make too much of this point, of course, but for Lichtenberg this costume arrangement was "worth the play of facial expression twice over."[42]

Whatever Garrick's reason for persisting in anachronistic costume, he was not aware of the impropriety. His library contained at least four works on historical costume.[43] The Folger Library holds a scarce two-volume work, published in London, 1773, entitled *A Collection of the Dresses of Different Nations, Antient and Modern, Particularly Old English Dresses*, the second volume of which is devoted to *The Habits of the Principal Characters on the English Stage*. The full-page illustrations which correspond to many of the existing theatrical prints of costumes on Drury Lane's stage would imply that some serious attempt had been made to approximate a modified historical accuracy, at least as the eighteenth century visualized it.

In the very early months of the new management *Albumazar* (October 3, 1747) was played "New Dress'd after the Manner of the Old English Comedy." Increased attention to historical accuracy, however inconsistent, seems to be suggested by periodic announcements. In the production of *Edward, the Black Prince* (January 6, 1750) the "English characters, dress'd in the Habit of those Days made an elegant Figure," and *The Chances*, revived November 7, 1754, was "Dress'd after the Old Italian and Spanish Manner."[44] Shakespeare occasionally was graced. Hopkins entered in the *Diaries* for *Richard III* on December 18, 1762, "the Play dress'd in the habits of the times," and for *As You Like It* on October 1, 1774, "The Play was New drest in the Habits of the Time & they look'd very well &c was applauded." But Ben Jonson apparently fared best. For the revival of *Everyman in his Humour*, on November 29, 1751, the bills announced the characters "dress'd in the Old English Manner." Similar announcements were made for the several revivals of *The Silent Woman* in the seasons 1752-53 and 1775-76. For the latter revival, noted the *Public Advertiser* (January 15, 1776), the "Dresses were new and elegant." Bills for *The Alchemist* frequently read, "Dress'd in the Habits of the Time." Perhaps the same costumes were used in all Jonson plays.

The "Account Books" disclose that when the new managers took over Drury Lane one of their first sizable expenditures went for costumes—historically accurate or not. In the first season they spent £1054 to build up the theatre's wardrobe, and from John Powell's statements in "Tit for Tat" it may be deduced that an equally substantial sum was put out the second year:

I shall find the greatest Difficulty of any yet, in making an Allowance for the nightly use of their Cloaths, Scenes, &c. there being a vast Number of Rich Cloaths brought into their Wardrobe within these Two Years, and large Sums paid to the Taylor, Mercer, and other Tradesmen, on Account of the same, but then the Stock remains and will serve for a Considerable Time with some little Addition, and it is well known the Wardrobe was never so rich before as at this Juncture, a great number of the Cloaths having been bought ready made as very great Bargains, and when they are no longer fit to appear upon the Stage, the Lace will burn to a considerable Part of their Money again.[45]

Costume expenditures for 1749-50 total £430. Some individual entries, such as payment of £12 and 12S to Mrs. Coleman for "a White & Gold Brocaded Robe," indicate that the performer on Drury Lane's boards was not always shabbily attired. No figures are available again until 1766-67 when the wardrobe was enriched with £1124 worth of material. Then from 1771-72 the figures increase considerably until they reach £1871 in the final season, topping in each year the expenditures on scenery and machines, and representing 6 to 8 per cent of the entire operating budget.

In addition to the expenditures Garrick was making directly for his wardrobe, his contracts with players also included allowances for clothes. In an agreement dated May 5, 1774, Mrs. Abington received an additional £60 for clothes, and in the same year we find Mrs. Yates informing Garrick she cannot accept less than £700 salary, plus. "For my Clothes, as I love to be well dressed, and the characters I appear in require it, I expect 200£." She finally settled for a total of £750. Spranger Barry's claim that he and his wife stood the expense of £500 per year for clothes will similarly indicate that not all of Drury Lane's costume money was going into spectacle and pantomime.[46] Although there were some complaints against costuming practice, for the most part it may be concluded that a regular dramatic performance at Drury Lane during Garrick's directorship was elegantly and stylishly clad.[47]

IV

Until Garrick introduced some new and more flexible lighting techniques at Drury Lane in 1765, the stage was illuminated by six chandeliers which hung over it. The chandeliers, which may be seen in several theatrical prints of the period, were hooped-shaped, each containing twelve wax candles in brass sockets, and they dripped their wax down upon the performers during all types of scenes, interior and exterior. The "Account Books" indicate that up to £400 annually was spent on candles (many of which were used for lighting passageways, lobbies, dressing rooms, and other areas of the theatre). The chandeliers could be lowered to be lighted and raised into the upper stage-house to darken the stage for an effect which the audience could readily see being created. Fire was a constant danger, but not the only one: on November 13, 1756, "the balance Weight of the Candles of the Branches fell from ye top of the house upon ye Stage, & broke a great piece in the Stage, the Weight was 200£. Mr Woodward had just mov'd from the Spot where it fell" (Cross-Hopkins).

Footlights were in use by 1715, and certainly sooner, despite the oft-held belief that Garrick introduced them in 1765. Items in the "Covent Garden Inventory" indicate that the footlights could be lowered into an apron trough when it was necessary to darken the stage, and we shall find in the Drury Lane prompt-books of The Provok'd Wife, Zara, and The Chances such notations as "Lamps down," and "Sink Lamps." The opera-tion of the lighting facilities may be visualized from an open letter to Garrick in 1761 finding fault with some aspects of The Coronation. Reminding the manager that much of the real pro-cession from the Abbey took place in the late afternoon dusk—to the exasperation of the thousands lining the streets—the critic sarcastically suggests that for the sake of accuracy Garrick should have ordered "the Lamps to sink under the Stage, and the Chan-deliers to rise till they are lost among the Clouds."[48]

In 1765, after his two years of grand-touring, Garrick returned to Drury Lane armed with lighting innovations which were to have far-reaching effects on future production techniques. He abolished the over-hanging chandeliers, improved the footlights, and devised a system of side-wing lights modeled after the French. "On the opening of Drury Lane playhouse for the ensuing winter," the Annual Register for 1765 reported (p. 130), "the audience were agreeably surprised to see the stage illuminated in a clear and strong manner without the assistance of the rings hitherto used for that purpose." The Universal Museum (September 1765) and the Public Advertiser (September 25, 1765) also noted the innovation, with the latter stating that "the Drury Lane Managers have absolutely created an Artificial Day . . . they seem to have brought down the Milky Way to the Bottom of the Stage."

In a letter from Jean Monnet, dated June 15, 1765, we are offered some further information on the lighting instruments whose models Garrick had requested from Paris. Along with some Boquet designs, Monnet advised he was forwarding "a reflector and two different models of the lamp with which you wish to illuminate the stage of your theatre." Of the two kinds of lamps, one was earthenware and biscuit-formed, with "six or eight wicks, and you put oil in them," and the other "are of tin; in the shape of a candle, with a spring and you put candles in them." The first type possessed the double advantage of being less costly and more brilliant, "but for them not to smell, you must use the best oil and keep the lamps very clean" (*Private Correspondence*, II, 441). Apparently the lamps could be used both in the footlights and winglights. Garrick seems to have chosen the first type, requiring the best oil, and the "Account Books" for 1766-67 most pointedly record the transition from candle to oil, although expenditures on wax and tallow were still considerable.

It is hardly likely, however, that this was the first season in which oil had been used for illumination purposes at Drury Lane. In 1761, the *London Spy* (September 12-19) performed the service of summarizing all the recent allegations against Garrick's management, and among them will be found the fact that "the Oil used in his Lamps stinks most abominably." The extant "Account Books" for the first several years contain no payments for oil; the records are not again available until after the new lighting innovations in 1765—but evidently at some point after 1750 and before 1761 oil lamps were put into operation at the theatre.

The new winglights consisted of a series of perpendicular lamps, either oil or candle, backed by reflectors, all mounted on iron posts or frames. Masked by the wings, this device could be turned away from the stage to diminish the light.[49] For the first time on the English stage it was possible to achieve with some control gradual darkness or dawn, effects now procurable by unseen means. A rash of sunrises burst over Drury Lane's horizon. Dow's *Zingis* (December 17, 1768) opened with "the Moon setting behind a Hill, and the Dawn of Morning." Perhaps the most striking effect achieved along these lines was De Loutherbourg's sunrise scene for "a grand Provencale Dance" presented before the King and Queen: "The drawing up of the Curtain discovered the Port of Marseilles, just before the Dawn of Day; the Sun rose with the Music; the various Tints which were thrown upon this Scene till the Entrance of the different Sailors and their Partners, had a most natural and pleasing effect."[50]

This ability to vary to a fine degree the intensity and color of his lighting was one of the Alsatian's special talents. In one of his first major efforts at Drury Lane, *A Christmas Tale*, De Louther- bourg "astonished the audience, not merely by the beautiful col- ouring and designs far superior to what they had been accustomed to, but by a sudden transition in a forest scene, where the foliage varies from green to blood colour." [51] Such a transformation was achieved by placing different colored silk screens in the flies and near the side wings. These turned on pivots, and when the lights were cast behind them they reflected their various enchanting hues upon the scenery and stage. The technique was not entirely new with De Loutherbourg. It had apparently first been used, along with scenic transparencies, on the English stage in Garrick's production of *Harlequin's Invasion* in 1759. Henry Angelo, the younger, credits his father with giving Garrick the idea. The elder Angelo had traveled much in continental theatrical circles, and as a frequent visitor behind Drury Lane's scenes he kept Garrick posted on all new developments. How Garrick came to use the transparencies and color reflecting silk screens, as told by young Angelo, is a long but interesting story:

> At a carnival at Venice, my father first saw that pleasing little pictorial drama, entitled *Le Tableau mouvant.* He was so delighted with its effect, the scenes being planted as transparencies, and the figures being all black profiles, that he constructed a stage on the same plan, and it was greatly admired by Gainsborough, Wilson, and other English landscape painters.
>
> The princes being informed of this ingenious exhibition . . . ex- pressed a desire to see it, and as the Princess Dowager urged him to gratify her sons, he promised to prepare a few scenes, and to render it more worthy a royal audience.
>
> Signor Servandoni at this time was employed as principal scene painter at the Opera-house, who being an old friend of my father's, he offered his assistance; and thus aided, a few very striking sub- jects were produced, a paste-board *dramatis personae* were pre- pared, a humorous little drama was written, and the dialogue was performed in the French language, to the entire satisfaction of the princes . . .
>
> . . . It was in consequence of the little stage that Garrick first seriously bent his thoughts to these pictorial reformations.
>
> One evening, after dining with my father, and sitting over the wine, Garrick, conversing upon a speaking pantomime which he had long projected, asked him to contrive a scene, such as would be likely to attract by its novelty.
>
> The projected piece was "*Harlequin's Invasion*," and Garrick, describing the various situations in which the character of the "*tailor*

in armour," was to be placed, it was suggested to lead him through an enchanted wood, in the pursuit of Harlequin . . .

Excited to exertion on this occasion, he [French, the scene painter whom Angelo mentions earlier] produced a very fine composition, which was painted with masterly execution; the slips or screens in the usual opaque manner, but the back scene was a transparency, behind which, visionary figures were seen flitting across, upon the plan of the *Tableau mouvant*.

That which rendered this scene apparently the work of enchantment, however, was a contrivance, which originated in the inventive faculties of my father.

He caused screens to be placed diagonally, which were covered with scarlet, crimson, and bright blue moreen, which, having a powerful light before them, by turning them towards the scenes, reflected these various colours alternately, with a success that astonished and delighted the audience. Indeed, the whole stage appeared on fire.

The success of this novel experiment gave rise to other scenes, in which transparent paintings were adopted.[52]

More important to the development of new staging techniques than the introduction of transparencies, sunrises, or changing colors, was the fact that this new lighting arrangement allowed the actors to step farther back into the scenic areas without becoming obscured by dark shadows. The light intensity from the winglights was now capable of illuminating many acting nuances that previously would have been caught by the spectator only if the actor was on the apron. Indeed, so bright and glaring had Drury Lane's stage become that Gainsborough advised Garrick to tone down the lighting in an effort to return to "modest truth" which would appear gloomy in contrast.[53]

Some picture of the progressively significant role played by lighting effects throughout Garrick's directorship may be visualized from the "Account Book" entries. In the early years, 1747-48 and 1749-50, the lighting expenditures were £421 and £414, respectively. Had we the ledgers which unfortunately are missing between 1750-51 and 1765-66, perhaps we would be allowed to follow the pattern of increasing expenses in lighting—and with scenery and costumes—until 1766-67 when we find allotted to illumination a total of £1240, or three times as much as the first season. Then during the years of De Loutherbourg's activities for Garrick, the amounts skyrocket to a final season figure of £1970, an expenditure which exceeds that for either wardrobe or scenery.

V

It becomes evident from the marked increases in expenditures for lighting, costumes, and scenery witnessed in the "Account Books" and manifested in the productions themselves, that by the last decade of Garrick's management (when he himself appeared but infrequently compared to earlier years, and when the rest of the giant race of actors had been reduced to a mere shadow of its former self) all the elements of the production were playing their significant roles. In the years for which comparative figures are available during this last decade, it will be enlightening, if not actually astonishing, to notice that the temple devoted to Shakespeare seems to have spent more money on scenes, costumes, and lights than had the house of Lun. By 1774, Garrick could boast with as much truth as complacency that "I never make any Objections to ye Expence of decorating a play, if I imagine that ye Performance will be of Service to the Author, & the Theatre."[54]

V

Draw the Scene

B EFORE PROCEEDING to an account of the productions of some specific plays under Garrick's directorship, it would be of value to set the Drury Lane stage, so to speak, by a consideration of prevailing staging practices and developments. While acting descriptions abound throughout the reign of Garrick, definite and specific details of staging are not easily found. Periodicals, newspapers, and the dozens of inevitable pamphlets, although slightly useful, for the most part yield precious little information about these matters. Charles H. Gray's research into the theatrical criticism of the period notes innumerable newspapers and periodicals, yet "the list of those which admit any sort of discussion of the theatre is, however, very much shorter." [1] More valuable certainly are the various chronicles of theatre men like Wilkinson, Chetwood, Victor, and Davies; but even these records seldom provide the particulars. In general, theatrical prints and portraits offer fairly faithful reproductions of faces and costumes. The trustworthiness of their scenic backgrounds and staging compositions is, unfortunately, often questionable. [2] There are few scenographic sketches or engravings to show staging and design. While we know the names of some designers and painters, with the exception of De Voto and De Loutherbourg, and later Capon, their work remains somewhat legendary. Obviously English scenographic sketches and designs must have existed; they did in copious numbers on the Continent at the same time. Garrick himself once owned many of them. Bound into Volume II of an extra-illustrated edition of *The Private Correspondence* at the Folger Library is a brochure entitled, *A Catalogue of a Valuable and Highly Interesting Collection of Engravings . . . the Property of the Late David Garrick, Esq. Which will be Sold by Mr. Christie . . . on Thursday, May the 5th, 1825.* Listed in this sales catalog under "Drawings" are items:

125 A parcel of Designs for theatrical dresses.
126 Various pen and pencil Sketches, by Loutherbourg.
127 Various Designs for Scenery.
128 Twenty-one ditto ditto, in black lead.
129 Twenty-seven large ditto, in ditto.
130 Eleven ditto, elaborately finished.

The whereabouts of these appears yet unknown.

In the reconstruction of staging practices the printed play texts are of some help. Whereas dramatic works in Cibber's day were published with little or no stage directions, the situation improved somewhat when the works and alterations of Garrick began to appear, "as they are now perform'd at the Theatres Royal in London." Even those advertised as "regulated from the prompt-book" must be approached with extreme caution, however. Some of these printed versions, such as Bell's edition of Shakespeare (1773-74), might well indicate actions and settings which actually appeared on the stage. Textually they seem quite valid for the most part, but theatrically speaking they simply fail to tell us enough. Except in the most obvious instances, if not dated, these editions could form the skeletal basis for a production anywhere in England, anytime between 1660 and 1850. Too often the scenic ascriptions are merely literary appendages rather than theatrical notations. This fact will become apparent in my subsequent discussions of specific scenes—for example, the early dawn parting of the lovers in *Romeo and Juliet*—where the availability of substantial documentary evidence points up the disparity.

Ideally, of course, we must work from the promptbooks, and fortunately there are at least fourteen promptbooks in America dating from Garrick's management. But with these we are often disappointed, for eighteenth-century promptbooks were not intended to be fully annotated production records. The Garrick promptbooks never offer any diagrams, nor do they in themselves disclose the arrangement of the characters on the stage during the playing of a scene. Completely devoid of symbols and offering little more than an accurate text of what was played, some of them do not even merit the appellation "promptbook." Several of them, however, like the prompts of *The Provok'd Wife, Macbeth, Zara, Alfred,* and *The Chances* provide us with insights into staging practices which we shall never find elsewhere.

These promptbooks are all at the Folger Library except the one for *King Lear,* which is in the Harvard Theatre Collection.

1. *Alfred* (David Mallet and James Thomson). This is an important, fully annotated playhouse book made on a 1751 edition of the play, which served for the revival of the production on October 9, 1773, with scenes by De Loutherbourg. The alterations are in Garrick's hand, and the prompter's hand is presumably that of William Hopkins.

2. *Antony and Cleopatra.* Made on a 1734 Tonson edition of the play, this document cannot really be regarded as a promptbook, since it contains no symbols whatever. Rather, it represents Edward Capell's cutting and arrangement of the play for Garrick, in the adapter's hand, and agrees in most respects with the edition published by Capell in 1758. For a detailed discussion of the text itself the reader is referred to an article by George W. Stone, Jr., "Garrick's Presentation of *Antony and Cleopatra,*" *Review of English Studies,* XIII (January 1937), 20-38.

3. *The Chances.* This is a rather fully annotated playhouse book made on a 1705 edition of Buckingham's version, and used as a promptbook at Drury Lane from 1754-55 through 1773-74. The prompter's hand is that of Richard Cross. The other hand, which has made the alterations in the text and added some other directions, is that of Garrick. The altered text itself agrees for the most part with that printed in the edition of 1773.

4. *Florizel and Perdita.* This is an annotated book made on a 1762 Tonson edition, with some Garrick notes, but mostly marked by a later hand. A Folger catalog notation identifies the copy tentatively as one used about 1780-90, probably at the Haymarket.

5. *Hamlet.* Made on a 1747 edition, this book contains in his own hand Garrick's alterations and the new last act introduced in 1772. It appears to be Garrick's personal working copy rather than the playhouse promptbook. This copy will be considered in the chapter on *Hamlet.*

6. *Henry IV, Part 2.* This is an annotated promptbook made on a 1733 Tonson edition. It contains notations for scene changes and entrances and exits in Garrick's hand. The alterations to the text are also Garrick's. The MS cast list attached agrees with the

cast printed on the bills for the first production of the play under Garrick on March 13, 1758.

7. *King Lear*. This represents a late and disappointing prompt-book made on a 1773 Bell edition. The few directions to be found are in Hopkins' hand, and they indicate mainly PS or OPS entrances or exits. There are no symbols indicating scene changes or scenic pieces. This book will be considered in the chapter on *King Lear*.

8. *Love's Labour's Lost*. This book, based on a 1735 Tonson edition, represents Captain E. Thompson's operatic arrangement of the play for Garrick. It is of no theatrical value whatever, containing merely textual cuts, and it was never produced. For a discussion of the literary adaptation see George W. Stone, Jr., "Garrick, and an Unknown Operatic Version of *Love's Labour's Lost*," *Review of English Studies*, XV (July 1939), 323-328.

9. *Macbeth*. This is a late and fully annotated playhouse copy made on a 1773 Bell edition. This copy has been worked over by three different hands, the earliest of which belongs to William Hopkins. The peculiarities of this promptbook will be considered in the chapter on *Macbeth*.

10. *A Midsummer Night's Dream*. This is a playhouse copy with notes and interlineations by Garrick on almost every page. Made on a 1734 Tonson edition, the text represents Garrick's stage version which was produced in 1763-64, during his absence on the Continent. The copy includes entrance and exit directions and symbols for scene changes. For a discussion of the textual version see George W. Stone, Jr., "*A Midsummer Night's Dream* in the Hands of Garrick and Coleman," *PMLA*, LIV (June 1939), 467-482.

11. *The Provok'd Wife*. This represents the most illuminating and completely annotated of all the promptbooks. Made on a 1743 Dublin edition, it contains numerous notes and directions in Garrick's hand for entrances, exits, scenery ascriptions and changes, light cues, and curtain cues. For the most part the promptbook agrees textually with the 1761 London edition of the play.

12. *The Rehearsal*. This is not really a prompt copy but Garrick's personal copy with the speeches of Bayes underlined. Made on a 1683 quarto, the copy has some cuttings in Garrick's hand, but no prompt directions or symbols.

13. *The Roman Father*. This is a disappointing copy made on a 1751 Dublin edition, containing only textual cuts and no other markings whatever.

14. *Zara.* This is a richly annotated promptbook containing many notes, directions, and scenic ascriptions. Made on a 1763 edition of the play, it therefore represents a promptbook used in the playhouse after Garrick's return from abroad in 1765.

II

The essential techniques of staging practiced in the first half of the eighteenth century differed little from those which had developed in the Restoration.[3] The apron still remained the site of most of the vague and unpropertied action, the proscenium doors for the most part still served as the principal means of entering and leaving, and the boxes above these doors continued to act as balconies and windows. The scenery consisted fundamentally of the groove-sliding wing-and-shutter system. Visual corroboration is now offered in a little-known engraving which served as frontispiece to a miscellany of prologues written by the provincial actor, James Cawdell, published in 1785 (plate 14).[4] The engraving shows Cawdell on the stage of the Sunderland Theatre standing amidst a setting of parallel wings and perspectively painted backscene. The engraving is unique: in no other theatrical print of the period are both wings and top borders together so unmistakably and clearly discernible. While no very startling changes occurred in this basic arrangement of scenery during at least the first half of the century, there was a gradual sophistication in many aspects of staging techniques at Drury Lane during Garrick's tenure.

During most of the first half of the century the curtain was seldom used once the play began. The practice persisted with some stubbornness throughout the Garrick period. Placed in strategic positions behind the proscenium, the shutters performed the services of a curtain by drawing or closing to reveal or hide a more elaborate or specific decor. Sometimes the actors remained on the forestage while the setting of wings and shutters changed, and then stepped back into the upstage area and into the new scene. This rather fluid staging technique may be seen in the Bell edition (1773) of *Richard the Third,* in which Act II opens with a scene in front of St. Paul's. As Richard soliloquizes:

Ha! Edward taken ill . . .

the direction reads, "Scene *draws* and *discovers,* Lady Anne in *Mourning,* Lord Stanley, Tressel, Guards *and* Bearers, with *King* Henry's *Body.*" Richard continues to speak:

But see! my Love appears . . .

and he steps into the scene to interrupt the progress of the funeral procession. Similarly in Garrick's promptbook of *Alfred,* a rustic cottage scene (III, 7) gradually opening, "discovers several triumphal arches, adorned with trophies and garlands. . . ." The prompter marks that here occurs the "Procession of Alfred," followed by "The Danish King & Procession." A marginal notation directs "as soon as the last Soldier are before the 2d gr. Shut on Wood" (close the backscene of a Wood in the second groove). Alfred who is still on the stage immediately commences the dialogue with a hermit.

Usually, however, the stage was clear of actors at the termination of a scene or act. The promptbooks almost always provide exit cues and directions. As the years progressed the employment of discoveries—that is, the drawing of shutter frames to reveal a new scene or actor—became more frequent. In Murphy's *Zenobia* (1767-68) Pharmanes "ascends the throne, and the backscene closes," and later "The backscene draws, and discovers the King's pavilion, with an altar, and fire blazing on it." [5] The process is seen in reverse in *The Desert Island* (1759-60): instead of the backscene opening to a new discovery, in Act II "the backscene closes, and presents a thick wood."

The Garrick promptbooks make evident that the use of front and back stage areas followed a generally consistent pattern of alternation. Examples could be cited from any of the playhouse copies which have cues for scene changes, but the promptbook of *The Provok'd Wife* will serve us best, being so fully annotated and representing at the same time the production procedure of this play over the entire twenty-nine years under discussion.

Act I opens in "Sir John Brute's House," with the prompt marking "Ch [amber] 2d gr," meaning that the painted backscene representing the chamber was located in the vicinity of the second shutter groove. (It should be noted that promptbook directions such as this one do not necessarily refer to the wings of the settings in the specified grooves. The English groove system gave us a method for naming certain areas of the stage. A scene in a "1st grove" might also indicate that a scene drop or a full shutter was placed in the area of this groove, and worked independently of it.) At the heading of scene 2 which is "A Dressing Room" we find the following prompter's markings: "(w) Pic & Ch^r Toilet 3 gr," which translated out of theatrical symbolism means "withdraw the previous setting [the chamber in the second groove] to reveal in the third groove the scene of a picture chamber with cosmetic table "for Lady Fancyful's dressing room." [6]

Act II, which begins in St. James's Park, is headed with the prompt markings: "(w) Old Pal 4th gr."—signifying that farther back on the stage is set a definitive shutter in the fourth groove, painted as the façade of an old palace (stock piece) which is revealed when the previous chamber setting in the third groove is withdrawn. The scene then changes back to the "P Ch[r] Table &c." in Lady Fancyful's house, presumably again in the third groove.

Act III begins in Sir John's house, but in a different room from the "Chamber" with which the play opens. This setting is noted as "Pal. 4th gr." and will serve as Brute's drawing room for the balance of the play. In this act the prompter has entered a scene change which is not evident in the 1753 edition of the play. After Lady Fancyful's exit, followed by Lady Brute and Belinda, we read "(w) Ch Ch[r] 1 gr.," indicating that the scene changes to a room with a fireplace. The next scene will find us in the tavern drinking with Sir John and his friends "(w) Tav Ch 3d gr." The procedure persists throughout the remainder of the promptbook:

Scene. A Bed Chamber	(w) Ch Ch 1st gr.
Scene. Covent Garden	(w) Street 2. gr.
Scene. A Bed Chamber	(w) Ch. Ch. 1st gr.
Scene. Spring Garden	(w) Wood 4th gr.
Scene. Lady Fancyful's House	(w) Pic. Ch. 3 gr.
Scene. Sir John Brute's House	Pal: Ch: on.
Scene. Lady Fancyful's House	P. Ch. 2 gr.
Scene. Constant's Lodgings	(w) Ch Ch 1st gr.
Scene. Sir John Brute's House	(w) Pal. 4th gr.

In Fielding's *Tumble-Down Dick; or, Phaeton in the Suds* (1736) the character of Machine instructs his crew: "Then draw the scene. Pray, let the Carpenters take care that all the Scenes be drawn in exact Time and Tune, that I may have no bungling in the Tricks . . ." [7] Bungling, to be sure, did occur on occasion. For a production of *Queen Mab* on October 16, 1751, Cross noted "a blunder in the Scenes of y[e] Entertainment & *great Noise* as [they] move." Two nights later: "a blunder in y[e] same place (the Giants) a great noise—Horse beans thrown—when y[e] Curtain was down, M[r] Woodward went on, & said—Gentlemen I am very sorry this Accident shou'd happen, but before this little piece is perform'd again, I'll take care to see it is so well practic'd that no Mistake can happen for y[e] future Great Applause—" Another time, October 12, 1763, "the last Scene in the Genii the Wings did not change on Account of the Barrel being broke," and on May 9, 1776, during a performance of *The Rival Candidates* "the whole set of Clouds fell down upon the Stage but did no Damage" (*Cross-Hopkins Diaries*).

In general, however, mishaps were kept at a minimum, and the comment of Edward Oxnard after viewing *Harlequin's Jacket* on October 11, 1775, that "the scenery was beyond anything I have ever imagined & was shifted with the greatest dexterity," is typical of many reports from visitors to Drury Lane.[8] Such intricate feats as those required in *Cymon* were carried off with *aplomb* ("the Machinery is admirably calculated to *elevate* and *surprize*").[9] Hopkins' entry for the opening night of *The Maid of the Oaks* (November 5, 1774)—"The whole Performance tho' the most complicated upon the Stage went off with uncommon Applause"—will stand as testimony to the fact that when the occasion demanded Garrick's stage crews operated in a conscientious and skillful fashion.

Already possessing what must be acknowledged as an extremely fluid and flexible technique for closing and discovering scenes, the theatre was slow to realize the usefulness of the act-curtain. In 1748 it was still infrequently if ever used. A pamphlet published that year, *Criticism of the Foundling, in a Letter to the Author*, complained that "the Act ended as I have seen many others do, with all the Performers leaving the Stage, and the Music striking up." In *Gentleman's Magazine* (May 1789) Dramaticus expressed "a wish that every dramatic author would so contrive the denouement . . . as not to cover the stage with dead bodies, except in the *finale*, or last scene of his play; whereby the specious representation will be supported, and the curtain may drop, to leave us in full enjoyment of the prosimilitude: for it cannot be denied that the carrying off stiffened counterfeit dead bodies is so laughable an artifice, it is sure to excite a risibility, and turns the whole into a tragic-comic farce." According to Dramaticus the situation had not much improved by 1789, which is precisely the reason he had been motivated to send his comments—supposedly written thirty years earlier—to the magazine.

Odell (I, 401) has suggested with some logic that the scene-drop probably was introduced before the act-curtain. The first notice of an unmistakable scene-drop known to Odell occurs in an account of *Harlequin Sorcerer* at Covent Garden found in *London Magazine*, February 1752: "a scene drops, and gives us a prospect of ruinous rugged cliffs, with two trees hanging over them, beautifully executed." [10] The only other definite reference to a scene-drop which I have succeeded in locating as early as the fifties is in *Ladies Magazine*'s review (January 6, 1753) of *The Genii*, first performed at Drury Lane December 26, 1752. In the midst of a long and full description of this pantomime (which bolstered every mainpiece for thirty-five consecutive performances that season) we read, "now drops a scene containing a rural prospect, which exceeds any landskip yet shown on the stage; a leather bottle hung out, the reapers enter, the scene rises and leaves them in a field where they dance."

In two theatrical prints which date slightly earlier than either example already cited, one certainly scents backdrops. The print of Woodward and Shutter in Drury Lane's revival of *Everyman in his Humour* (November 29, 1751) renders the background in reduced and disproportionate perspective, strongly suggesting that the characters are standing before a drop lowered at the forward grooves (plate 21). The same may be concluded of the rather unusual illustration showing the arrangement of the leading characters in *The Roman Father* (February 24, 1750), in which the backscene, apparently placed at the proscenium line, bears definite resemblance to a drop (plate 19). If only the promptbook of *The Roman Father* provided some corroboration perhaps a nice conclusion could be offered, but this prompt is one of those frustratingly devoid of symbols. Whether drops or shutters are illustrated, these prints allow us some visual impression of what the actors looked like before a terminating backscene placed in the forward stage area.

The fact that the scene-drop technique is noted in several instances as early as the fifties would perhaps indicate that its use may well have been common, although generally unrecorded. However, in the nine promptbooks containing any symbols whatever, only two drops are indicated. Both are in late promptbooks, after 1773. In the final scene of *Macbeth* is found the notation, "Drop Street 2d gro," a strange choice of setting for the demise of Macbeth. The other instance, which occurs in *Alfred*, is most provocative indeed. At the opening of III, 6 appears the marking, "Drop Carver," and at the beginning of the next scene, "raise Carver." Both notations have been crossed out by the same hand, implying that on second thought some other scenic piece was employed. The fascinating thing about these notations, however, is the labelling of a drop with the name of its painter, Robert Carver.

(In the "Covent Garden Inventory," 1743, "Harvey's Hall" and "Harvey's Pallace" were similarly identified.) If Carver executed this drop for Garrick while still employed at Drury Lane he would have had to do it prior to 1750, the year he switched his affiliation to Covent Garden.[11] Such a circumstance would of course imply that this stock scene-drop had been hauled out of the scene room for frequent service between 1750, or earlier, and 1773. By 1819 it is evident from Rees's *Cyclopaedia* that the roller back-drop had in most instances replaced the shutters. How truly prevalent the innovation was between 1747 and 1776 is difficult to determine. The appearance of two back-drop palaces and a drop-wood in the "Crowe Street Theatre Inventory" of 1776, implies that by the close of this period the employment of drops was no longer novel.[12]

As the drops began gradually to supersede the familiar drawing frames, it was only a short step to the realization of the usefulness of an act-curtain. Although only a short step, the century seems to have paced it with some hesitation. Professor Nicoll has pointed out the "irritating tardiness" with which the curtain came more and more into use.[13] Odell (I, 402) claims that by 1750 new plays are marked by the omission of tag-lines—for example, Thomson's *Coriolanus* (1749)—indicating that the act-curtain made them by now unnecessary. Actually the fall of the curtain at act intervals was not unknown to the Restoration; however, the technique seems not to have been widely practiced.[14]

All too few contemporary notices of the act-curtain may be offered as evidence. In *London Magazine's* review (January 1756) of *The Apprentice* at Drury Lane, January 2, 1756, we are informed that at the opening of Act II "the curtain rises and discovers the Spouting Club, the members seated, roaring out bravos! drinking, &c." That the act-curtain was in frequent employ by 1760 is implied in Goldsmith's No. 21st *Citizen of the World*, in which a Chinese visitor describes his playhouse impressions. "After thus grieving through three scenes," he says of the heroine, "the curtain dropped for the first act." Then "after the queen had fretted through the second act, the curtain was let down once more," and so on for the other three acts.

There are some fruitful references to curtains in the promptbooks which are illuminating yet puzzling by their ambiguity. Several pages before the end of Act II of *The Provok'd Wife* is found the marking "*Ring*," standing as a reminder to the prompter that the close of the act approaches. After the final exits of the scene is the bold statement *"Curtain down."* A similar warning, *"Ring,"* is entered several pages before the conclusions of acts I, III, and IV, but no call for the curtain accompanies them.

Likewise, act-end warnings occur rather consistently in *Zara, The Chances,* and *2 Henry IV,* but in none of these is the curtain specified. While it may have fallen, it is probably wiser to conclude that these warning cues are mainly designed to alert the musicians. A French visitor in 1765 noted, "the last scene of every act is constantly interrupted, and sometimes in the most interesting part, by the tinkling of a little bell, which apprizes the music to be ready to play in the interval between the acts."[15] It was customary for the musicians to retire backstage during the acts, but finally in 1774-75 Garrick required them to remain in their places in the orchestra because their constant coming and going proved to be too distracting.[16]

In the original manuscript of Garrick's *Harlequin's Invasion* (December 31, 1759), there are several references to the curtain falling between the acts.[17] A page prior to the conclusion of Act I the marking "ACT" occurs, and at the close, *"Drop: Bar Bell. Act ends."* In the middle of II, 2 again is entered *"Curtain Bell,"* and at the close of this first scene of the act, *"Cur: Bell,"* implying that on this occasion the curtain fell in the middle of an act. In the second scene of Act II there is another "ACT" warning, with the concluding *"Act Ends. Drop.* Abram *Dresses."* The production also closes with *"Ring. Curtain. Finis."*

Another reference to the act-curtain is discovered in an unidentified eighteenth-century promptbook of *Jane Shore* (made on a 1713 edition) now at the Folger Library, where at the end of Act IV is the entry, *"Curtain down.* Give out the Play"—referring to the practice of announcing the next day's bill from the stage. In Wilkinson's promptbook of *The Brothers,* also at the Folger Library, will likewise be found at the end of the fourth act, "Speak to give out the Play." The manner in which the act-curtain in combination with the scene-drop seems to have come into gradual but more general use during Garrick's management is reflected in the promptbook which served for the 1773-74 revival of *Alfred.* At the end of the first act is the prompt note, "as the Fryer is going up to his cell *Drop Landskip."* At the close of the next act is similarly marked, "Drop Landskip." Evidently act-curtains were sometimes painted with appropriate landscape

views. Such a "Landscape curtain" is specified in Garrick's personal notes for the scenic requirements in *Cymon*. And in "An
Address to the Managers of both Theatres," which offered a satirical and ridiculous proposal for a new pageant to end all pageants, a serviceable wit in *Oxford Magazine* (October, 1773)
suggested that "your curtain should be painted with a view of
some public place, (as I have observed it upon other occasion)."

III

It has been put forth that the box-set, using lateral flat scenes,
became a definite development in the last half of the eighteenth
century.[18] If so, then the cause of theatrical realism would have
been advanced by a good number of years. But there seems to be
no recorded example of anything insinuative of a box-set in the
century. No newspapers or periodical accounts (almost certain
to report such an innovation) mention it, nor does any of the late
eighteenth-century promptbooks I have perused suggest it. In
Changeable Scenery (pp. 236-37) Dr. Southern has called attention to a print of Bickerstaffe's *Padlock* (DL, October 3, 1768)
which seems possibly to yield a backscene composed of a narrow
centerpiece and two short raking flats set at an angle to it, but
this arrangement is a far cry, indeed, from a box-set or even a full-
fledged lateral scene. Furthermore, no inference of either a box-set
or a side flat positioned perpendicular to the front of the stage
can be adduced from the very thorough and detailed account of
early nineteenth-century staging practices included in Rees's *Cyclopaedia*. At this writing the closest that modern scholarship has
pin-pointed the introduction of an unmistakable box-set on the
English stage is its use by Madame Vestris in 1832 at the Olympic
Theatre.[19]

During Garrick's management, however, new techniques—or
rather the modification of old techniques—in the arrangement of
scenic components resulting in improved playing methods were
on foot.

One of the more interesting developments at Drury Lane
especially evocative by the implications of its subsequent evolu-
tion into fully realized lateral flats was the occasional turning of
the parallel wings to oblique positions. This manner of wing
placement was utilized in Aaron Hill's *Merope* in the season
1749-50. In a letter dated July 11, 1749, Hill wrote to Garrick

about the technical problems to be encountered in the last act
of *Merope:*

> As to the last act of *Merope,* I rather chuse to *break* the scene,
> than *lose* an added beauty, of such striking force, as that will carry.
> . . . The chief *difficulty* will be found your *painter's;* For, consider-
> ing, how crowded a confusion, has, before, been represented to the
> *audience,* in the speech of *Euricles,* 'twill call for all the *pencil's* art,
> to fill the temple (through side openings, seen twixt columns, stand-
> ing separate from the slanted scenes, which are to be set back as far
> as possible) with such significantly busied groupes of interested peo-
> ple, as were spoken of in the description, and to lessen off their
> view, in gradual depth of *keeping,* so as to extend the prospect with
> scarce a sensible distinction, from the real life, before, and near the
> altar; such as the kneeling *queen* and *prostrate* guards, together
> with the *priests* and *virgins. . . .*[20]

The speech of Euricles referred to by Hill came at the close of
the preceding scene. It is important because it describes in vivid
detail the tableau the audience was to see when the shutters
parted:

> The Altar, strew'd with Flow'rs, was ready dress'd,
> And smoking Incense rose, in fragrant Curls,
> And *Hymen's* lambent Torches flam'd, serene,
> Silence, and Expectation's dreadful *Stillness,*
> Doubled the solemn Horror of the Scene!
> . . .
> The dreadful *Prince* [Eumenes] . . .
> Leapt, from the Altar, to the Tyrant's Breast—
> And plung'd the sacred *Axe* of Sacrifice,
> Snatch'd, like a Lightening's Flash! and reach'd his *Life.*
> —He fell—and o'er him while with pendant Eye
> Th' indignant Hero hung, the Arm new-rais'd,
> Base, from behind, pale *Erox* pierc'd his Side.
> —Red, in his mingled Blood, and raising Anger,
> He heard the *Crowd's protective Cry*—turn'd short,
> And buried in his Brow the rapid Steel.
> Then to the Altar's Height sublimely sprung,
> Stood, Monarch, all confess'd; and *wav'd* the Throng.
> Come, let me guide you to this Work of Heav'n.
> Hast, and partake it—fly—

The shutter then parted to reveal the Temple of Hymen,
"Eumenes discover'd on the Altar with the Axe of Sacrifice in his
Hand. Merope kneeling, Priest, Attendants and Guards." Hill's
letter indicates that part of this tableau was live, part was painted
on the wings and shutter. The altar was certainly a practical set-
piece: Eumenes was required to stand upon it, and the bodies of

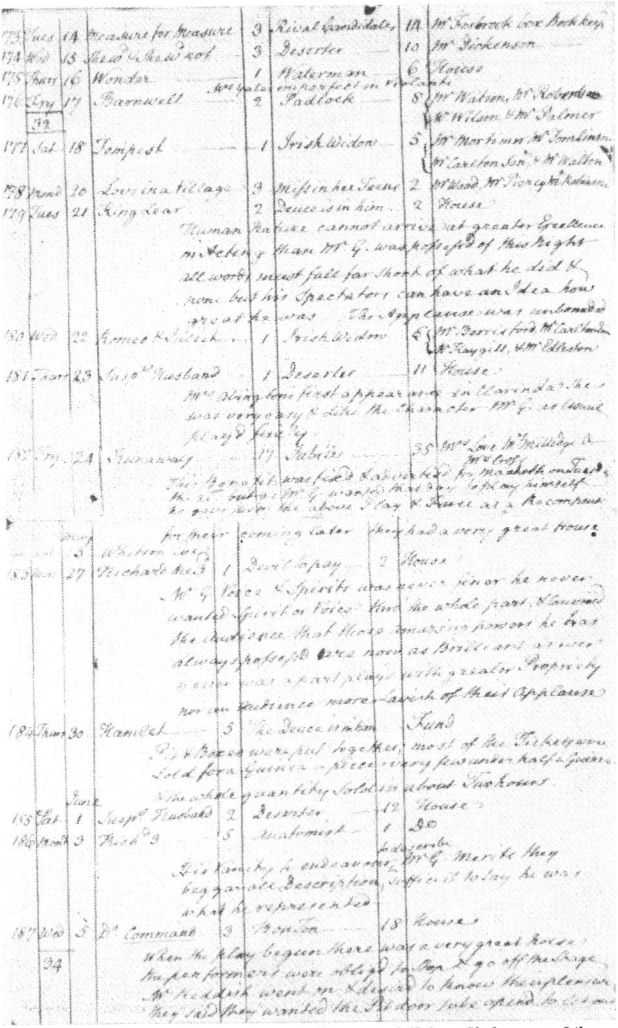

173 Tues 14 Measure for Measure 3 Rival Candidates 10 Mr Fosbrook box Bookkeep[er]
174 Wed 15 Know ... 3 Deserter 10 Mr Dickenson
175 Thurs 16 Wonder 1 Waterman 6 Houses
Mrs Yates imperfect in Violante
176 Fry 17 Barnwell 2 Padlock 8 Mr Watson, Mr Roberts / Mr Wilson & Mr Palmer
32
177 Sat 18 Tempest 1 Irish Widow 5 Mr Mortimer Mr Tomlinson / Mr Carleton Jun & Mr Walton
178 Mond 20 Love in a Village 3 Miss in her Teens 2 Mr Wood, Mr Pierce, Mr Robinson
179 Tues 21 King Lear 2 Deuce is in him 2 House
Human Nature cannot arrive at greater Excellence in Acting than Mr G. was possess'd of this Night all words must fall far short of what he did & none but his Spectators can have an Idea how great he was. The Applause was unbounded
180 Wed 22 Romeo & Juliet 1 Irish Widow 6 Mr Berrisford Mr Carleton / Mr Haygill, & Mr Eddleston
181 Thurs 23 Susp[icious] Husband 1 Deserter 11 House
Mrs Abington first appearance in Clarinda she was very easy & like the Character Mr G. as usual play'd finely
182 Fry 24 Runaway 17 Jubilee 35 Mrs Love Mr Milledge & Mr Cotts
This Benefit was fix'd & advertis'd for Macbeth on Tuesday the 21 but as Mr G wanted that day to play himself he gave them the above Play & Farce as a Recompence for their coming later they had a very great House.
May 3 Whitsun eve
183 Mon 27 Richard the 3 1 Devil to pay 2 House
Mr G Voice & Spirits was never finer he never wanted Spirit or Voice thro' the whole part, & convinced the Audience that those amazing powers he has always possess'd are now as Brilliant as ever never was a part play'd with greater Propriety nor an Audience more Lavish of their Applause
184 Thurs 30 Hamlet 5 The Deuce is in him Fund
Pit & Boxes were put together, most of the Tickets were sold for a Guinea a piece very few under half a Guinea & the whole quantity sold in about Two hours
June
185 Sat 1 Susp[icious] Husband 2 Deserter 12 House
186 Mond 3 Rich[ard] 3 5 Anatomist 1 Do
Tis Vanity to endeavour to describe Mr G. Merits they beggar all Description, suffice it to say he was what he represented
187 Wed 5 Dr Command 3 Bon Ton 18 House
34
When the play begun there was a very great Noise the performers were oblig'd to Stop & go off the Stage Mr Hopkins went on & desired to know their pleasure they said they wanted the Pit door to be open'd to let ...

Courtesy of Folger Shakespeare Library

PLATE 2. Drury Lane Diary—William Hopkins (May-June, 1776)

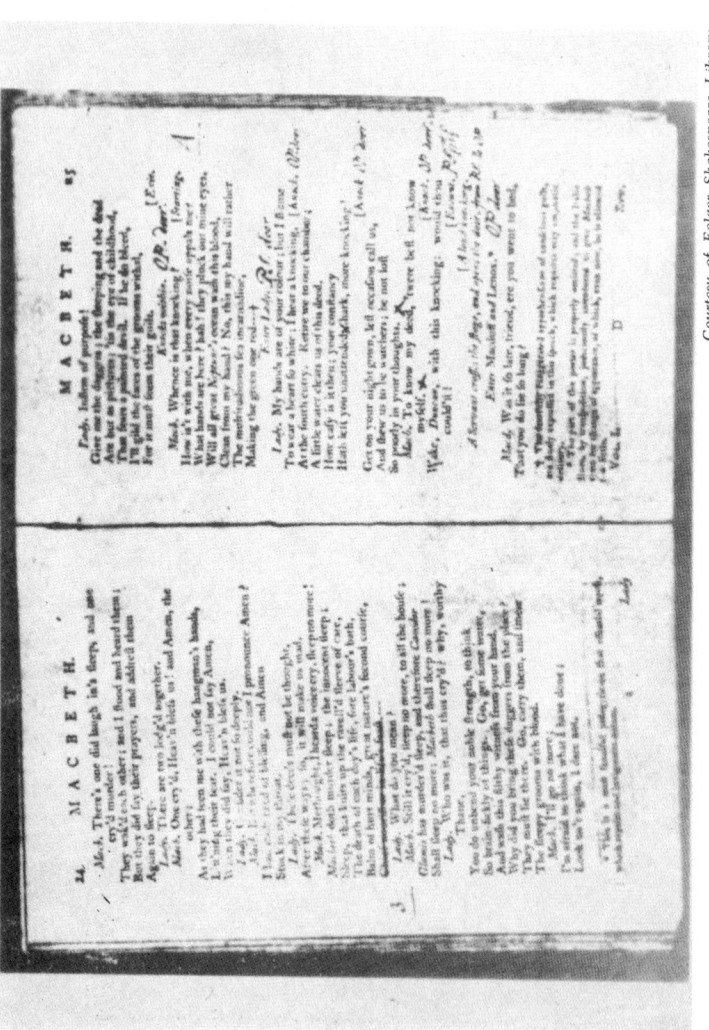

PLATE 3. Drury Lane Theatre Promptbook of *Macbeth* (Showing the cutting of the drunken porter)

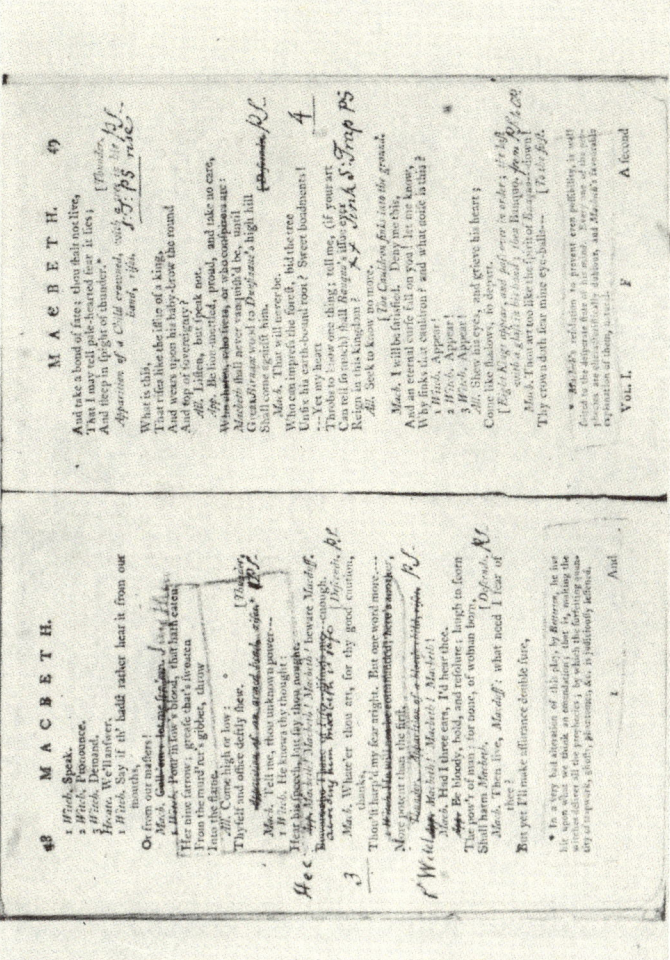

PLATE 4. Promptbook of *Macbeth* (Scene in the Witches' Cave)

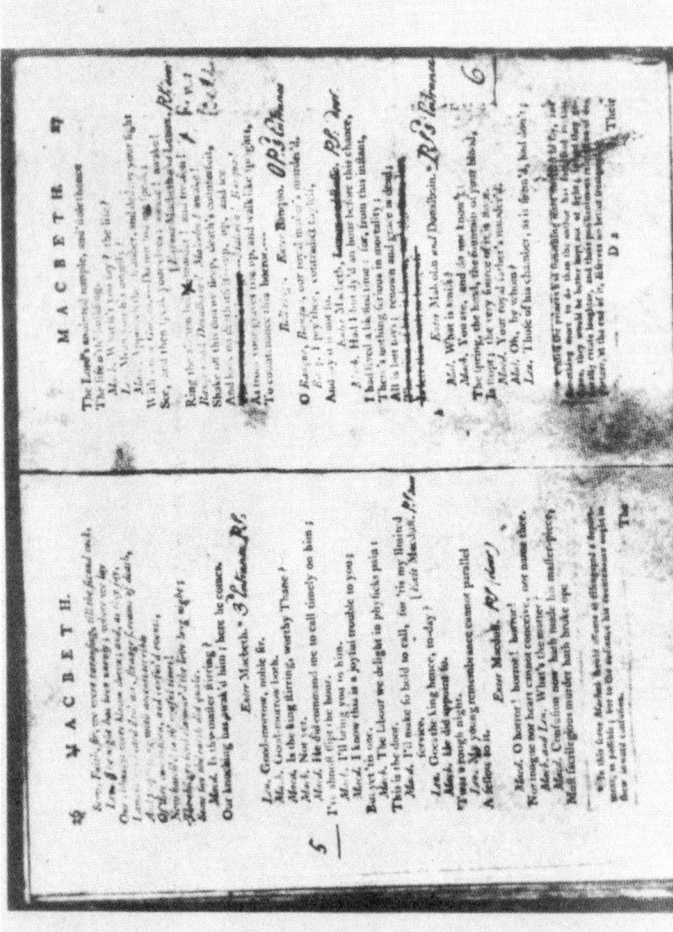

Courtesy of Folger Shakespeare Library

PLATE 5. Promptbook of *Macbeth* (Discovery of Duncan's murder)

PLATE 6. Garrick in the Witches' Cave—Engraving by Bannerman after Dawes, 1772

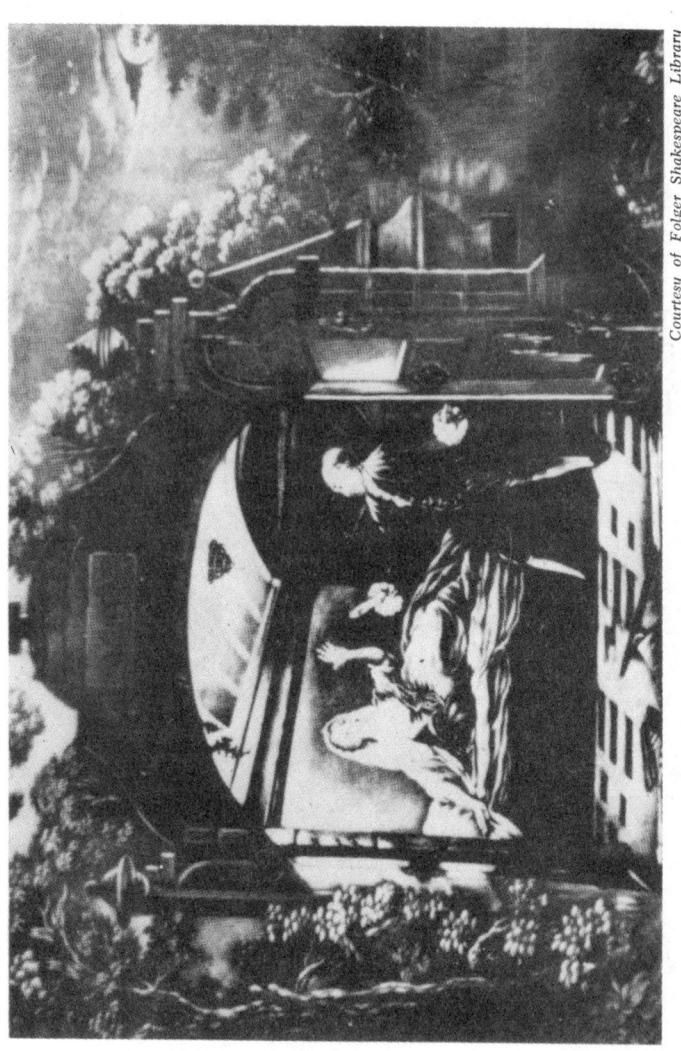

PLATE 7. Garrick and Mrs. Bellamy in *Romeo and Juliet*

PLATE 8. Barry and Miss Nossiter in *Romeo and Juliet*

PLATE 9. Henry Woodward as The Fine Gentleman in *Lethe*

PLATE 10. Lear in the Storm—Engraving by McArdell after Benjamin Wilson, 1762

PLATE 11. Francis Hayman's frontispiece to Othello—Jennens'
edition, 1771-1774

PLATE 12. Garrick as Hamlet—Engraving by McArdell after
Benjamin Wilson, 1754

PLATE 13. Barry in *King Lear* at the Haymarket Theatre—*The Universal Museum,*
Sept. 1767

PLATE 14. Stage of the Sunderland Theatre—frontispiece to *The Miscellaneous Poems of James Cawdell, Comedian* 1785

The London Theatre

Hamlet Act 3 Scene 7

Engraved for ÿ Universal Museum

PLATE 15. *Hamlet*, the play scene, *Universal Museum*, March 1769

PLATE 16. *Hamlet,* the closet scene, by Francis Hayman

PLATE 17. Frontispiece to *The Provok'd Wife*, 1753

PLATE 18. Francis Hayman's frontispiece to *King Lear*, engraving
by Ravenet, Charles Jennens' edition

PLATE 19. Scene from *The Roman Father*, Drury Lane

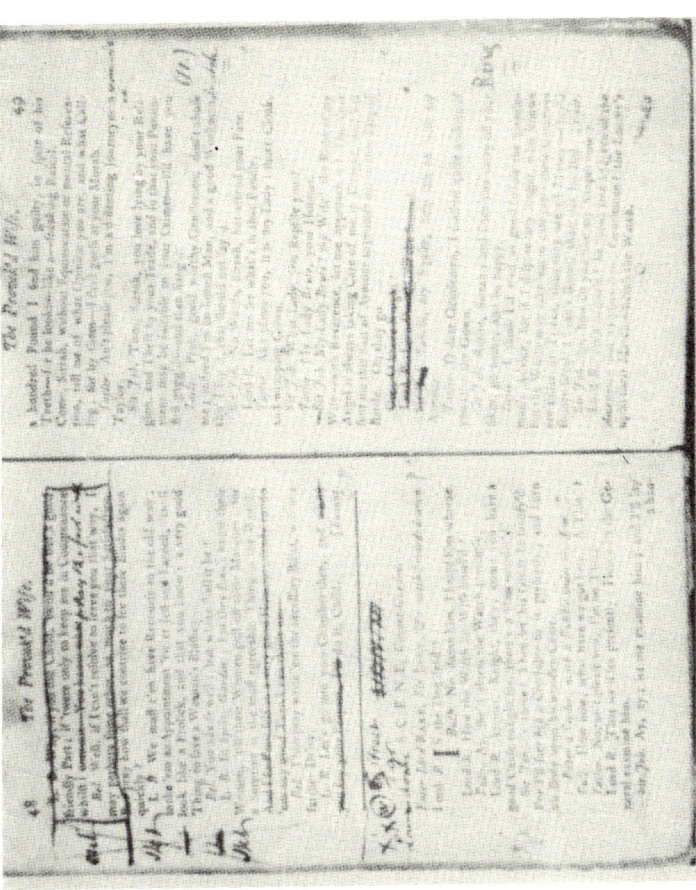

PLATE 20. Promptbook of *The Provok'd Wife*, Drury Lane

PLATE 21. Scene from *Every Man in His Humour*, Drury Lane

the tyrant and Erox were strewn about it. The problem exists with the placement of the crowd. The tortuous ambiguity of Hill's letter to Garrick may be deciphered as follows. The temple was represented by wings and shutter; some of the side wings depicted columns and painted people who seemed to stand between the columns. So skillfully were these wings to be painted that the people on them would scarcely be distinguishable from the real life in the forward area and around the altar.

The most interesting part of Hill's letter, however, is the unique mention of *slanted scenes*. Since the word *scene* at this time almost invariably referred to scenery components, it is clear, I think, that Hill was discussing obliquely positioned side wings. This letter must contain one of the earliest, if not the earliest reference to oblique wings in the English theatre, although their use had been rather popular with earlier Italian designers of the seventeenth century. Dr. Southern has already pointed out that Andrea Pozzo, in the first volume of his book on perspective (1692), consistently drew the side wings obliquely.[21] By the second volume, published in 1700, Pozzo acknowledged the alternative of the straight wing, which then became standard procedure for the eighteenth-century designers. About a decade later, in *L'Architettura Civile preparata sulla geometria e ridota alle prospettiva* (Parma, 1711), Ferdinando Bibiena described in chapter IV, operation 70, "how to design scenes on oblique frames, not parallel to the front of the stage." Bibiena's treatise has yet to be translated into English, but Pozzo's first volume was so rendered in 1707 by John James.[22] So for Hill to mention *slanted scenes* as late as 1749 is not revolutionary in itself, but since he writes about them in such a matter-of-fact manner perhaps this technique was more common in English staging than previously assumed.[23]

Another feature of maturing staging methods was the cultivation of a new flexibility in the placement of doors, arches, and other means of access to the stage. As long as the decorations had remained primarily a background for action, the two proscenium doors served nicely for most situations. (A good example is found in the 1773 Bell edition of *Coriolanus*: II, 1 is set in a "Wood," and we read, "Enter at one door Cominus, with the Romans: at the other door Martius with his arm in a scarf.") But as the action abetted by Garrick's new lighting techniques withdrew more and more into the frame of the proscenium, it was inevitable that more natural mediums for entrances would be required if the correctness of the illusion was to be maintained.

Indeed, fear of destroying the illusion had not prevented actors from entering between the wings, even if the doors were not present. Dramaticus (our informer in *Gentleman's Magazine*, October 1789) commented on how ridiculous it was "to behold the actors making their *entrees* and *exits* through plastered walls and wainscot panels." In Act III of Murphy's *The Apprentice* (January 2, 1756), for example, is found the direction, "Enter Watchmen from all Parts, some drunk, some coughing, &c." The various places of egress between the wings were designated according to their contiguous wing grooves: in the promptbooks are occasional references like "Enter 3 spirits 2ᵈ Ent. O P" (*Alfred* I. 7), "Exeunt Banquo and Fleance 3ᵈ Entᵉ O P" (*Macbeth* II.1), and "Enter Seyton OP—1st Wing" (*Macbeth* V. 3).

During Garrick's management, however, a new taste was developing in his audience for a decor that was both literal and romantic. Trees and rocks were to look like trees and rocks, and Charing Cross or Westminster Hall was to be seen on stage as a likely copy of the original.[24] Reviewing *The Institution of the Garter*, the *Town and Country Magazine* (October 1771) lamented that the painter had presented the stalls of St. George's Chapel as nearly straw color, rather than the deepest brown which they really were. So more and more capricious movements through wing intervals were being superseded by unmistakably practical doors set between the wings, which served to maintain the illusion of realistic interiors.[25] In the promptbook of *Jane Shore*, at the Folger Library, the symbols MDOP appear frequently (middle door opposite prompt side). Similarly, Macklin's rambling and often incoherent notes which he wrote in preparation for his ill-received production of *Macbeth* in 1773 direct that for the beginning of the dagger scene "Macbeth should enter m.d.P.S. or O.P.," implying obviously that he intended to have three doors on either side of the stage.[26]

Practical doors and open flats are also clearly evident on the backscenes during the Garrick period. There was that setting for *Fop's Fortune* used at Covent Garden from 1747 until at least 1790, described by Wilkinson as having "wings and flat, of Spanish figures at full length, and *two folding doors in the middle*."[27] In a review of *Cross-Purposes* at Covent Garden in 1772, the *Morning Chronicle* (December 8) while describing the action in the parlor scene reports, "Mr. *Grubb* and his wife then return at opposite doors . . . and a few minutes after Miss brings on Captain *Bevil*, through a door in the middle of the scene." That same season at Drury Lane found Arcas comforting Euphrasia during the first act of *The Grecian Daughter:*

> —I will unbar the dungeon,
> Unloose the chain that binds him to the rock
> And leave your interview without restraint.

Arcas then "opens a cell in the back scene," an action which discloses Evander on the floor of his dungeon. The prisoner "Rises and comes out." This action is an unmistakable parallel to Romeo's breaking open the Capulet tomb to reveal Juliet on her funeral bier; Wilson's painting, published in 1753, portraying Garrick and Mrs. Bellamy in the tomb scene of *Romeo and Juliet* certainly suggests that double doors on a shutter backscene were used in this play.[28] (plate 7)

Obvious variations of doors in the backscene were practical gates and arches, which appear with ever-increasing frequency on Garrick's stage. During Act II of *The Orphan of China* (1759) "Two large Folding-gates in the Back-scene are burst open by the Tartars, and then enter Timurkan, with his Train." The promptbook of *Zara* calls for "Gates W.W." (with wings) in the final act. A most interesting use of gates occurs in *Timon* (1771) where in Act V the scene changes "to the Walls of Athens." The senators on stage before the walls are directed to exit "in the gate" and in a moment after the sound of a parley they "appear upon the walls." The utilization of built-up set-pieces for stairways may also be noted in the final scene of this play, whose setting depicts "the prospect of a rude wild country, to a considerable extent, with the ruins of the temple of Faunus." During the action of the scene Timon "sinks down the steps of the temple, being supported in his fall by Evanthe and Flavius."[29]

Another play by Cumberland, *The Fashionable Lover* (DL, January 20, 1772) enlists a combination of arch and stairway setting which is suspiciously evocative by its modernity. The play opens in "A Hall in Lord Abberville's House, with a Staircase seen through an Arch." In the course of the action the ladies decide to pay their courtesies to Lady Caroline, who is "above stairs." Dr. Druid directs a servant to "show the Ladies up," while Mr. Bridgemore remarks "Ay, ay, go up and show your clothes. I'll chat with Dr. Druid here below." The direction in the text reads, "Exeunt Ladies"—and if the text may be trusted to reflect the actual action on the stage (remember our caution on such matters) the ladies retired back through the arch and up the stairs.

An open practical arch is evident in Hill's *The Fatal Vision* in 1716. Actually the employ of profile flats even in 1716 is not too startling. Jones and Webb used them frequently in the seventeenth century. How such a combination of scenic pieces was arranged on the stage may be gathered from the promptbook of *Alfred,* where the opening of the second act discovers "Lethe's open flat 3^d & 5 gr," indicating that the arch or profile flat was in the third groove and the backing piece in the fifth groove. Of course, the method, *sans* grooves, is still being used. From the notation in *Alfred* it is also clear that this scenic piece was a stock item, probably first built for use in Garrick's *Lethe,* a little play which Garrick had written as early as 1740 and which appeared in several revised versions throughout his management.

Although practical doors and arches were fairly common, windows presented somewhat more of a problem. For the most part, windows—as doors often were—were merely painted on the wings and shutter as part of the decor of the interior setting. If a character was required to appear in an upper window or balcony, as in *Romeo and Juliet,* the boxes over the proscenium doors served very well in most instances. An excellent example of the staging technique is demonstrated in the promptbook of *The Chances,* where Richard Cross's notation for the opening of Act IV reads, "Town. Sign of Bush." During the action the 1st Constantia enters into a tavern (O.P.) and presently appears above "at the window." Then the 2nd Constantia "Goes up to her mother," and she also looks out the window. Don John decides to join the party upstairs and as he moves to the entrance of the tavern on the stage level, the 2nd Constantia, having come down again, meets him at the door.

The specification of the "Sign of Bush" to be found in this scene on the exterior of the tavern suggests a fascinating sidelight which points to the use of realistic, topical, and recognizable locales. The oldest sign borrowed from the vegetable kingdom to be placed on inn signboards is the bush. Even today it remains a very general sign for inns and public-houses in England. However, the *Beggar's Bush* was a notorious house in Southwark during the seventeenth and eighteenth centuries, and since this tavern in *The Chances* is designated by another prompt marking as a "bagnio," the sign appears to have been used with special purpose.[30]

There seems to be little indication that anything but the proscenium boxes ever served as upper windows or balconies on

Garrick's stage, although perhaps practical windows were achieved in some built-up effects. Transparent or practical windows on the stage level, however, were certainly possible, being simply reduced variations of larger backscene profiles and transparencies. In November 1762, a correspondent identified only as "J.H." told Garrick about a new window technique which the manager undoubtedly was already aware of:

> A few Months ago I happened to be at one of ye Portuguese Theatres in Lisbon, where I saw a little Improvement in point of Scenery that had a pretty Effect. The Intention of it was to give a View of a number of Gallants passing before a Window of a Lady; for this purpose there was two Large Windows made in ye Scene in ye Venetian taste, & coverd with white Gauze, which besides its transparency & resemblance to Glass, has an air of elegance that the Latter can not come up to. There are likewise a number of cross Barrs in imitation of Casement, which is the fashion in those Countrys. I imagine this hint might be made use of in ye Last Scene of ye 2d Act of the Wonder; & if on that or any other occasion you find it of service, it will give me great pleasure.[31]

In Drury Lane's production of *King Arthur* (December 13, 1770) there was a gothic stained-glass window whose effect was achieved by lighting from behind. Horace Walpole was there: "This scene, which should be a barbarous temple of Woden, is a perfect cathedral, and the devil officiates at a kind of high mass. I never saw greater absurdities."[32]

IV

These new insights into eighteenth-century theatrical production methods offered especially by the Garrick promptbooks and correspondence must be judged as unequivocal as they are fascinating. The protracted but ever-increasing appearances of new staging procedures such as the act-curtain and practical stage openings and doors imply that the focus of action in Drury Lane's plays was gradually being removed from the forward apron-stage area and pushed farther back into the stage picture beyond the proscenium arch. Such a conclusion is substantiated by numerous revealing stage directions in the promptbooks and printed texts, some of which I have already presented in the course of this chapter. One especially illuminating prompt entry to be found at least once in *Zara* and many times in *Macbeth* is "enter from the top," signifying the rear of the stage. The same direction oc-

curs in the last act of *The Grecian Daughter*—Dionysius "Goes to
the top of the stage." According to James Messink's manuscript
"Order of the Pageant in the Jubilee," which describes that event
in the 1769-70 production at Drury Lane, all the various groups
made their entrances "P.S. at the Top." [33] Frequently, I suspect,
after such entries the actors continued in the tradition of advancing to what they considered a more advantageous position on the
forestage (for example in I. 4 of *Timon*, "Evanthe advances from
the backscene, attended by a train of Ladies") but as we shall
observe in our subsequent discussions of the individual plays, it
is quite certain that very much of the action, indeed more than
previously assumed, occurred within the proscenium frame in
areas where the newly developed techniques of both lighting and
scenery could be brought to bear with greatest advantage.

VI

Macbeth

ON JANUARY 7, 1744, at Drury Lane, under the stewardship of Garrick, Shakespeare's *Macbeth* was brought back to the theatre for the first time since the earliest days of the Restoration. Twenty-seven and not yet manager, Garrick was making his first essay at the title role. His reputation and talent being such, he was allowed complete directorial control over the venture. Garrick's portrayal of the Scottish tyrant attracted immediate and unparalleled acclaim, and subsequently was a most persuasive factor in making *Macbeth* the third most popular tragedy in Drury Lane's repertory during his career. The play was offered some 96 times in Garrick's version between 1744 and 1776; it was first played under Garrick-Lacy auspices on March 19, 1748. The following discussion attempts to convey a composite account of the tragedy as it was produced during Garrick's career.[1]

Garrick's announcement in January 1744 that his *Macbeth* was to be played "as written by Shakespeare" moved James Quin to ask, "Don't I play *Macbeth* as Shakespeare wrote it?" Indeed, Quin never did, for although the story received some 200 performances in the first 43 years of the century, it had always been presented in the adaptation by William Davenant which had so gratified Pepys in the 1660's by its divertissements.

Brief notice of some features of Davenant's version will emphasize the service Garrick performed by restoring most of the original. Described by Downes "as being in the nature of an Opera," which recompenced double the expenditures made by the managers of Dorset Garden on "its Finery, as new Cloath's, new Scenes, Machines, and flyings for the Witches," [2] Davenant's text barely manages to retain the structural threads of the original masterpiece. Davenant heightened the parts of Macduff and his wife, and included a triple prophecy to them on the heath to parallel the one received by Macbeth. Act I contains a new scene in which Lady Macbeth consoles Lady Macduff, who pines for her husband off at the wars. The dagger scene is considerably reduced, the Porter is omitted, Banquo and Macduff are slain offstage, and although Macbeth dies on stage, at the end his sword, not his head, is brought forth. The nature of Davenant's numerous verbal "improvements" may be judged by Macbeth's unhappy expiring line, "Farewell, vain world, and what's most vain in it, ambition."

When Garrick decided to restore the original text he consulted Warburton and Johnson concerning dubious and controversial passages in an effort to make his rendition as authoritative as possible. A comparison of Johnson's *Miscellaneous Observations on the Tragedy of Macbeth* (1745) with Garrick's acting version as published in the first volume of Bell's *Shakespeare* (1773) indicates Johnson's intimate association with Garrick in forming the text.[3] However honorable Garrick's intentions may have been, the suggestion that he truly restored Shakespeare's text must be accepted with some reservations. Thomas Davies gives the impression that a scene or two "not conducive to the action" had been deleted, while others had been pruned. [4] Actually Garrick cut about 269 lines from the text, and then added explanatory passages where he considered Shakespeare's meaning obscure. Decorum and propriety still prevented the inclusion of many passages which Davenant also had excluded. A more respectable servant was substituted for the drunken porter, most of the scene with Lady Macduff and her son, including their murders, was omitted, and eighty lines of Malcom's description of his own intemperance were eliminated as unsuitable for refined taste. Although there was less flying about than in Davenant's opera (all except Hecate were grounded) the witches still danced and sang several of Davenant's songs. Since Garrick excelled "in the expression of convulsive throes and dying agonies, and would not lose any opportunity that offered to shew his skill in that profession," he composed an ample dying speech for Macbeth.[5] But despite its omissions, additions, and a few alterations, it must be admitted that the core of greatness in Shakespeare's creation is to be found here. Dr. Stone considered Garrick's text on the whole "the most accurate stage version of a Shakespearian play which had appeared since 1671."[6]

II

Garrick was always sensitive to critical examination; consequently wits like Samuel Foote, aware of his fear of ridicule, lost few opportunities to attack him where he was most vulnerable. Realizing that his production of *Macbeth* promised to be different both in text and concept from anything previously seen, Garrick hoped to blunt possible attacks by writing a satirical pamphlet against his own intentions in advance of the opening. Published anonymously, this pamphlet is entitled *An Essay on Acting: in which will be consider'd the mimical behaviour of a certain faulty actor, and the laudableness of such unmannerly, as well as inhumane proceedings. To which will be added, A short criticism on his acting Macbeth* (London, 1744). The *Essay on Acting* represents some of Garrick's most delightful writing, and at the same time, if one can determine when the author is serious, offers some interesting insights into the production of *Macbeth*. Here Garrick assumes the role of a petulant critic who finds fault with almost everything about the projected *Macbeth*. Deriding his own small stature, he questions his own physical qualifications for assuming the role of the six-foot Scottish king. He decides he is suited neither externally nor internally for this character, but "could he *Speak* the *Part,* is well form'd for Fleance, or one of the *Infant Shadows* in the Cauldron Scene" (p. 14). Perhaps with this production Garrick first substituted the shorter tye-wig for the more tragical flows previously worn—"I shall leave it to the Consideration of the Publick, whether or no a *Tye Wig* is more eligible than a *Major,* or a *plain Hat,* than a lac'd one" (p. 15).[7] He criticizes his own eye movements and his gestures as too orderly and immoveable, and then proposes a preposterous manner of playing the dagger scene, designed to satirize Quin's ridiculous clutching and convulsive actions:

> Now in this visionary Horror, he should not rivet his Eyes to an *imaginary* Object, as if it *really* was there, but should shew an *unsettled Motion* in his Eye, like one not quite awak'd from some disordering Dream; his *Hands and Fingers* should not be *immoveable,* but restless, and endeavouring to dispense the Cloud that overshad-

ows his optick Ray, and bedims his Intellects . . . *Come let me clutch thee!* is not to be done by *one* Motion only, but by several *successive Catches* at it, first with one Hand, and then with the other, preserving the same Motion, at the same Time, with his Feet, like a Man, who out of his Depth, and half drowned in his struggles, *catches* at *Air* for *Substance:* This would make the Spectator's Blood run cold.[8]

In his discussion of the banquet, Garrick offers his opinion of those directors—like the one at Covent Garden—who would litter the stage with the impressively realistic accoutrements of a royal feast, yet lose in this grandeur the dramatic purpose of the action. Criticising the meanness of his own banquet, which is to be "compos'd of a few *Apples, Oranges,* and such like *Trash,*" he ironically pronounces that such a regal meal should have "*hot* costly *Viands,* and large Pyramids of *wet Sweetmeats,* and *Savoy Biscuits;* this would cast an inconceiveable Grandeur upon the Scene, and add greatly to the Horror of the Ghost" (p. 21).

He then sets his sights upon those critics who would damn an entire production because of some few insignificant breaches of decorum. At the banquet, for example, the ghost of Banquo "ought to rise in a *Red Cloak,* as he was seen to cross the stage in one, immediately before his Murder; this would throw a great solemnity upon the Figure of Banquo, and preserve the Decorum of the Stage" (p. 20). But the most exquisite cut of all is the criticism of some details in the scene following the murder of Duncan: "the *Daggers* are near an Inch and half too long, in Proportion to the Height of the Murderer. The Nightgown, he appears in, after the Murder, ought to be a *Red Damask,* and not the frippery-flower'd one of a Foppington; but when Taste is wanting in *Trifles,* and *Judgment* in *Essentials,* how can we hope to see the *THEATRE* flourish?" (p. 18).

How well Garrick succeeded in thwarting his attackers perhaps may be judged by the general lack of carping criticism. When he was called to task for his acting of Macbeth over the years such criticisms usually assumed the guise of constructive suggestions which were softened by flattery. For example, after just witnessing a performance of *Macbeth*—"a play in which the unlimited genius of Mr. Garrick seems to have found scope for entire exertion"—the anonymous "H. H." wrote on January 22, 1762, congratulating him on his excellence in the scene with Lady Macbeth before the murder, the dagger scene, and the scene in which the murder is discovered. The correspondent nevertheless

was obliged to present a long list of line readings, with suggestions for proper emphasis. In the air-drawn dagger speech, he
observed, "you lay a prodigious emphasis on *was* in this line,
      And such an instrument I was to use.
which I do not see the reason of, and rather think that *use* is the
word to be marked" (*Private Correspondence,* I, 132). In his
diplomatic reply, Garrick agreed in some points, disagreed in
others, and on the proper emphasis of the line just quoted he
compromised: "I think, Sir, that both the words *was* and *use*
should be equally, though slightly impressed as I have marked
them: and if you will please consider the passage, you will find
they are both emphatical" (*Private Correspondence,* I, 135).[9]

Generally, however, Garrick was accorded another triumph
with *Macbeth*. Francis Gentleman's introduction to the play in
the Bell edition reflects the typical approbations:

> We should deem ourselves ungrateful to Mr. Garrick's unparalled
> merit, if we did not here remark that he sustains the importance,
> marks the strong feelings, and illustrates the author's powerful
> ideas, with such natural, animated, forcible propriety, that the
> dullest heart must receive impressions from him, which the clearest
> head cannot adequately express.

Gentleman, of course, seldom had anything unfavorable to report
about Garrick, and the above statement, in one form or another,
seems to preface every play he edited. Yet other gentlemen with
more important matters on their minds also found time to praise
Garrick's Macbeth, among them William Pitt, who wrote to a
friend after viewing a command performance, "Inimitable Shakespeare! but more matchless Garrick! always as deep in Nature as
the Poet, but never (what the Poet is too often) out of it" (*Private Correspondence,* II, 364).

Of the other performers who filled out the cast of *Macbeth*
little can be recorded other than their names, with the exception
of Mrs. Pritchard whose portrayal of Lady Macbeth stood as a
peerless model for the age.[10] According to Gentleman, in the
Dramatic Censor (I, 111), Ryan and Havard had done "great
justice" in the role of Macduff, but Reddish, whose feelings were
"manly, yet tender," was superior to all. Similarly Gentleman
regarded Ross's playing of Banquo "the most striking, picturesque
appearance we have seen." [11]

III

The promptbook of *Macbeth* now at the Folger Library, attributed to Garrick's management, is an illuminating but often puzzling playhouse document.[12] Made on a 1773 Bell edition of the play, it had been worked over by two distinctly different hands. In the first hand, that of William Hopkins, are stage directions, cuts, and some emendations, in ink. The later and unidentified hand in red crayon has cut some additional passages and restored some of those originally eliminated by Hopkins. By 1773 when the Bell edition on which the promptbook is made was published, Garrick had long since given up the part of Macbeth, having played it for the last time on September 22, 1768.[13] Between his giving up the role in 1768 and his retirement in 1776, *Macbeth* was played at Drury Lane only 10 times; 5 of these performances occurred after the publication of the text on which the prompt copy in question was fashioned. After Garrick's retirement, his prompter William Hopkins continued in his position until his death in 1780, in which interval *Macbeth* was played 12 more times. It is then possible that this Folger promptbook may not represent a playhouse copy in use during Garrick's management. Actually there seem to be only three possibilities: the promptbook represents a transcription made by Hopkins in 1773 or later of an earlier promptbook which had worn out with use; it is a promptbook made anew after 1773 for the remaining productions under Garrick's management, and perhaps used later as well; or it is a playhouse copy made by Hopkins after Garrick's retirement. Significant are the facts that only the hand of Hopkins—Drury Lane's prompter from 1760—has made the entries for stage directions and scene changes, and that the text itself is Garrick's acting version. In addition, the promptbook as a Drury Lane document reflects many aspects of traditional Garrick staging which can be corroborated from other sources. For these reasons I suspect it is safe enough to assume that in deciding upon any of the three possibilities above we shall not be far off in the total impression received. (plates 4 and 5)

In the discussion which follows I shall be dealing with two different but generally complementary sets of stage directions: those printed in the Bell edition ("as regulated by the Prompter") and those entered in ink by Hopkins. For the convenience of recognizable differentiation between them, I have italicized all of the prompter's manuscript entries and put the printed directions in regular type, never italicized, regardless of what form either originally appears in. This procedure will be followed in all subsequent discussions of promptbooks in this book.

ACT I. The tragedy of *Macbeth* first unfolds on Garrick's stage, as it nearly always has, with the Weird Sisters meeting to decide when the hurly-burly will be done. The scene is "an open Place," set according to the prompter's entry at the "*1st Grove.*" The stage is "*Dark*" and there is "Thunder and Lightning."

The only additional prompt notation made in this short twelve-line scene is a sound cue—"*Owl within*"—where the text reads, "Padocke calls within." There is no indication how the witches effected their entrance (text: "Enter three Witches") although traditionally they rose up through the traps. This is the method by which they disappear in the Bell text: "Thunder. The Witches sink." Commenting editorially, Francis Gentleman found an impropriety in the witches sinking under the stage after just having pronounced.

> Fair is foul, and foul is fair
> Hover through the fog and filthy air.

Garrick broke with staging tradition here by keeping his witches on the ground. In Davenant's version they "Ex. flying," and similarly in Rowe's edition (1709) they "rise from the stage and fly away."

In his editorial annotation Francis Gentleman advised that the expression of the witches "should be outrè, their appearance as far as decorum will admit, hagged and squalid." Garrick's witches usually wore blue-checked aprons, torn mobs upon their heads, topped with high crowned black hats, thus giving them an appearance more like basket women and trulls than creatures of enchantment. Traditionally played by men, they were always represented in what Walpole termed "a buffoon light . . . which must make the people not consider them as beings endowed with supernatural powers." [14] According to Richard Aldsworth, a minor skillful politician of the period whose chief enterprise was the producing of plays and pantomimes for an English diplomatic colony in Geneva, Garrick had once approved the idea of converting the burlesque characters and their birch brooms into magicians with long beards and black gowns, an alteration he thought designed to produce awe and horror, but which he dared not carry into execution "for fear of offending the Gallery." [15]

After the sinking of the witches the scene then changes to a palace at Foris; although the promptbook provides no stage location, the scene was probably played on the apron. In Gentleman's editorial opinion King Duncan, "having nothing of consequence to say or act, if he looks like a monarch, on the stage, may do well enough."

To the accompaniment of more thunder, the witches appear again, upon the heath, for scene 3 set in the "*1st Grove.*" The Bell text has them "rise from under the stage," but Hopkins has crossed out this direction and substituted instead "*OP & PS.*"[16] According to the promptbook Macbeth and Banquo enter with their soldiers "*from the top,*" or upstage area, to the tune of a "*Scotch March.*" We learn elsewhere, however, that Garrick's army did not actually appear on the stage for this scene. In an open letter addressed to Garrick in *St. James's Chronicle,* October 28-30, 1773, which compares Garrick's traditional business with the recent staging of the play by Macklin at Covent Garden, the writer complains of Macklin's stage arrangement in this scene on the heath:

> The advanced Guards of the Army ought to have remained . . . without the Door; and not to have been placed between *Macbeth, Banquo,* and the *Weird Sisters.* I have always regarded the spurious Line with which hitherto you have begun your Part [i.e. Garrick], as an Apology for the Non-appearance of the Soldiers: Macklin spoke the same Line, but his Army followed within Sight.

Garrick had retained Davenant's reading, "Command they make a halt upon the heath!" His business in the scene became traditional, despite Macklin, and in *Macbeth* productions in the nineteenth century the command "Halt, halt, halt," could still be heard off-stage as it was supposedly passed down the ranks.[17]

At the termination of the prophecies there was more "*Thunder,*" and the witches vanished, "*OP.*" In this first encounter with the spirits, we are told by the *Universal Museum* (January 1762) that Garrick, as he revealed "the traits of ambition opening in his mind by degrees . . . was peculiarly natural and great." After the subsequent entrance of Ross and Angus ("*OP*") who now hail the new Thane of Cawdor, everyone withdraws back "*to the top,*" again to the "*Scotch March.*"

Several scenes of little note may be passed over until scene 7 of this first act, the arrival of Duncan at Macbeth's pleasant site. We read: "Scene before Macbeth's Castle-gate." To the accompaniment of a flourish the king enters from the stage right *("OP")* with his two sons, Banquo, Lenox, Macduff, and other attendants. The prompt notation indicates that practical gates were here set in the backscene—*"Castle Gate open"*—and in a moment Lady Macbeth enters through them *("top")* to greet the royal entourage. They all proceed back through the gates as a front scene closes in the *"2d Grove"* to present a *"chamber"* within the castle. Macbeth entering *"OP"* delivers the "If it were done" soliloquy. He is later joined by his wife *("OP")* who urges the bloody deed upon him, and as they both leave the room *("OP")*, determined in their course, the act concludes.

ACT II. In the long scene which opens Act II—consisting of the dagger soliloquy, the after-murder dialogue, and the discovery of the deed—the prompt notations are exceedingly informative, although not always easy to follow.

One of the characteristics of Hopkins' directions in this scene is that when the proscenium doors are to be used, they are generally specifically identified *"OP Door"* or *"PS Door."* Sometimes, however, only *"OP"* or *"PS"* is marked, though it is clear from the action that the proscenium doors are intended.

Other places of egress are delineated *"3d Ent.ᵉ OP," "PS 3d Entrance,"* and *"PS 1st E."* [18]

From the circumstances of the action and the prompter's notations the stage plan may be reconstructed as follows: The setting is "a Hall in Macbeth's Castle," designated by the prompter as *"Palace."* The remainder of Hopkins' notation reads, *"Table on. 2 Candles. ready a Torch."* On the prompt side, stage-left, are found three entrances: the proscenium door *(PS Door)*, which leads to Duncan's chamber; an entrance above that labeled *"PS 1st E,"* which leads to Macbeth's and Lady Macbeth's bedchamber; and yet a third entrance above that, designated *"3d Ent. PS,"* which leads to the chamber shared by Malcom and Donalbain. On the stage right side *(OPS)* are found two more entrances: the *"OP Door"* leading to the more public areas of the castle, and through which anyone entering from the outside must pass; and an entrance set above that, designated *"OP 3d Entrance,"* which leads to the bedchamber shared by Banquo and Fleance. The groundplan must have looked something like this:

Backscene

3rd Ent. OP

3rd Ent. PS
3rd Wing
2nd Wing
PS 1st Ent.
1st Wing

(Right) OP Door

PS Door (Left)

Proscenium
Apron

The action begins in simulated stage darkness as Banquo
and Fleance enter from Duncan's chamber at the "PS Door."
Fleance carries the torch which has been listed as a property by
the prompter at the heading of this scene. In a few moments
Macbeth and a servant with a light ("2 Candles") appear "OP
[Door];" they all chat awhile, Macbeth wishes his guests good
repose, and Banquo and Fleance leave for their bedchamber "3
Ent.ᵉ OP." Immediately Macbeth orders his servant

> Go, bid thy mistress, when my drink is ready,
> She strike upon the bell. Get thee to bed.

and the servant exits back out the "OP:Door" to deliver the mes-
sage. (Macklin implies that the traditional staging was for the
servant to take both candles off with him, leaving Macbeth in
the dark—"a breach of manners even to absurdity.")[19]

Certain stage business of this first sequence of events with
Banquo and Fleance is recorded in an undated letter to Garrick
from Arthur Murphy. Although Murphy regarded the performance as "greatly superior to your former outdoings," he was
obliged to call Garrick's attention to several instances where the
actor seemed "not to have executed so happily as before." One
example is the short conversation with Banquo just prior to the
dagger scene, which Murphy found too "disengaged, too free,
and too much at ease." Why had not Garrick played this bit as
he usually had, with considerably more apprehension, forced
gaiety, and frequent furtive looks toward the door beyond which
slept the unsuspecting king? After bidding his visitors goodnight,
usually he reposed a while, eye fixed on the door, and in a broken
tone dismissed his servant (*Private Correspondence*, II, 363).

The dagger soliloquy, which immediately follows in the action, was a climactic acting moment for Garrick. "The sudden
start on seeing the dagger in the air,—the endeavour of the actor
to seize it,—the disappointment—the suggestion of its being only

a vision of the disturbed fancy,—the seeing it still in form most palpable, with the reasoning upon it,—these are difficulties," Davies relates, "which the mind of Garrick was capable of encountering and subduing." [20] So legendary did his rendition of the soliloquy become that while on the grand tour he was frequently requested to perform it for a distinguished assembly. *Sans* costume and all other externals which may credit an actor, Garrick would oblige. Although his words were seldom understood, his face, body, and vocal tones so vividly portrayed every sentiment and passion that his audiences on these occasions "beheld him with astonishment." [21]

At the conclusion of the dagger speech, the bell inviting Macbeth to murder rings *"OP"* and he exits out the *"PS Door"* into Duncan's chamber. Lady Macbeth now appears for the first time in the scene *("OP")* to wait for her husband's return to the stage. Their assignation at this point, now that the deed was done, afforded Garrick and Mrs. Pritchard the opportunity to display their manifold talents. When Garrick returned from the murder he presented the very epitome of mortal fear—"he looked like a ghastly spectacle, and his complexion grew whiter every moment." [22] How Garrick accomplished this amazing feat of blenching is difficult to say, but it appears to have been one of his favorite tricks. The practical *Connoisseur*, September 1, 1754, suggests he simply wiped the make-up from his face before entering. His wig was awry and one of the tyes to it undone. The *Connoisseur* labels this arrangement ridiculous: "The player would have us imagine that the same deed, which has thrown all that horror and confusion into his countenance, has also untwisted one of the tails of his periwig." The first time that he played the role, he entered upon the stage with his coat and waistcoat unbuttoned, a fortunate stroke of discomposure which "added greatly to the resemblance of nature in that part of his character." [23] For some reason, Garrick never again resorted to this disarray of costume.

Davies describes the mood of tremulous horror which Garrick and Mrs. Pritchard created at this moment:

> The representation of this terrible part of the play, by Garrick and Mrs. Pritchard, can no more be described than I believe it can be equalled. I will not separate these performers, for the merits of both were transcendent. His distraction of mind and agonizing horrors were finely contrasted by her seeming apathy, tranquillity, and confidence. The beginning of the scene . . . was conducted in ter-

rifying whispers. Their looks and actions supplied the place of words. You heard what they spoke, but you learned more from the agitation of the mind displayed in their action and deportment. . . . The dark colouring given by the actor to these abrupt speeches, makes the scene awful and tremendous to the auditors. The wonderful expression of heartful terror, which Garrick felt when he shewed his bloody hands, can only be conceived and described by those who saw him! [24]

The awesome moment has been recorded in a well-known mezzotint by Green, after Zoffany, dated 1775. Garrick stands in a frozen but studied posture of fear, with his feet set in ballet-like position, and his expressive hands thrown out in front. He wears the traditional Windsor uniform, a scarlet coat, a waistcoat laced with silver, a wig and breeches of eighteenth-century cut. Mrs. Pritchard, similarly clad in fine contemporary garb, with daggers in hand, is starting out the double-paneled door which allows light to be shed into an otherwise darkened gothic palace hall. The illustration bears some theatrical validity. The large window in the backscene, backed by a moonlit sky, would offer no technical problem, nor would the double doors shown down stage-right.

Upon Lady Macbeth's return from Duncan's chamber where she has planted the daggers, the knocks commence at the "OP Door" down-right. Husband and wife, partners in murder, now retire to their chamber—"PS 1st E"—where, they delude themselves, a little water will clear them of their deed. The knocking persisting, "A Servant crosses the Stage, and opens the door" to admit Macduff and Lenox. The prompt notation advises that the servant crosses "From PS to OP," and at this point we seem to have run out of logical entrances. He hardly comes from "PS 1st E" through which Macbeth and his wife have just exited. If he comes from the door above, the "3d Entrance PS," it would seem that his entrance would be so marked. Unless our prompter has been less than accurate in his task, we must take him at his word and accept the fact that the servant enters from the down-left proscenium door which has been designated quite clearly throughout this scene as Duncan's chamber. Why he does is inexplicable.

The mention of the servant at this point in the action reveals of course the omission of the porter at the gate. "To what end Shakespeare could introduce so incongruous a character as the porter . . . we believe no mortal can tell," wrote Gentleman in comment typical of eighteenth-century reaction to the porter; "At such an interesting period to turn the most serious feelings into laughter, or rather into distaste, by a string of strained quibbles is an insult upon judgment, and must fill the imagination with chaos of idea." [25] As a result of the deletion Garrick found it necessary to insert nine lines of his own in order to allow Macbeth some time to change—very rapidly indeed—from the fine dress of an eighteenth-century court gentleman into a costume more suitable for a man who was supposed to be sleeping all night. When he does return to meet Macduff and Lenox he enters, according to the prompt notation which may be an error, not from his own chamber "*PS 1st E,*" as would be expected, but from the egress above, "*3d Entrance PS.*" With our stage plan in mind, we are allowed to follow the subsequent action quite easily as the principals converge upon the stage (plate 3):

MACDUFF.   Is the king stirring, worthy Thane?
MACBETH.   Not yet.
MACDUFF.   He did command me to call timely on him; I've
almost slipt the hour . . .
MACBETH.   . . . This is the door.
MACDUFF.   I'll make so bold to call, for 'tis my limited service.
[Exit Macduff. *PS Door*

He discovers the murder and returns

Enter Macduff. *PS Door*

MACDUFF.   O horror! horror! horror!
Nor tongue nor heart cannot conceive, nor name thee . . .
Confusion now hath made his master-piece,
Most sacrilegious murder hath broke ope
The Lord's appointed temple, and stole thence
The life o' th' building.
MACBETH.   What is't you say? the life?
LENOX.   Mean you his majesty?
MACDUFF.   Approach the chamber, and destroy your sight
With a new Gorgon—Do not bid me speak;
See, and then speak yourselves: awake! awake!
[Exeunt Macbeth and Lenox.
PS Door
Ring the alarum bell—murder! and treason!
Banquo and Donalbane! Malcolm! awake!
Bell rings. Enter Banquo. *OP 3d Entrance*
O Banquo, Banquo, our royal master's murdered.
BANQUO.   I pry'thee, contradict thyself,
And say it is not so.
Enter Macbeth, Lenox, and Rosse.
PS Door

MACBETH. Had I but dy'd an hour before this chance,
I had lived a blessed time; for, from this instant,
There's nothing serious in mortality . . .

Enter Malcolm and Donalbain.
PS 3rd Entrance

and all the characters are now on stage.

During the business attending the discovery of the murder, Garrick, "struggling to assume the appearance of innocence and deep concern," dared not meet the eye of any one on stage. The rest walked up and down in grief. But Macduff and the sons of Duncan, by their looks, appeared to point out Macbeth as the murderer.[26]

Traditionally, Lady Macbeth did not reappear for her fainting bit in this scene. Davies relates an earlier eighteenth-century production in which she did enter as the original specifies, only to be hooted off by the upper gallery. Although Garrick had once made a brave attempt to restore the entrance, not even Mrs. Pritchard, favorite that she was, could carry it off successfully. It was Macklin's opinion that only Mrs. Porter—Mrs. Pritchard's predecessor—could have sufficient control over an audience "to induce them to endure the hypocrisy of such a scene."[27] Probably the real reason the omission persisted, however, was that Lady Macbeth was too occupied with dressing for her regal appearance as queen.[28]

The promptbook concludes its fascinating account of this scene with *"Exeunt severally."*

The prompt entries in the last scene of this act and the first four scenes of the third act reveal nothing of special interest except the traditional employment of the proscenium doors in alternating sequence.

The Banquet. For the fifth scene of Act III the setting "Changes to a room of state in the castle. A banquet prepar'd." Although the Bell text indicates all the banquet participants enter to the flourish of trumpets, the prompt notation—*"Palace. Throne. 5 Chairs. Banquet on. Trap* ready"—and the omission of any prompt direction for a grand entrance suggests the scene was discovered, with all in place. Accommodations at the banquet table are provided for six characters: Macbeth, his wife, Rosse, Lenox, and two other lords—a rather meagre company for such an affair. There is no reference in the promptbook to the seating arrangement, or to the number and positions of the attendants. In his *Essay on Acting*, it will be recalled, Garrick had poked fun at the "few *Apples, Oranges,* and such like *Trash*" which would characterize the meanness of his feast. Although his table did not approach the magnificence of Macklin's, John Powell's testimony in "Tit for Tat" indicates that some expenditure was allotted to Drury Lane's version—"The play of Macbeth, requires more incidents, than a Common Play, such as Wine and Fruit made use of in the Banqueting Scene; also Spirits of Wine for the Cauldron . . . Rosin for Lightening." [29]

Macbeth's conversation with the first murderer occurs aside, down at the *"OP Door."* So intense was Garrick's acting here, as legend has it, that when he said to the murderer, "There's blood upon thy face," the startled actor (perhaps an extra) put up his hand and blurted, "Is there by God!" However effective the acting may have been, the *Dramatic Censor* (I, 94) could only wish that decorum "had not suffered such a ragamuffin's entrance to a room of state, amidst the whole court." Hippisley, sometime Murderer at Covent Garden between 1733 and 1741, used to appear with chalked-white face, large whiskers, and a long black hat.[30] The "damnable faces" made by the mugging actor usually were anticipated by the gallery as moments of comic relief in the otherwise tragic decorum.

After the murderer's exit, Macbeth starts back to his throne. Meanwhile "the Ghost of Banquo rises, and sits in Macbeth's place." Two prompt markings at this point *("Rise Trap OP,"* and *"OP 1st W")* make it clear that the ghost's entrance is effected on a rising trap found near the first OP wing.

There was some contemporary opinion that the actual appearance of the ghost was a rude device, and that Banquo's image should be seen only in Macbeth's imagination. What offended Robert Lloyd most, for example, was the slip-door and the slowly rising ghost:

> Why need the Ghost usurp the Monarch's Place,
> To frighten Children with his mealy Face?
> The King alone should form the Phantom there,
> And talk and tremble at the vacant Chair.[31]

A similar complaint was registered by Bonnell Thornton, who would confine all ghosts except that in *Hamlet* beneath the traps —"Their mealy faces, white shirts, and red rags stuck on in imitation of blood, are rather objects of ridicule than terror." The ghost, it was argued, was really as much a figment of Macbeth's imagination as the airy dagger, which as yet had not made its appearance on a wire over the distracted head of Macbeth. "At present I am sure by far," concluded Thornton, "the greatest part of the audience is chiefly taken up in contemplating the odd figure of Macduff *[sic]* and marking the opening and closing of the trap-doors." [32]

Despite the corporeal embodiment of the ghost, Garrick and Mrs. Pritchard managed to make the spectre's appearance memorable:

> The admirable scene was greatly supported by the speaking terrors of Garrick's look and action. Mrs. Pritchard shewed admirable art in endeavouring to hide Macbeth's frenzy from the observation of the guests, by drawing their attention to conviviality. She smiled on one, whispered to another, and distantly saluted a third; in short, she practiced every possible artifice to hide the transaction that passed between her husband and the vision his disturbed imagination had raised. Her reproving and angry looks, which glanced towards Macbeth, at the same time were mixed with marks of inward vexation and uneasiness. When, at last as if unable to support her feelings any longer, she rose from her seat, and seized his arm, and, with a half-whisper of terror, said, "Are you a man!" she assumed a look of such anger, indignation, and contempt as cannot be surpassed. [33]

The ghost vanishes on the lines

> If charnel houses and our graves must send
> Those that we bury, back, our monuments
> Shall be the maws of kites.—

[The Ghost vanishes. *Sink T:OP*]

but he rises again after Macbeth's toast. In 1762, Mr. H. H. criticized Garrick's reactions to the second appearance of the ghost. "You recollect a degree of resolution, and advancing upon the Ghost, pronounce the passage ['Be live again, And dare me to desart with thy sword'] in a firm tone of voice. I apprehend the whole situation supposes a fixed immoveable attitude of horror and amazement." In his reply Garrick politely but firmly disagreed with his correspondent's notions, stating that by the second appearance of the spectre Macbeth has gained strength. Either the critic saw incorrectly or Garrick did not realize exactly how he was playing the scene, for in answer to the criticism of advancing on the ghost during these lines, Garrick asserted, "I never advance an inch, for, notwithstanding my agitation, my feet are immoveable" (*Private Correspondence*, I, 132-135). Perhaps by 1762 Garrick had altered his manner of playing this sequence. An earlier correspondent (he was beset by them) saw the play shortly after the opening in 1744. Expressing the opinion that this scene was acted "to very little advantage," he politely takes Garrick to task for interpreting the action in exactly the manner that the later critic of 1762 wishes he would. This earlier critic, however, allows that Garrick was not alone responsible for the poor effect of the scene. Drury Lane's Banquo (Havard in 1744) performed his part "very poorly," especially in the excessively slow retreat at the close where the motions were preposterous and unnatural. The anonymous writer suggests that Macbeth should have followed Banquo step for step: "I remember to have seen it acted in that manner, and it had a very good effect" (*Private Correspondence*, I, 20). On the line, "Hence horrible shadow, away," it had been customary for previous actors to draw their swords and bully Banquo off.[34] Garrick had ridiculed the tradition in his *Essay on Acting*, and although H. H.'s observations imply Garrick may on occasion have indulged in this business himself, for the most part he stood transfixed.

Banquo made his retreat walking backwards, returning not to the trap area OP from which he had risen for both his entrances, but rather vanishing somewhere between the wings promptside ("The Ghost vanishes. *PS*"). This business in one instance at least was cause of great mirth for the audience, when "the Ghost of Banquo . . . fell upon his Rump, to the great Surprise and Astonishment of Macbeth, and all his Train."[35]

Garrick's *Essay on Acting* elucidates one more piece of business which probably dates back to the original staging of the banquet scene at Shakespeare's Globe. On the second coming of the ghost, the glass of wine in Macbeth's hand, Garrick writes, "should not be dash'd upon the Ground, but it should fall *gently* from him, and he should not discover the least Consciousness of having such a Vehicle in his Hand." Witness now the lines in the last act of Beaumont's *Knight of the Burning Pestle* which almost certainly parody the situation in Shakespeare's play. Disguised as a ghost Rafe threatens Jasper:

> When thou are at thy table with thy friends,
> Merry in heart, and 'fild with swelling wine,
> I'll come in midst of all thy pride and mirth,
> Invisible to all men but thy self,
> And whisper such a sad tale in thy ear,
> Shall make thee let the cup fall from thy hand,
> And stand as mute and pale as death it self.

When all have departed from the banquet hall, the "Scene changes to the Heath" *(1st Grove)* for the very brief interlude with the three witches and Hecate which terminates the third act. At the end of the witches' chorus in the Bell text is the direction, "Symphony, whilst Hecate places herself in the machine," and then Hecate takes to the air. Heading this scene is a most provocative prompt marking that provides a fascinating insight into the solution of a staging problem which itself is not immediately evident. In the prompter's hand is written, *"Drop the Street to take off"*—a most puzzling direction to find here, to be sure. We must return to the banquet before the meaning of the notation will become obvious. The banquet, according to Hopkins' direction, transpires in the setting identified as *"Palace."* It is the same setting which served earlier for the events surrounding Duncan's murder. Clearly it is a combination of wings and shutter which allows for the utilization of the full stage area, for it must accommodate three entrances above the proscenium doors in the murder scene, and it must later contain the banquet table, the throne, the five chairs, and all the accoutrements and people concerned as well. After the banquet concludes, the setting must change to the heath. In almost all similar instances, eighteenth-century staging procedure would call for the shutters to close in at the proscenium line and cover the previous banquet setting from view; and the action in front on the heath would continue unimpeded while the properties and setting behind the shutter were being removed. In this particular sequence of events in *Macbeth,* however, such a simple procedure was hardly probable; for, in the scene which follows the banquet Hecate must fly away in a machine. In order to accomplish this the heath scene must also be played within the scenic area behind the proscenium where the flying apparatus was found.

We can now, I believe, interpret the direction, *"Drop the Street to take off."* A street-drop acting in the capacity of a front curtain fell here to allow the crew *"to take off"* the properties and scenery of the banquet, so that Hecate could use the same stage area for the act-closing aeronautical departure. It is the only logical explanation for the prompt notation. Why a street-drop, of all things, would be employed when the curtain itself would have served the purpose is not easy to explain. We have previously noted, however, several other instances of "landskip" drops being used at act intervals, and one time, in *Harlequin's Invasion* (1759), a curtain dropped for a scene change in the middle of an

act. This revelation by the promptbook, which we never should
have discovered from the printed text alone, must strongly recom-
mend that throughout the Garrick period the lowering of a drop
or curtain to effect a change while the action of the play waited
was a recognized sophisticated staging procedure.

ACT IV. The first scene of Act IV represents from a production point of view the most exciting sequence of events in the
play. Betterton had eliminated most of the trap-work in Davenant's version by having the witches deliver all the prophecies;
Garrick offered the audience the full spectacle. At the opening
of Act IV the Bell text reads, "Scene a dark cave: in the middle
a great Cauldron burning. Thunder. Enter the three Witches . . .
They march round the Cauldron, and throw in the several Ingredients, as for the Preparation of the Charm." This direction
is accompanied by the prompter's markings, *"Cave with Transp:
Scene up. Cauldron on."* [36] Since the term *scene* in this connection
almost always referred to a scenic piece, usually a flat scene, it
seems that here the witches and their cauldron are discovered in
the cave by the raising of a scene drop at the beginning of the
act. If so, then a scene drop probably fell at the close of Act III
(but there is no notation to this effect), and another example of
an actdrop may be added to a surprising number of instances
revealed by the promptbooks. I reserve for the moment my consideration of the term *"Transp*[arency]."

After the witches have mixed their baleful brew Hecate and
three more witches enter *"PS"* to the strains of *"Witch Music."*
There is a knocking at the *"OP Door."*

> *2 Witch.* Hold by the pricking of my thumbs,
> Something wicked this way comes.
> Open looks, whoever knocks.

"Enter Macbeth. Not from the O.P. door whence the knocking
comes, but from the *"OP 1st W."*

A letter writer in *St. James's Chronicle* supplies some intri-
guing information about Garrick's entrance and the cave itself.

> When you precipitate down the Steps which lead to the Cavern,
> you have never appeared enough struck with the Solemnity of a
> Scene concerning which *Macbeth* could have no previous informa-
> tion. . . . A Pause of silent Wonder, when you descend . . . would
> not be thrown away on your audience.
>   . . . The last Dress in which you played *Macbeth*, was that of a
> *modern fine Gentleman*, so that when you came among the Witches
> in the 4th Act, you looked like a Beau, who had unfortunately

slipped his Foot and tumbled into a Night Cellar, where a Parcel of old Women were boiling Tripe for their Supper. The very Door in the Rock, by which you enter . . . ought to fly open. . . . I am convinced that a greater Dignity of Habit, and a little more Attention to Decorations, would effectually enhance the Terrors of this powerful Scene.[37]

The setting which this correspondent saw on Garrick's stage had a practical door at the top of some practical steps down which Macbeth descended into the cave. This built-up set-piece was located, according to the promptbook, at the position behind the 1st O.P. wing. (It is interesting to note here that Macklin's specifications for the cave scene in his "Scottish" production called for "high rocks all round So as to form the stage into a deep cave and down the back part must be a winding way for Macbeth." [38])

During the action the various apparitions rise and sink at a trap located prompt side *("S:T:PS rise"),* and on the admonition of the witches to Macbeth to "Seek to know no more," the cauldron as well sinks into the ground *("Sink S:Trap PS").* Then, according to the Bell text, "Eight Kings appear, and pass over in order; the last with a glass in his hand; then Banquo." The notation that the procession passes *"from PS:to OP"* is added by the prompter.

A line engraving by Alexander Bannerman, dating from 1763, after a painting by Dawes, captures precisely this moment in the witches' cave during Garrick's production (plate 6). Here we seem fortunately confronted with an illustration of special theatrical validity, and one which, I suggest, offers a solution to the appearance of the prompter's notation *"Transp:"* that heads the scene. Garrick stands center-stage in his familiar ballet posture, with the left hand characteristically projected in front of him in the same manner that we find it in Hogarth's famous rendition of the tent scene in *Richard III.* At stage-right is a conclave of five witches, with the sixth witch seated upon the ground center. Hecate is pictured in the forecorner stage-left. The cavern setting rises all about, and the whole rendering must be regarded as excellent dramatic composition.

Perhaps most interesting, however, is the procession of the kings in the background upstage-left. I believe it is evident that although the kings appear to be hovering *into* sight, we are viewing actually the *end* of the procession, as it paused in its passage from stage-left to right *("from PS: to OP").* The last king "with a glass in his hand" is pictured as the foremost monarch, and at the extreme left stands Banquo who is supposed to tail the procession. We may now find some employment for the transparency —a translucent backscene behind which the procession took place. With proper lighting the hazy supernatural nature of the transparency would have created an effective atmosphere. The technique appears to be strikingly modern, but transparencies were not strangers at Drury Lane even before De Loutherbourg. The method was in use, if not in vogue, earlier than assumed. Garrick's production of *Harlequin's Invasion* in 1759 may be cited as the prototype of the effect, in which the designer, French, created an enchanted wood whose backscene was a transparency "behind which, visionary figures were seen flitting across, upon the plan of the *Tableau mouvant*." [39]

The cave scene concludes with a dance of furies, at the end of which everyone on stage except Macbeth vanishes, according to the prompter, "*PS.*" No traps are here indicated.

The following scene, the murders of Lady Macduff and her son, found disgracefully horrid to eighteenth-century sensibility, is curtailed in Garrick's version, ending in the Bell text with Angus' warning to Lady Macduff to flee. Curiously enough, the prompter has eliminated the scene in its entirety. Similarly, in the following scene at the King of England's palace (*"1st Grove"*), Malcolm's deprecation of his own character is omitted.

ACT V. Lady Macbeth's sleepwalking scene, which opens the final act, was carried off superbly by Mrs. Pritchard, her acting resembling "those sudden flashes of lightening which more accurately discover the horrors of surrounding darkness." [40] Francis Gentleman has undoubtedly used her as his model in his footnote instructions that the actress of this difficult scene must speak "in a low, anxious voice, keep moving slowly about, with fixed, glaring, open eyes, and horror-struck features." A print in the Folger Library shows the celebrated actress in the sleepwalking scene wearing voluminous night clothes and carrying a taper, a property which must have precluded any of the hand-wringing that later became associated with the soliloquy. The costume evidently is highly conventional: James Messink's manuscript "Order of the Pageant in the Jubilee" (at the Folger Library) specifies Lady Macbeth is to walk in the procession "in hir mad Dress." The illustration evokes further interest by the positions of the doctor and gentlewoman before an open door in the backscene. The lack of corroborating accounts and the absence of prompter's notations for this scene do not allow us to determine with any success the theatrical validity of this print.

There is, however, at the heading of the scene the prompter's notation, "*Stage Cloth on*," signifying that the tragic carpet required for Macbeth's death at the conclusion of the play was placed on the stage floor before the act began. The theatres used no groundcloths—bare boards formed the foreground of any scene—so in order to protect the actor's costly vestments from being soiled, a six-foot square green baize cloth was spread before all death scenes. The promptbook of *Zara* requires that two carpets be put out at the opening of the last act to accommodate the double tragedy of that play.[41]

Other incidents in this final act of *Macbeth* may be passed by without detailed notice, until the fourth scene, before Dunsinane ("*2d Grove*"), where Malcolm, Siward, Macduff, and their army enter with boughs from "*PS Top*." From this point the promptbook markings must be followed with close attention if we hope to visualize these last hectic moments of the production.

"A grand battle is fought across the stage," but its pattern of action is in no way revealed to us by the promptbook.[42] In the midst of the fray, Macbeth enters "*OP W.W.*"—a localization which, I confess, escapes my interpretation (perhaps W.W. designates wall or wood wing). Young Siward now enters from the opposite side of the stage ("*PS*"), the two engage in mortal combat, after which the victorious Macbeth departs at the upper wing prompt-side ("*U.P.W.*"), that is, the last wing in the series on the stage. At this point a "*Drop-Street 2d gro*" transfers us to a more secluded part of the battle area before Dunsinane Castle.

> Alarums. Enter Macduff. *PS*
>
> *Macduff.* That way the noise is. Tyrant, shew thy face;
> If thou be'st slain, and with no stroke of mine,
> My wife and children's ghosts will haunt me still.
> I cannot strike at wretched Kernes,
> Let me find him fortune!

and Macduff dashes off stage in search of Macbeth, who almost immediately appears at the opposite side, at the "*OP U*[pper] *W*[ing.]"

> *Macbeth.* Why should I play the Roman fool, and die
> On mine own sword? whilst I see lives, the gashes
> Do better upon them.
>
> To him enter Macduff. *PS*

and the two combatants now confront each other from opposite diagonal corners of the stage. They engage, Macduff lays on, and Macbeth falls. Macduff takes his sword and leaves. In the agony of his death throes Macbeth delivers Garrick's painful interpolation:

'Tis done, the scene of life will quickly close.
Ambition's vain, delusive dreams are fled,
And now I wake to darkness, guilt and horror.
I cannot bear it! let me shake it off—
'Two' not be; my soul is clogg'd with blood—
I cannot rise! I dare not ask for mercy—
It is too late, hell drags me down. I sink
I sink—oh!—my soul is lost forever!

[Dies.

Despite the insipidness of the ridiculous farewell death rattle, Macbeth's demise represented one of Garrick's supreme acting triumphs. Noverre provides an exceptionally vivid account of the great Roscius' writhing and flouncing on the tragic carpet:

I have seen him represent a tyrant who, appalled at the enormity of his crime, dies torn with remorse. The last act was given up to regrets and grief, humanity triumphed over murder and barbarism; the tyrant, obedient to the voice of conscience, denounced his crimes aloud; they gradually became his judges and his executioners; the approach of death showed each instant on his face; his eyes became dim; his voice could not support the efforts he made to speak his thoughts. His gestures, without losing their expression, revealed the approach of his last moment; his legs gave way under him, his face lengthened, his pale and livid features bore the signs of suffering and repentance. At last, he fell; at that moment his crimes peopled his thoughts with the most horrible forms; terrified at the hideous pictures which his past acts revealed to him, he struggled against death; nature seemed to make one supreme effort. His plight made the audience shudder, he clawed the ground and seemed to be digging his own grave, but the dread moment was nigh, one saw death in reality, everything expressed that instant which makes all equal. In the end he expired. The death rattle and the convulsive movements of the features, arms and breast, gave the final touch to this terrible picture.[43]

After Macbeth finally expired, another *"Drop-Street"* fell to facilitate the removal of the body without impropriety. "A Retreat and flourish" sound and we are returned to the main battle ground before Dunsinane *("2d Grove")*. Macduff makes the presentation of the dead tyrant's sword to Malcolm, and the tragedy concludes.

IV

Garrick last played Macbeth on September 22, 1768, although the tragedy remained in the repertory with Barry, Reddish, and William Smith alternating in the title role. On Good Friday, 1767, Davy told his brother George that rich food and drink had made him too fat to undertake Macbeth that season (*Private Correspondence*, I, 253). A more sentimental explanation offered for his never playing the role again was his reluctance to appear opposite any Lady Macbeth other than Hannah Pritchard, who retired in 1768. Why he should give up the role so early in his career is a puzzle, especially since he continued to play parts which were more physically demanding and for which he was less suited. In his final round of characters before retirement he had intended to dress both *Macbeth* and *King Lear* in historical costume.[44] *King Lear* was presented as planned, but *Macbeth* never did materialize, perhaps because Roscius did not feel physically up to resuming the role after an eight-year lapse. In a letter on December 17, 1775, to Sir Gray Cooper, he excused himself from a command performance: "I am really not yet prepar'd for Macbeth, 'tis the most violent part I have, & I don't think myself yet able to obey his Lordship's Command as I ought besides We are not yet prepar'd with our Matters for I have a design to exhibit ye Characters in ye old dresses."[45] He never did oblige.

By clearing the play in 1744 of the rubbish and trappings which had plagued it over the previous eighty years Garrick allowed *Macbeth* to assert its pristine vibrancy. It is true that not even Garrick could resist the temptation to die by gasps and spasms, but it was his peculiar genius that he could, even here, stride that delicate balance point which distinguishes tragedy from melodrama and maintain his footing. What had been for too long the plaything of enterprising machinists and fustian-spouting actors was now restored, for the most part, in form and spirit as a supreme human expression.

VII

Romeo and Juliet

IN THE SECOND SEASON of the management, on November 29, 1748, Garrick's alteration of *Romeo and Juliet* was first performed. Immediately popular, it received 21 performances that season, 13 of them in consecutive run, and then reached a total of over 140 performances between 1748 and 1776. *Romeo and Juliet*, "Wrote by Mr. Shakespeare," had first been revived in the Restoration, March 1, 1762, shortly after the opening of the first theatre in Lincoln's—Inn-Fields. Samuel Pepys saw the opening night and judged it "a play of itself the worst that ever I heard in my life." Shortly thereafter James Howard altered the drama, preserving the lovers alive at the end. The two versions, according to Downes, were then played alternately, "Tragical one Day, and Tragicomical another; for several Days together."[1] Despite Pepys discommendation, he had the distinction of being among the last for almost two hundred years to see the play as written by Shakespeare. In 1680 both the original and Howard's adaptation were superseded by Otway's *Caius Marius* which then held the stage for 64 years. Although Otway did not preserve the lovers as Howard had done, he allowed Lavinia (Juliet) to awaken in the tomb before Marius (Romeo) expired, a revision which both Theophilus Cibber and Garrick later adopted in their respective versions, and which was until well into the nineteenth century preferred by most audiences as an ending superior to Shakespeare's original.[2]

The year 1744 found the cantankerous and rancorous Theophilus Cibber again in rebellion from the patent houses. Theophilus had taken up at that refuge for rebellious actors, the "late Little Theatre in Hay-Market," which he announced was now converted into an "Academy" for fledglings of the histrionic profession. The familiar concerts were to be offered for a small fee, and in addition, in order that the Town could be judges of the progress being made by his students, play rehearsals "with proper *Habits, Decorations,* &c." were to be exhibited *gratis*.[3] It was under such circumstances that Cibber's alteration of *Romeo and Juliet* was first presented on September 11, 1744. Romeo was played by Cibber himself, and Juliet by his daughter Jenny, who at barely fifteen "shewed a happy genius." Garrick was among those who attended the "rehearsal" and reported that he had never heard so vile and scandalous a performance in his life. He was convinced that

> nothing could be more contemptible. The play was tolerable enough, considering Theophilus was the hero. The rest of his company were gathered from Southwark and Mayfair. Mrs. Charke played the Nurse to his daughter, Juliet; but she was so miserable throughout, and so abounded in airs, affectation, and *Cibberisms,* that I was quite shocked at her: the girl, I believe, may have genius; but unless she changes her preceptor, she must be entirely ruined.[4]

Cibber's version, although announced as "Not acted these hundred years," was far from the original, but rather a hodge-podge of Otway's *Caius Marius* and the Bard's *Romeo and Juliet* and *Two Gentlemen of Verona*. First published in 1748 and ironically dedicated to John Rich, the text offers little of interest in the way of staging hints.

Perhaps the abuses wrought by Otway and Cibber prompted Garrick to work on the play. It may be said with some justice that except for some minor deletions and some additions, including a funeral procession for Juliet, Garrick's acting version was essentially faithful to the original. Lady Montague is omitted and there is no mention of Rosaline. As in Otway and Cibber, Romeo is in love with Juliet at the outset: his first lines are inspired by her, and he goes to the ball to see her, not to be smitten by her. Although Garrick did not retain Otway's lines for the tomb scene, unable to deprive his audience of this unhappy moment, he wrote in some 65 lines of his own, in which Juliet awakens to take leave of her lover before the poison finally kills him.

In the Advertisement to the printed text, Garrick announced that his "chief Design of the Alterations . . . was to clear the original as much as possible from the Jingle and Quibble which were always the Objections to the reviving it." Lest he be considered presumptuous by his modifications of the work of his professed diety, Garrick added that "The sudden Change of *Romeo's* Love from *Rosaline* to *Juliet* was thought by many . . . to be a blemish in his Character; an Alteration in that Particular has been made more in Compliance to that Opinion, than from a Conviction that *Shakespear,* the best Judge of human Nature, was faulty." His alibi for changing the ending was that Bandello, from whom he explains Shakespeare borrowed the subject, had Juliet awaken before Romeo dies; but since Shakespeare did not read Italian, having taken the story from French and English translations—"both which have injudiciously left out this Addition to the Catastrophe"—he did not know the ending, to which certainly his better judgment would have given approval. Garrick furthermore felt obliged to compose his own conclusion because Otway's did not possess sufficient "Nature, Terror, and Distress." [5]

This arrangement of the play by Garrick held the stage until the late nineteenth century. His addition to the tomb scene, used as late as 1875 by Charles Wyndham, apparently was not abandoned until Irving's 1882 production.[6] There must have been something inherently dramatic in the remodeled scene for it to have been popular for so long.

II

Actually, Garrick never fancied himself in the role of Romeo when he decided to revive the play. Spranger Barry and Susannah Cibber were his original lovers, and not until the season of 1750-51 was Garrick forced into the part after a series of events which finally resulted in the most famous theatrical rivalry of the century.

Before the season 1750-51 opened, Barry, Macklin, and Mrs. Cibber quit Garrick for Covent Garden, where Rich already had Quin, Ryan, and Peg Woffington in his employ. The rival company now presented a substantial threat to the supremacy previously enjoyed by Drury Lane. Garrick countered by attempting to lure Quin from Rich, but succeeded only in obtaining for that actor a raise to £1000, which boosted his salary for acting higher than Garrick's.

Capitalizing on his new stars' reputations in the play, Rich decided to offer *Romeo and Juliet*—in Garrick's version—on September 28, 1750. In a calculated risk, Garrick determined to test the drawing power of his own personality by presenting the same play on the same night, with himself and Miss Bellamy in the title roles. It is not known when Rich had made his decision to offer the play, but from a letter to Lacy on July 27, 1750, it is evident that Garrick, himself, had been preparing his September production for some time. Garrick's letter offers additional information about historical costuming, and makes clear that the alteration of having Romeo in love with Juliet at the beginning of the play was not in Garrick's original 1748 revival, but was added here in the season 1750-51:

> I shall soon be ready in *Romeo* which we shall bring out early: I have altered something in the beginning and have made him only in love with Juliet—I believe you'll like it—if Bellamy agrees with us, she may open with it. Then if we can get *King John* before 'em (as we certainly may) and dress the character half Old English half modern as in Edward the black Prince, we shall cut their combs there too.[7]

Both plays opened on schedule. The duel lasted for 12 consecutive evenings. At first the novel and intense rivalry captured the imagination of the Town, but as the potential audience exhausted itself, the houses began to thin, and both theatres began to lose money. A brief poem in the *Daily Advertiser* bespeaks the final boredom and irritation of the Town:

> "Well, what's today," says angry Ned,
>   As up from bed he rouses.
> "Romeo again!" and shakes his head,
>   "Ah, pox on both your houses." [8]

Garrick, however, expressed the "Impartial opinion" that his house had "yᵉ advantage" in the battle. On October 4 he wrote to an unidentified lady-friend, "Our house tonight was much better than their's, & I believe 'tis generally thought that our Performance is best." [9] On October 21, Mrs. Cibber weakened, Covent Garden capitulated, and Drury Lane triumphantly added a thirteenth performance. "Our Antagonists yielded last thursday Night & we play'd yᵉ Same Play (Romeo & Juliet) on yᵉ Fryday to a very full house to very great applause," Garrick wrote to the

Countess of Burlington. Both Barry and Mrs. Cibber came incognito to Drury Lane to see the performance and Garrick was "well-assur'd they receiv'd no little Mortification.—"[10]

Both productions, apparently each of the first rank, stirred a controversy which raged for days in the coffee houses over the relative merits of the two casts. Most critical opinion favored Barry, the actor Garrick had originally trained in the role, especially in the love scenes. Charles Macklin, violently prejudiced against Garrick at this moment, thought Barry the "best lover that ever appeared on the stage," and Garrick not at all qualified for Romeo. "The amorous harmony of Mr. Barry's features, his melting eyes, and unequalled plaintiveness of voice, and his fine graceful figure gave him a great superiority."[11] It was Wilkinson's opinion that Barry "was as much superior to Garrick in *Romeo,* as York Minster is to a Methodist Chapel."[12] Barry's performance was universally admired, but Garrick's fertile genius was in turn not to be outdone in its own right. "He struck out so many new lights and raised such terror and pity in the catastrophe, that the public opinion was much divided, and the palm of victory hung in suspense between the two competitors," is the way Arthur Murphy saw it.[13] With his natural physical and vocal advantages along with his undeniable gift for tragedy, Barry was more ideally suited to the role. But Garrick's genius, hampered by his small size and heavy features but extended to its fullest qualities by the challenge, allowed him nearly to equal Barry's performance. The virtuosity of Garrick's acting—with his masterly command of attitudes and emotions—almost compensated for Barry's love scenes. In fact many loyal followers of Roscius judged Garrick the better Romeo. The *Dramatic Censor,* whose editor Francis Gentleman was generally partial to Garrick, advised that he drew the most applause while Barry drew the most tears. It judged Barry better in the balcony scene, in the early morning parting of the lovers, and in the first part of the tomb scene; Garrick was untouchable in Friar Lawrence's cell and in the tomb scene from the point at which the poison began to operate (I, 189).

In general, the critical compromise was to award Barry superiority in the first three acts, Garrick the final two. Some spectators, to be sure, made a practice of leaving Covent Garden after Act III to catch the wind-up at Drury Lane. Perhaps the most astute comment made on the respective performances, and the one which best summarizes the tenor of critical reports, was that of a practical female who announced that "Had I been Juliet to

Garrick's Romeo,—so ardent and impassioned was he, I should have expected he would have *come up* to me in the balcony; but had I been Juliet to Barry's Romeo,—so tender, so eloquent, and so seductive was he, I should certainly have *gone down* to him!" [14] The observations of another woman, these written in a style and spelling reflective of her halting English, are exceedingly interesting, stemming as they do from Mrs. Garrick herself. Needless to say, she preferred the more mature performance of Romeo being exhibited at Drury Lane, but like the rest of the public wished for an end of the contest: "I was at the Play Last Saturday at Coven-garden, all what I can Say of it is, that Mr Barry is to jung (in his ha'd) for Romeo, & Mrs Cibber to old for a girle of 18 . . . I wish thie woold finish both, for it is to much for My Little Dear Spouse to Play Every Day." [15]

A less-fevered controversy was raged over the relative merits of the contending Juliets. Generally Mrs. Cibber's grander beauty and forceful tragic expression of distress and despair at Covent Garden bore the palm from Miss Bellamy's amorous rapture and natural loveliness. The comparative excellences of the two actresses were delineated in some detail by a reviewer:

> Miss *Bellamy*, if she possesses not Mrs. *Cibber's* softness, she makes a large compensation by her variety. Mrs. *Cibber* succeeds in those parts in which the soul is to be melted by tenderness: she utters the soliloquy before she drinks the draught given her by the friar, with all imaginable terror: the scene of parting, and the news of *Romeo's* banishment, are inexpressively moving; but her judgment greatly fails in the tombscene, when she rises as it were instantaneously, which prevents a great part of that alarming distraction which *Romeo* discovers in finding life returning to *Juliet* by slow degrees. Miss *Bellamy* rises more gradually; she keeps the audience longer in amazement, while the astonishment of *Romeo* rises in proportion, and is finely heightened and wonderfully affecting as perform'd by Mr. *Garrick*, whose attitudes through the whole play are so inimitably excellent, as to bid defiance to the other *Romeo*. Mrs. *Cibber*, when she gives herself the mortal stab, has introduced a shudder that affects the whole audience, but in all other parts of the distress upon the body of *Romeo*, I think she has no claim to superiority. For my own part, I shed more tears in seeing Mrs. *Cibber*, but I am more delighted in seeing Miss *Bellamy*.[16]

There was little question, however, as to the better Mercutio. At Covent Garden the role was played by Macklin, who, miscast, contrasted oddly with Mercutio's attractive personality. Macklin for some reason considered this role one of his best performances, but actually he was only tolerably well received. Henry Woodward, already famous as a superb pantomimist, achieved one of his triumphs in the role at Drury Lane. A comic actor of great natural ability, Woodward possessed the necessary qualities of elegant rascality and brazen impertinence. (Bobadil in *Every Man in his Humour* was accounted his supreme performance; as Touchstone he excelled all his contemporaries.) Arthur Murphy relates that Woodward in Mercutio "was a tower of strength; a character so highly finished, so whimsical, yet natural, so eccentric, yet sensible, and altogether so entertaining, cannot be found in any play whatever, and no actor ever reached the vivacity of Woodward." [17]

III

Garrick's arrangement of *Romeo and Juliet* was first published by Tonson in 1748, "As it is performed at the Theatre Royal in Drury Lane." Another printing appeared in 1750, "With Alterations, and an additional Scene," the additional scene being the funeral procession for Juliet which had been added by both theatres during the rivalry. Another edition of 1766 and Bell's edition of 1773-74 are essentially reprints of the 1750 edition. By combining information offered in these texts with scattered notices, several significant aspects of a typical production of the play at Drury Lane can be reconstructed.

ACT I. The opening action of *Romeo and Juliet* takes place in "The Street in Verona," where the familiar battle between the two families erupts anew. The setting then shifts for scene 2 to "Before Capulet's House," for a transposed scene in which Capulet expresses his approval of Paris as suitor to his daughter. Scene 3 occurs in "A Wood near Verona," where we have the first appearance of Romeo (already in love with Juliet), Benvolio, and Mercutio. The direction at the opening of the scene reads, "Romeo *crosses the Stage*," ostensibly in melancholy dumps, and after he exits his two friends enter to comment upon his new love. Romeo re-enters in a moment, conveys his dilemma at being in love with a Capulet, and at the advice of Mercutio, the three decide to crash the Capulet's party. An excellent print (plate 9) survives of Woodward in this scene delivering the Queen Mab speech. He is apparelled in the dress of a fine eighteenth-century gentleman, with knee breeches, ruffled shirt, tye-wig, and three-cornered hat.[18] Since the index finger of his right hand rests at the tip of his nose, the print evidently captures the moment when he speaks the line, "Athwart men's noses as they lie asleep," or "Sometime she gallops o'er a lawyer's nose." The rustic background offers a glimpse of what one of Drury Lane's stock "wood" backscenes looked like. Scene 5 is at Capulet's house again, on the forestage area, and then the shutters part for scene 6—"A Hall in Capulet's House. The Capulets, Ladies, Guests, and Maskers are discovered." For some curious reason, details for the staging of the first act—in a play so popular as this was—are conspicuously absent.

ACT II. Macklin considered ridiculous the manner in which the rival Romeos made their entrances into the garden: "Barry comes into it, Sir, as great as a Lord, swaggering about his love, and talking so loud. . . . But how does Garrick act this? . . . he comes creeping in upon his toes, whispering his love, and looking about him *just like a thief in the night.*"[19]

According to the text, "Juliet appears above at a window," presumably in the stage-box over the proscenium door. Professor Sprague has suggested that a window alone served the purpose, and that the now familiar balcony was not provided until much later by Kemble. Indeed, Shakespeare's original text requires but a window. However, the anonymous adulatory *Letter to Miss Nossiter,* occasioned by that actress's debut as Juliet at Covent Garden, October 10, 1753, speaks of "the favourite Scene of the Balcony," although to be sure the author relates that Juliet "appears at the Window."[20] But there is pictorial evidence for the balcony, as well. Plate 8 is a theatrical print which has been recently identified as the balcony scene from *Romeo and Juliet,* as played at Covent Garden in 1754.[21] The principals are Barry and Miss Nossiter. Here we find a low-hung balcony, ostensibly not in the position of the proscenium box. No window is evident. Romeo stands below in a patio section of the garden which is curiously illuminated by a chandelier suspended from an open evening sky, a detail which confirms dating of the picture before 1765, the year Garrick's lighting innovations were effected. The entire rendering appears to be theatrically valid, and one certainly scents scenery in the background. The rather substantial set-piece of the balcony found in the side wall is suspect, perhaps, even though such set-pieces were not unknown at this time. The point to be gathered, nevertheless, is that the balcony as a stage tradition is clearly within the scope of reference of the artist.

The scene of the lovely love duet is followed by scene 3, "A

Monastery," and then scene 4, "The Street" where the Nurse (seeking Romeo) and her man Peter always indulged in a traditional bit of broad farce. The nurse's crutch-stick was a favorite property used for cudgeling Peter. It was invariable stage policy, "to please the upper regions," that Peter entered bearing an enormous fan before the nurse, "skipping also and grinning like a baboon; the beating which he gets, for not resenting Mercutio's raillery, is a very mean pantomimical, yet sure motive of laughter." [22]

ACT III. Little of interest may be reported until scene 3, the pre-dawn parting of the lovers, where the text reads, "The Garden. Enter Romeo and Juliet above at a window; a ladder of Ropes set." No stage direction is provided for Romeo's descent. This circumstance excellently illustrates that eighteenth-century acting texts cannot always be trusted, for it seems that in actuality this parting was played not at the window at all, but in the garden below. A letter dated October 20, 1750, in *The Student: Or, the Oxford and Cambridge Miscellany* criticizes the prosaic arrangement whereby the lovers were obliged to play the scene "on the platform of the stage; whereas in SHAKE-SPEARE they are supposed to converse together from a window." [23] Twelve years later in the *Universal Museum* (October 1762) the same complaint is registered in verbal echoes of the earlier criticism: "They are brought *tête à tête* on the platform of the stage, whereas in *Shakespear* they are supposed to converse together from the window. . . . In Shakespear's original, *Romeo* descends from his mistress's window by a ladder of ropes; but by the present management, as he is made to walk off the stage cooly, a circumstance is destroyed." The *Letter to Miss Nossiter* describes how Barry's young protégée played the scene and at the same time confirms the locale:

> In the Morning Scene, after the stolen Consummation of their Nuptials, nothing could be more delicate and sweet. She looks at him, as they come in Hand in Hand, with such an Excess of Fondness, that every Heart melted at the Sight. Then leaning, with the most winning, familiar Innocence upon him, she throws so much tender Persuasion into her Voice and Looks, that we sicken with Delight, too exquisite to bear. . . . And her exit, though she speaks nothing as she goes off, a Circumstance very embarrassing to the Player, was remarkably graceful and expressive.

ACT IV. Of special interest in Act IV is the sequence of scenes surrounding the drinking of the potion by Juliet. Scene 3 represents "Juliet's Chamber," set with a bed. At the conclusion of the famous soliloquy, Juliet drinks the potion and then "She throws herself on the bed." At this point the Bell edition advises "The scene shuts on her." Scene 4 begins immediately in front of the shutters in "A Hall. Enter Lady Capulet and Nurse." Soon Capulet enters, instructs the nurse to "Go waken Juliet," and then he and his wife leave the stage. The text now reads, "Scene draws, and discovers Juliet on a bed." Immediately the nurse advancing from her forward position on the apron begins to speak to Juliet, ignoring the dissolving walls—an extremely plastic staging technique which we have noted on other occasions.

Act V. The action of this final act commences "inside of a Church. Enter the funeral procession of Juliet." Critical reaction to Garrick's interpolated funeral was always mixed. Some observers, like the *Theatrical Review* (1772, I, 63), acknowledged it as a fine piece of pageantry but felt it added little to "the importance of the tragedy." A reviewer in *Universal Museum* (October 1762) asked, "what end is all this pomp, shew, and farce to answer? [for after all the audience knows Juliet is not really dead] If it be calculated to please the eye and ear only, and not designed to have a proper theatrical effect on the mind of the audience, nor contribute to the carrying out of the *denouement* of the plot, it is absurd and ridiculous." On the other hand, the *Dramatic Censor* (I, 85), while agreeing that the funeral was not absolutely essential, expressed the opinion that "nothing could be better devised than a funeral procession to render this play thoroughly popular," for after all, "three-fourths of every audience are more capable of enjoying sound and shew than solid sense and poetical imagination."

The best contemporary account of the funeral scene is offered by Count Frederick Kielmansegge, who saw the play at Drury Lane, December 26, 1761.

> In the play an entire funeral is represented, with bells tolling, and a choir singing. Juliet, feigning death, lies on a state bed with a splendid canopy over her, guarded by girls who strew flowers, and by torch-bearers with flaming torches. The choristers and clergy in their vestments walk in front, and the father and mother and their friends follow. The scene represents the interior of a church. To my feeling this appears rather profane, but putting this aside, nothing of the kind could be represented more beautifully or naturally. The funeral dirges and the choirs made the whole ceremony too solemn for theatrical representation, especially on the English stage, which has no superior in the world, and on

which everything is produced with the highest degree of truth. This effect can be attained more easily here than upon any other stage, owing to the quantity of actors, including dancers and singers, of whom fifty are sometimes to be seen on one night, whilst there are probably as many absent, and the quantity of different decorations, machinery, and dresses, which are provided regardless of cost and with thorough completeness.[24]

Contrary to Kielmansegge's reaction to the funeral at Drury Lane is an unfavorable report of the similar event at Covent Garden. Christlob Mylius, cousin of Lessing, saw Rich's spectacle sometime between September and March 1754, and recorded his impressions in his *Tagebuch:*

> This merry tragedy, very faulty both in form and content . . . was performed according to its merits. Most of the actors, including Mr. Barry and Miss Nossiter, who are supposed to be the best, played with arrogant pomposity. The newly added scene, the burial of Juliet, is stupid and ridiculous. A bell is actually tolled on the stage. The costumes are mediocre and the decorations positively bad.[25]

Despite Mylius' candid remarks, we are told generally that Rich's funeral procession was "very grand." George Anne Bellamy (II, 195) relates that after her desertion to Covent Garden in 1754, Garrick "tried to stem the current of our success by purchasing a new *Bell* at an enormous expence; but finding that its harmonious notes during the procession did not congregate the numbers expected," he discontinued its use. The same bell was now to toll for the execution of Pierre in *Venice Preserv'd.*

The action of the play concludes in "a Church-yard; in it a Monument belonging to the Capulets." From the various accounts of this scene and from Benjamin Wilson's painting of Garrick and Bellamy in the tomb (plate 7) we can deduce the precise manner of staging. Backscene shutters placed in some advantageous groove position separated the graveyard from the interior of the monument. In the center were the double doors in a profile flat. When these doors sprung open, Juliet was revealed on her bier. Another backscene, drop or flat, formed the definitive background of the inner tomb. In the light of my previous citations of practical doors and profiled flats, Wilson's painting must be considered a highly valid theatrical rendition, as valid perhaps as a photograph. Dating from 1753 this illustration represents one of the first pictorial records of practical double doors in a backscene.

One of the many interesting aspects of Wilson's painting is the appearance of the moon breaking through the clouds and trees. The familiar engraving of Garrick and Mrs. Cibber in a scene from *Venice Preserv'd* bears a similar moonlight effect. In actual production perhaps the moon was painted on the backscene in both instances, but the informative Rees *Cyclopaedia* tells of "An apparatus, rather optical than mechanical," which was designed to give the effect of a full moon. It had, according to the *Cyclopaedia*, been employed with great success at Drury Lane during the eighteenth century.

It is a conical case of tin, the lesser diameter of which is a concave reflector. . . . The greater diameter . . . is covered with taffeta, or any transparent coloured cloth, to give the shade required; and a lamp is suspended within the case, which is perforated in many places to admit the air. Simple as this apparatus is, it gives a very striking resemblance of a full moon when suspended by three cords, and when the back part of the stage is darkened.[26]

The events surrounding Romeo's breaking open of the tomb perhaps formed the most discussed moment of the play. The action has been preserved by several cynical versifiers, one of whom describes Barry in the scene:

> When *Barry* fraught with all the rage of woe,
> His accents broken, and his paces slow,
> Tow'rds *Juliet's* tomb in desperation moves,
> Each look, each motion, shows how much he loves:
> But, when, by *Paris* challeng'd to the fight,
> With hollow voice he warns the am'rous knight,
> Starts back erect, and aims the crow on high,
> Shudders the audience, and attempts to fly . . .[27]

In *The Actor* Robert Lloyd ridiculed the traditional posturing:

> When Romeo sorrowing at his *Juliet's* Doom,
> With eager madness bursts the canvas Tomb,
> The sudden Whirl, stretch'd Leg, and lifted Staff,
> Which please the Vulgar, make the Critic laugh.

Garrick held the "Cyclopedian Attitude" with iron crow on high (actually a piece of wood) long enough—according to Theophilus Cibber—to allow Paris more than sufficient time "to run him thro' the Body." [28]

John Hill similarly deplored as false this attitude in which Romeo intends to dash out Paris' brains, emphatically stating that Romeo rather should have recourse to his sword—"the weapon of a gentleman." [29] The moment was played in this same manner not only by Garrick and Barry, but by everyone else as well, for the whirling about with the iron crow was a truly fine bit, well calculated to draw applause from the gallery.[30]

After the breaking open of the tomb, the discovery of the inanimate Juliet must have been effective. Romeo enters the tomb, and drinks the poison just as Juliet awakens. In his joy, Romeo forgets his fate, and a love duet follows, during which he "brings her from the tomb" out to the graveyard—closer to the audience. But the poison begins its deadly task, and Romeo cannot help but remember his doom:

> My powers are blasted,
> 'Twixt death and love I'm torn—I'm distracted!

he cries out in words supplied by Garrick. After a striking rendition of death's agonies, which Garrick prolonged in order to exhibit his famous skill at such things, Romeo expires and Juliet faints over his body. Upon her revival she stabs herself.[31]

Shakespeare has Juliet dispatch herself with Romeo's dagger. For several seasons after Garrick's revival there was no change in the prescribed business until in one performance, Wilkinson relates, Mrs. Cibber at Covent Garden "fumbled and fumbled, but no dagger was to be found; at last, evidently much distressed, she held up her delicate fist . . . and ideally plunged the weapon to her heart." [32] From that night eighteenth-century Juliets carried their own daggers as insurance. Curiously not too many in the audience regarded it strange, or even slightly humorous, that Juliet should draw a dagger from her funeral robes after having been prepared for internment.

The entire tomb scene, when played by any competent combination of stage-lovers, was always extremely effective in the eighteenth century and well into the next century. "The waking of Juliet before Romeo's death," declared Francis Gentleman as editor of the Bell edition, "is exceedingly judicious; it gives an opportunity of working the pathos to its tenderest pitch, and shows a very fine picture, if the performers strike out just and graceful attitudes." The same critic, writing now in the *Dramatic Censor* (I, 187), observed that nature was brought to its "most critical feelings" by the awakening of Juliet, "and her husband's affectionate transports, forgetting what he has done, fills the audience with a most cordial sympathy of satisfaction, which is soon dashed in both, by the poison's operating." In his less trenchant days, Arthur Murphy went so far as to suggest that "the catastrophe, as it now stands, is the most affecting in the whole compass of the drama." [33]

Garrick gave up the part of Romeo in 1761-62, and was followed at Drury Lane by a series of inferior replacements including Holland, Ross, Fleetwood, and Cautherley. Barry also played Romeo again under Garrick's management when he returned to the fold in 1767-68, but he was woefully beyond his prime at this point. By 1771, the *Theatrical Review* (I, 67), reporting a production on October 10 of that once excellent stock piece at Drury Lane, thought that "nothing can be more contemptible"—Cautherley was completely unsuited to Romeo, and Mrs. Barry, although possessing "great Merit," could not approach the excellence of Miss Bellamy's interpretation.

The tragedy of the star-crossed lovers became on Garrick's stage a true tale of woe, first in alteration, and then finally in playing. To borrow a title from a collection of Garrick's letters, those "Pineapples of Finest Flavour" in *Romeo and Juliet* had mellowed, by the last act, into a demulcent saccharinity. Although our palates may now prefer pineapples of a different taste, as historians at least, we cannot objectively regret the success of Garrick's version. The popularity of *Romeo and Juliet* bred sufficient contemporary comment to allow us to reconstruct in part some of the play's most exciting moments at Drury Lane.

VIII

King Lear

OF THE NEAR ONE HUNDRED ROLES which Garrick created, his supreme achievement was King Lear. His portrayal of this difficult, indeed almost unplayable character, reputedly unsurpassed by any actor before or since, transcended all praise in its own day. Hannah More, who saw the great actor in his last magnificent performance as Lear, had not yet recovered four days later from the emotional shock of "one of the greatest scenes ever exhibited." [1] Throughout Garrick's entire career, so very high was his reputation in the part that when a performance of the play was announced, the mobs often filled the theatre several hours before curtain-time. On May 12, 1763, Boswell went to Drury Lane and found the pit teeming with people shortly after four o'clock, but he was rewarded for his discomfort and patience during the two hour wait for *King Lear* to begin—"I was fully moved, and I shed abundance of tears," he wrote in his *London Journal*.[2] In her *Diary* Fanny Burney confided she knew not whether she had received "*pain or pleasure*" in seeing Garrick's Lear, he was so "exquisitely great." [3] Mr. Tighe paid similar homage with a description of the effect the performance had on the Montgomery sisters:

> The expression of the eldest was wonderful. . . . She gazed, she panted, she grew pale, then again the blood rose in her cheeks, she was elevated, she almost started out of her seat, and *tears began to flow &c. &c.*[4]

Garrick's Lear struck to every soul: on May 22, 1773, Dr. Beattie expressed his uncertainty of "outliving the distresses of Lear" when personated by him, and after seeing another performance wrote in his *Diary,* "The many tears shed by the audience bore ample testimony to his and to Shakespear's merits." [5]

The merit indeed was mostly Garrick's, for the play itself was, for the most part, Nahum Tate's hopeless dilution of Shakespeare's sublime effort. Although the original had been revived for a few performances in the early years of the Restoration, it was soon neglected "as unprofitable to the players," and replaced by Tate's adaptation in 1681 which then held the stage until 1823, when Elliston performed the blessed service of again restoring the original, freed of its accumulated mutations. [6] Successfully played by Betterton, Booth, Quin, and then Garrick for fifteen years, the Tate version reflects the violence wrought on the Bard's work in methods most typical of the Shakespearean adaptors.

The principles of decorum and sensibility were Tate's guides. These dictated a virtuous happy ending with Lear, Gloster, and Kent retiring to a monkish cell for reflection. An insipid love affair between Edgar and Cordelia is brought to a logical conclusion with both becoming the co-monarchs of the once disrupted kingdom. Consequently the King of France is omitted, as is the Fool, considered indecorous to tragedy. Gloster's jumping from the cliff is rejected as too improbable. Edmund's illicit affairs with Goneril and Regan are elaborated upon, and he is shown lusting for Cordelia in the bargain.

Tate's adaptation, especially the unhappy happy ending, satisfied the demands of the age for greater unity and poetic justice. Except for the one weak voice of Addison protesting that in this now "chimerical notion of poetic justice" Shakespeare's admirable tragedy had lost half its beauty, the adaptation was accorded the highest praise by eighteenth-century moralists. [7] The play now presented the distinct advantage of rewarding every instance of virtue and punishing every instance of vice, an arrangement so completely negating the dark intention of the original masterpiece as to be more pitiable than appalling. And it was approved by Dr. Johnson who could not bear to read the last act of the original. The critical approbation of the period is summarized in *The British Journal,* December 12, 1730:

> While *Lear* and the Companions of his Wretchedness are almost without Hopes, unerring Nature is pursuing her Course; the

Vices of *Goneril, Regan,* and *Edmund,* are working their own Ruin, and the Uprising of those whom their Cruelty had reduced to the lowest State of Misery. Here is a Lesson *that administers Comfort to the poor and distressed . . .*

I have read many Sermons, but remember no one that contains so fine a Lesson of Morality as this Play. Here is Loyalty to a Prince, Duty to a Parent, Perseverance in a chaste Love, and almost every exalted Virtue of the Soul, recommended in the lovelyest Colours; and the opposite Vices are placed in the strongest Light in which Horror and Detestation can place them.

Garrick first played Lear at the age of 24, on March 11, 1742, at Goodman's Fields. He had requested Macklin, then still his close friend, to sit as a first-night critic. Although he was dressed very appropriately for Lear, Macklin judged him not especially successful at portraying the infirmities of an eighty-year-old man. In the delivery of the curse at the close of the first act, Macklin thought he began too low and ended too high, and finally, that he did not exhibit dignity enough for a king in the prison scene. Garrick was most obliged for the criticism, made the suggested changes at rehearsals, and within six weeks played the role to Macklin's amazement:

> it exceeded his imagination, and the curse had such an effect that it seemed to electrify the audience with horror. The words 'Kill-kill-kill' echoed all the revenge of a frantic king, whilst he exhibited such a scene of the pathetic discovery of his daughter Cordelia, as drew tears of commiseration from the whole house.

Macklin was enraptured—"the little dog made it a *chef d'oeuvre,* and a *chef d'oeuvre* it continued to the end of his life." [8]

As a result of the impetus now provided by Garrick the play became the fourth most popular tragedy at Drury Lane during the period 1741-1747, playing 101 times (twice the number of productions than between 1702-1740), with 83 of these performances during Garrick's management.[9] Not all the performances, however, were given in the "pure" Tate version. In *An Examen of the New Comedy, Call'd the Suspicious Husband* (1747), to which was appended a "Word of Advice to Mr. G-rr-ck," Samuel Foote bestowed high tribute on the actor and then appealed to him to effect some significant changes in his playing of *King Lear.* Foote requested among other things—such as changing his costume in the fourth act, abolishing the handkerchief during the curse, and abandoning the fainting bit in the last act—that Garrick put aside Tate's "execrable Alteration" and give "*Lear* in the *Original,* Fool and all." Other "Admirers of unsophisticated

Shakespeare" had also urged upon the manager the restoration of the original. Finally, Garrick propitiated the god of his idolatry on October 28, 1756, by announcing "KING LEAR—with restorations from Shakespeare." [10] In Garrick's new arrangement of the play, the liaison between Edgar and Cordelia, although much abbreviated, and the happy ending were still to be found; for as originally written the final distress "would have been more than any audience could bear." Garrick had thought of restoring the fool but decided against "so bold an attempt." [11] Although the new version retained much of Tate, the restoration of Shakespeare's original lines in scene after scene was most refreshing. [12] Garrick must be credited with sustaining even in this mutilated form perhaps the theatre's greatest tragedy.

II

Garrick's Lear was a "little, old, white haired man . . . with spindle-shanks, a tottering gait, and great shoes upon his little feet," with face made up with a remarkable skill to show old age. [13] In his own words the actor characterized Lear as "a *weak* man . . . violent, old & weakly fond of his daughters," whose weakness proceeds from his age and whose unhappiness stems not from his vices but from good qualities carried to excess of folly. [14] His madness emanated more from the cruelty of his daughters and the loss of their love than from the loss of his kingdom and privileges. Flowing tears and surging passions were the keywords of the performance. In the cursing of Goneril he started a tradition which persisted until recent years, when as Foote told him in *An Examen of the New Comedy,*

> You fall precipitately upon your Knees, extend your arms—clench your Hand—set your Teeth—and with a savage Distraction in your Look—trembling in your Limbs—and your Eyes pointed to Heaven . . . begin . . . with a *broken, inward, eager* Utterance; from thence rising every Line in Loudness and Rapidity of Voice,

and at last, "bursting into tears." Just before the curse he threw away his crutch as he knelt. [15] The general tenor of Garrick's overwhelming Lear is captured in Dr. Fordyce's letter to him on May 13, 1763:

> Such violent starts of amazement, of horror, of indignation, of paternal rage, excited by filial ingratitude the most prodigious; such a perceptible, yet rapid gradation, from those dreadful feelings to the deepest frenzy; such a striking correspondence between the

tempest in his mind, and that of the surrounding elements. . . .
Those resistless complaints of aged and royal wretchedness, with
all the mingled workings of a warm and hasty, but well-meaning
and generous soul, just recovering from the convulsion of its faculties . . . till at length the parent, the sovereign, and the friend shine
out in the mildest majesty of fervant virtue. . . . These, Sir, are some
of the great circumstances which so eminently distinguished your
action two nights ago. They possessed by turns all your frame, and
appeared successively in every word, and yet more in every gesture,
but most of all in every look and feature; presenting, I verily think,
such a picture as the world never saw anywhere else; yet such a
one as all the world must acknowledge perfectly true, interesting,
and unaffected. . . . But what struck me most, was the sustaining
with full powers, to the last, a character marked with the most di-
versified and vehement sensations, without ever departing once, so
far as I could perceive, even in the quickest transitions and the
fiercest paroxysms, from the simplicity of nature, the grace of attitude, or the beauty of expression.[16]

As it was with *Macbeth*, so rapturously did the critics sing
the praises of Garrick's wonderwork in *King Lear* that there is
precious little to record of the other Drury Lane performers in
the cast. Barry, who sometimes played Lear at Drury Lane but
more often at Covent Garden, was but "a faint apology" compared to Garrick.[17] Dignified and impressive, but unequal to the
mad scenes in which Garrick excelled, Barry was characterized
as "Every Inch a King," while Garrick was "Every Inch King
Lear." The character of Edgar was supported by Havard "with
great abilities," but the role was accounted Reddish's masterpiece,
especially in the mad scenes where, taking care not to overplay,
he made his portrayal a foil "to the serious, and truly passionate
Parts." As Gloster, Sparks was "extremely respectable," Berry not
far behind, and Burton "feeble." Palmer played the Bastard with
some merit but with too much levity, while Bensley's rendering
was "just." The *Dramatic Censor* refrained from commenting on
the performers of Goneril and Regan, female monsters of whom
it would be "a coarse compliment to say any ladies looked or
played them thoroughly in character." In Cordelia, Mrs. Cibber
was marked pleasing, Miss Bellamy monotonous, and Mrs. Barry,
who spoke and felt the part very well, afforded much satisfaction
"although she rather over-figures the Character."[18]

III

Although there were numerous accounts offered in tribute to
Garrick's acting of Lear, in few instances only can we find specific

details of the staging of the production. It is frustrating to think that the wealth of contemporary comment on this portrayal—in which the frantic part of Lear "seems never to have been rightly understood till this Gentleman studied it"[19]—has left us with little more than a vacuous legacy.

The Garrick promptbook for *King Lear* in the Harvard Theatre Collection, for example, when compared to the rich yieldings of the *Macbeth* promptbook already discussed must be regarded as a document of relatively little value. Made on a Bell edition (1774) of the play, it confronts us with precisely the same problems of assignment which the *Macbeth* promptbook offers. *King Lear* was produced only six times between the publication of the Bell text and Garrick's retirement. The three alternatives posited in my earlier discussion of the playhouse copy of *Macbeth* also apply here, but they are hardly worth consideration in this instance. There are very few markings in the Harvard copy of *King Lear*, all in the hand of William Hopkins, and they specify only P.S. or O.P. entrance and exit directions. There are no directions for scene changes, and with the exception of some cues for thunder and lightning on the heath there is nothing else. All notations, in fact, cease after the second scene of Act V, leaving the last nine pages of the text to fend for themselves. For these reasons, and because of the general scarcity of staging information, a scene-by-scene account of *King Lear* on Garrick's stage is not yet possible. But the existence of several contemporary illustrations, a fortunate letter, and several revealing eye-witness accounts allow in part the reconstruction of some of the exciting moments on the heath and in the prison.

Garrick's madness, coming upon him during the storm, evidently was an unforgettable sight to behold. Although his final acting version had cleared away a good deal of Tate's absurdities, the storm scenes remained still somewhat blurred; for the Fool was still omitted and Kent was Lear's companion on the heath. Fortunately, Lear's apostrophizing of the storm remained in Shakespeare's imagery. The effect of Garrick's actions with his Lear now on the verge of madness is described by Thomas Wilkes:

> I never see him coming down from one corner of the stage, with his old grey hair standing, as it were, erect on his head, his face filled with horror and attention, his hands expanded, and his whole frame actuated by a dreadful solemnity, but I am astounded, and share in all his distresses. . . . Methinks I share in his calamities, I feel the dark drifting rain, and the sharp tempest.[20]

In this delicate and almost imperceptible working up of the madness Garrick was remarkable, as his lines darted forth "like Flashes of Lightening in a stormy Night, making the Horrors more visible." "It steals so gradually," marked Pittard of the madness, "the Difference grows like a Colour, which runs on from the highest to the darkest Tint, without perceiving Shades . . . the King is never one Moment forgotten; it is Royalty in Lunacy." [21] In the insanity Garrick indulged in no sudden starts, no violent gestures, but his movements were slow and feeble, and during the whole time "he presented a sight of woe and misery, and total alienation from every idea but that of his unkind daughters." [22]

McArdell's mezzotint after Benjamin Wilson's painting, dated 1762, captures Lear upon the heath with Kent and Edgar (plate 10). Garrick as Lear stands in regal costume in his familiar distraught historical stance. The whole seems to be a valid theatrical rendition of III.3, as printed in the Bell text, which opens: "Storm continued. The Heath. Enter Lear and Kent," P.S. according to the promptbook, followed later by Edgar, "disguis'd like a Madman." The promptbook here bears cues for *"Thunder"* and *"Rain."*

A unique letter to the artist-scenographer Francis Hayman and a little-known engraving document the staging of a later moment in the storm. Hayman had executed a series of frontispieces for the Hanmer edition of Shakespeare in 1743-44. Among these was one for King Lear, which in grouping and staging anticipates the much later McArdell engraving. In costume and concept Hayman's illustration for Hanmer is highly suggestive of a stage performance, except in one conspicuous manner—the inclusion of the cowering Fool who has no stage counterpart in the eighteenth century. [23] Subsequently Hayman was commissioned to paint among other decorations for the Prince's Pavilion at Vauxhall Gardens four Shakespearean subjects: the Play Scene from *Hamlet*, Prospero and Miranda, a scene from *Henry V*, and Lear in the Storm. During the course of this project upon which Hayman labored in the forties and fifties, the artist apparently turned to Garrick for advice. In October of 1745, while biding his time at Bath before accepting offers to appear in Dublin, Garrick wrote a most illuminating letter to Hayman on the subject of the Lear illustration (plate 18):

> I should have perform'd my promise of writing to you sooner, could I have sent you a Letter either of Fun or Business. The dullness of this place does not afford for the first, & I have been too much harried by Fishing Feasting &c. to sit down to the last. M^r

Windham is now with me, we have had much talk about you and your performances & both agree the scheme of the six pictures from Shakespear will be an excellent and advantagious one . . . if you intend altering the scene in Lear (which by the by cannot be mended either in design or execution) what think you of the following one. Suppose Lear mad, upon the ground, with Edgar by him; his attitude should be leaning upon one hand & pointing wildly towards the Heavens with the other. Kent & Footman attend him, & Gloster comes to him with a Torch; the real Madness of Lear, the frantick affectation of Edgar, & the different looks of concern in the three other carracters, will have a fine effect. suppose you express Kent's particular care & distress by putting him upon one knee begging & entreating him to rise & go with Gloster. but I beg your pardon for pretending to give you advice in these affairs, you may thank yourself for it, it is your Flattery has made me impertinent . . .[24]

Unfortunately Hayman's painting of Lear in the Storm for Vauxhall Gardens seems not to have survived, nor have any details of its composition been recorded. Hayman, however, was also engaged in book illustrating for some thirty years after the appearance of the Hanmer edition, and in 1770-74 provided six frontispieces for the single-volume editions of Shakespeare by Jennens. Among these was one for *King Lear*—executed in precisely the manner Garrick had advised by his letter of 1745, with the single exception that the footman is absent. Being almost as much a creation of Garrick's mind as it is of Hayman's, it would seem to offer a valid rendition of the director's staging. The engraving delineates the second storm scene (III.3) as presented in the Tate-Garrick version, where Gloster seeks to carry Lear to shelter.

> *Kent.* Good my Lord, take his Offer.
> *Lear.* First let me talk with this Philosopher . . .
> *Glost.* Beseech you, Sir, go with me . . .
> *Kent.* His Wits are quite unsettled; good Sir, lets force him
> hence . . .
> *Glost.* Now, I prithee, Friend, let's take him in our Arms, and
> carry him where he shall meet both Welcome and Protection. Good Sir, along with us.

At this point in the action Garrick had introduced the business of falling asleep which required Gloster and Kent to carry him off the stage (P.S. according to the promptbook) for an effective exit. Macklin termed the falling asleep "a mere trick in acting," devised by Garrick to gain the advantage over Barry, who was too big a man "to be carried off the stage with the same ease that he could." [25] In a production for which staging details are few, the fortunate letter to Hayman, the subsequent plate in the Jennens edition, and the Tate-Garrick text all happily conspire to render a unique tableau of the action.[26]

The last great moment for Garrick came in the prison scene (V.3) when Lear in a final triumphant burst of strength fights off the soldiers who have come to execute him and Cordelia. In the scuffle, according to the Bell text, Lear "Snatches a Sword, and kills two of them; the rest quit Cordelia, and Exeunt." In what was perhaps Garrick's supreme tragic moment, after he had slain the two soldiers his face radiated exultation and pride, which, an instant later, as if exhausted by the superhuman exertion, gave way once again to the weakness and infirmity of age. The action is described by Hugh Kelly, who found some fault with Garrick's sudden transition from weakness to rage then back to weakness again:

> Ev'n in his Lear, where desperately wild,
> He stabs the ruffians to preserve his child,
> And quite worn out with tenderness and rage,
> Leans, wholly spent, and breathless on the stage;
> Then, while the tide of sympathy has rose,
> And every bosom labour'd with his woes,
> Than have I seen him negligently fall,
> Full with his face against the prison wall,
> Snatch every feature strangely from our sight,
> And check the flood of exquisite delight.[27]

Kelly's complaint concerned Garrick's hiding "the wond'rous workings of his face" by turning upstage against the prison wall. Tate Wilkinson, who as an under-actor at Drury Lane must have witnessed the performance many times, corroborates Kelly's account of Garrick's action, without the criticism, and at the same time provides in fortunate detail the general layout of the prison setting:

> On the P.S. side he slept on Cordelia's knee, and when with parental phrenzy, he had slain the two ruffians, he fell breathless against the MIDDLE pillar of two high arches that stretched across the stage, (behind which was spread a quantity of straw, but none towards the front, in the slovenly manner I have often seen it); consequently, on turning round to pronounce 'did I not, fellow?' he was in the centre; the characters equally divided, and the figure open to command the whole theatre: it was not higher up than the second wing from the frontispiece.[28]

Wilkinson's account becomes especially significant when studied in the light of an engraving (plate 13) which appeared in the *Universal Museum,* September 1767, depicting Barry and Mrs. Dancer (later to be Mrs. Barry) in the prison scene as it was performed that previous summer at the Haymarket Theatre. Centre-stage, with sword in hand, Barry sinks against the middle pillar of two arches which span the stage. Cordelia is within one arch stage-left (P.S. where Wilkinson said we would find her) and the two soldiers are beneath the right arch on straw which indeed overspreads in the slovenly manner so disliked by Wilkinson. The entire rendering reflects in precise detail Wilkinson's description of *Garrick's* staging of the scene. The fact that Barry also played it in the same manner should not be too surprising, for theatrical convention of the period would almost dictate that he do so. It will be recalled that Barry had perfected his Romeo under Garrick's directorship and then deserted in 1750 to mount the play on Covent Garden's boards in a like manner. Although Barry had not attempted Lear during his apprenticeship at Drury Lane, after his defection to the rival house he challenged his former mentor with a production of *King Lear* in the season 1755-56. As it had been with their Romeos, the two actors were compared scene by scene, with Garrick this time decidedly coming off the victor. In order to score their respective performances it seems fairly certain that the audiences would have demanded that both productions be staged in essentially the same fashion, point for point. Indeed, Davies called Barry's Lear "a lively copy" of Garrick's.[29] Furthermore, after Barry's summer performance of Lear at the Haymarket in 1767, which occasioned the engraving under discussion, he returned to the Drury Lane fold and played the role more frequently between 1767-68 and 1773-74 than did Garrick himself.[30] We must therefore regard this print from the *Universal Museum* as a highly authentic pictorial record of the manner in which this particular moment in *King Lear* was traditionally staged not only at Drury Lane, but at the other London theatres as well.

IV

In that round of brilliant performances with which Garrick took his last bows from the stage, *King Lear* seems to have held a special significance, perhaps because the swelling emotion Garrick evoked in the part was so appropriate to the final events. On May 13, 1776, the crowd who came to offer its final tribute flocked about the doors of old Drury by two o'clock. Never had there been such an overflow, never had Garrick seemed happier in

Lear. "The Applause was beyond description 3 or 4 loud Claps succeeding one another at all his Exits & many cry'd out Garrick for Ever &c &c." [31] A week later, on May 21, Garrick fulfilled his ambition to bring out the play in historical costumes and new scenery. "The play received considerable improvement last night," reported the *London Chronicle*, May 21-23, 1776, "from the characters being judiciously habited in Old English Dresses. Lear's was more majestic than usual, and in our opinion much more in character. The disposition of the scenery was likewise varied on the occasion, so as to produce a pleasing effect, and heighten the general representation of the piece." Steevens had prevailed upon him to play the genuine text of the play in honor of the occasion but Garrick, already under considerable strain, dared not risk the confusion which could result in unlearning a text he had been playing for so many years.

The performance was incomparable. "Human nature cannot arrive at greater Excellence in Acting than M^r G was possess'd of this Night," Hopkins wrote into the *Diaries*, "all words must fall far short of what he did & none but his Spectators can have an Idea how great he was—The Applause was unbounded." In the scenes of highest phrenetic emotion the house was dissolved into tears, and on stage even the characteristically unfeeling Goneril and Regan were seen to weep throughout the exquisite performance. Later that evening another scene of pathos was played out in the Green Room. With emotions running high, Garrick took his leave of his Cordelia, Miss Younge, whom despite all the heartache she had caused him in real life, he called his "daughter," and in a solemn manner bestowed his blessings upon her.

On June 8, 1776, Garrick played Lear for the last time, the next to last theatrical performance of his life. It took Joshua Reynolds three days to recover from this final *King Lear*, whose wonder it was—like Lear's heart itself—that it hath endured so long.

IX

Hamlet

BY THE EIGHTEENTH CENTURY Hamlet had become legend in theatrical lore.[1] Although Lear was Garrick's supreme tragic rendition, his Hamlet was the most popular, the one most readily shared between actor and audience as joint tenants of a single theatrical concept. Such a communization bespeaks a fairly well accepted interpretation of the dramatic situations and the title role of the play. The catholicity of the appeal of *Hamlet* is given impressive testimony by its 152 performances at Drury Lane between 1741 and 1776 (more than any other tragedy) and its previous record of appearances at both houses in every year but two between 1710 and 1740.[2]

Hamlet had first appeared on the Restoration stage in the summer of 1661, in an alteration which was probably the work of Davenant. The alteration, based on Q6 printed in 1637, did no great structural violence to the play, but it "being too long to be conveniently Acted," many passages and incidents were eliminated. Omitted from the acting version were Voltimand and Cornelius, all the Fortinbras material except the ending, the king's address from the throne on the state of government, Polonius' advice to Laertes and his scene with Reynaldo, and Hamlet's advice to the players. Greatly reduced were Horatio's explanation of the preparations for war, the king's reproof of Hamlet's excessive mourning, Laertes' and Polonius' advice to Ophelia, Hamlet's dissertation on drinking, the conversation with the first player, the Mouse-Trap, and the closet scene. In all, some 816 lines and parts of lines were lopped off, mostly from the lyric and sententious passages. This was the text which Betterton acted until his death in 1710. When Robert Wilks succeeded him as the accepted Hamlet of the London stage, he sought the literary assistance of his friend John Hughs in an effort to arrive at a text which would be closer to Shakespeare than was the Davenant version. The result was an edition in 1718 which restored old readings, significantly the "Angels and Ministers of Grace defend us" speech and Hamlet's advice to the players. Additional allowances must be made for some changes in interpretation and vocabulary, but in essence this text, which then served as the official acting version up to the early years of Garrick's management, did not differ in theatrical terms very much from the Restoration *Hamlet*.[3]

Garrick performed Hamlet for the first time in his career, in Dublin, August 12, 1742. From the outset he received many letters from friends and anonymous critics suggesting possible changes in the interpretation and the text. He had begun with the Wilks-Hughs text, and then gradually added, deleted, and revised as the occasion suited him. He had always been reluctant to allow his acting text of *Hamlet* to be published. When Garrick left for the Continent in 1763, and it seemed that in all probability he would never play the role again, Colman—left in charge of the theatre—released the text to Haws and Company for printing. Published that year, and then reissued again some six times, the edition differs somewhat from the Wilks-Hughs text, but only in the matter of excisions. It is a shorter play, but essentially the same in terms of action and situation.[4] Save for some more minor excisions and alterations, it is also the same text published by Bell in 1774. Since the Bell edition was the last acting version of the play published in Garrick's management, it will serve as the foundation for my stage reconstruction.

Garrick played this comparatively harmless arrangement for the greater part of his career. Then in the season 1772-73, for reasons almost as unfathomable as they are unpardonable, he foisted yet a new alteration upon an unwilling public. This alteration has been traditionally characterized as a "travesty of *Hamlet*" wrought by Garrick "in an evil moment." [5] The scholarship of Dr. Stone, however, who brought to light the true nature of the alteration—never printed in its own day—somewhat vindicates Garrick. The promptbook for the alteration, at the Folger Library, was made on a 1747 duodecimo edition of the play, and contains in Garrick's hand numerous notes, cuttings, and emendations. Although Garrick divided the acts differently, actually he made no serious changes in the action until the last act. The fate of Rosencrantz and Guildenstern was omitted, as was the funeral of Ophelia—thereby leaving her end uncertain and the grave-diggers unnecessary. In compensation for cutting the last act, Garrick restored some 629 lines of Shakespeare to the earlier parts of the play. "There is here no evidence of Bottom the Weaver—an actor mutilating all parts but his own," concludes Dr. Stone. "With the exception of Osric and the Grave-diggers, every character in the play is made richer by the restorations." [6] But the violence done to the last act is inexcusable. James Boaden, who claimed to have seen Garrick play the alteration, offers an accurate account of the final action:

> Hamlet bursts in upon the King and his court, and Laertes re-proaches him with his father's and his sister's deaths. The exasper-ation of both is at its height, when the King interposes; he had commanded Hamlet to depart for England, and declares that he will no longer bear this rebellious conduct, but that his wrath shall at length fall heavy on the prince. 'First,' exclaims Hamlet, 'feel you mine'; and he instantly stabs him. The queen rushes out imploring the attendants to save her from her son. Laertes, seeing treason and murder before him, attacks Hamlet to revenge his father, his sister, and his King. He wounds Hamlet mortally, and Horatio is on the point of making Laertes accompany him to the shades, when the prince commands him to desist, assuring him that it was the hand of Heaven, which administered by Laertes 'that precious balm for all his wounds.' We then learn that the miserable mother had dropt in a trance ere she could reach her chamber-door, and Hamlet im-plores for her 'an hour or penitance ere madness end her.' He then joins the hands of Laertes and Horatio, and commands them to unite their virtues (a coalition of ministers) 'to calm the troubled land.' The old couplet, as to the bodies, concludes the play.

All this, Boaden concludes with good reason, "was written in a mean and trashy common-place manner, and, in a word, sullied the page of Shakespeare, and disgraced the taste and judgment of Mr. Garrick." [7]

In the last months before retirement Garrick finally admitted to Sir William Young that his alteration of *Hamlet* was "the most impudent thing" he had ever done in all his life, yet he had sworn to himself that he "would not leave the stage till I had rescued that whole play from all the rubbish of the fifth act." [8]

Garrick's alteration was first presented at Drury Lane on December 18, 1772, when Hopkins wrote, "The Tragedy of Hamlet having been greatly Alter'd by D. G. was performed for the 1st time Mr Garrick playd divinely & merited the great Applause he receivd. It is alterd much for the better in regard to the part of Hamlet & I think the alterations very fine & proper."

Although fastidious critics were appalled, and rightly so, the immediate reaction of the press was for the most part extremely favorable. It was reported that "this brilliant Creation of the Poet's Fancy is purged from the Vapours and Clouds which obscured it,"[9] and "in short, instead of the critical part of the audience being obliged to deduct, the absurdities and improbabilities of this piece from its real merits, the chain of entertainment is now conducted, unbroken and connected."[10] The alteration held the stage until Garrick's retirement, sometimes with considerable opposition, but with much support. But when it no longer had the bribe of Garrick's own performance to enhance it, no English audience could be prevailed upon "to sit patiently and behold the martyrdom of their favorite author."[11] The spectators called for their old friends the grave-diggers and the fencing match, and it is hardly coincidental that both Garrick and his version of *Hamlet* died at about the same time.

II

The materials at hand for a study of Drury Lane's production of *Hamlet* are plentiful, for the center of vitality in the play was Garrick. His interpretation followed what has been termed "a most vigorous dramatic—a theatrical—tradition," which traced back to Shakespeare himself.[12]

Almost everyone who tried his hand at writing memoirs in the eighteenth century had something to say of Garrick's Hamlet; so the characteristic features of his interpretation are not difficult to define. Garrick was a splendid mouthpiece for Shakespeare's eloquence—so splendid, indeed, that he could eliminate the music that traditionally had accompanied Hamlet about the stage.[13] He subtilized where Betterton had been more robust, and he infused the role with more delicacy and sentimentality. The melancholy which was in later years to become the overwhelming characteristic of Hamlet performances was emphasized in Garrick's performance. But Garrick's Dane was still a man of action, no unmanly prince paralyzed by the tragic flaw of irresolution. From the accounts I shall soon offer, it will be clear that, indeed, Garrick conceived of the whole play in terms of action. His madness, never comic, always feigned, followed in the tradition of Betterton. Filial reverence and awe were emphasized qualities, and he showed a "real tenderness for Ophelia."[14] His interpretation fixed for the century a picture of Hamlet which was then painted in less brilliant strokes by a host of slavish imitators.[15]

The potency of Garrick's Hamlet had weakened but little by the final years when his age and body would normally have presented extreme disadvantages. Several late observers, to be sure, commented upon the signs of age which had become visible in his characterization. Edward Oxnard, the exile from New England, saw *Hamlet* on November 27, 1775, and although he was "highly entertained" by Garrick's admirable acting, he noted in his *Journal* the tacit reflection that "In his younger years, I think he must have been entitled to all the merit, which is ascribed to him in tragedy."[16] Johann Friedrich Grimm saw a performance in May, 1774: Garrick put him in *"einen kalten Todeschweiss"* during the interview with the ghost in which the clear voice of the actor, even in a whisper, could be heard in every corner of the theatre. But Grimm noticed as well the gray hairs on Garrick's head which marked this Hamlet as one who had lived over 55 years.[17] Even so, the performances continued to captivate. John Taylor describes the reactions of his friend, Farrington, who in Garrick's last season entered Drury Lane flushed with the excitement of seeing the great Roscius for the first time. The play was *Hamlet,* and Farrington sat bored until the Dane's first entrance:

> He then bent forward with eagerness. . . . Observing his painted face, which but ill concealed the effects of time, his bulky form and high-heeled shoes to raise his figure, Mr. Farrington drew back with disappointment and dejection, thinking that a man who at an earlier period might fully deserve all his celebrity, was going to expose himself in the attempt to perform a character for which from age, he was totally unfit. At length Garrick began to speak in answer to the King. Mr. Farrington then resumed his attention; and such was the truth, simplicity, and feeling . . . that my friend declared he lost sight of Garrick's age, bulk, and high-heeled shoes, and saw nothing but the 'Hamlet' which the actor had designed.[18]

Friedrich Günderode, a German visitor the year before, had a similar experience, first premature disappointment to discover Garrick so old, then amazement at the aura of youthful verve which he radiated.

I was all eyes and ears during the performance and was amazed at the extraordinary acting of this man. He was over sixty years of age [actually 57], yet he played . . . with all the verve and sensibility of youth. The melancholy which marked every feature of his face when he made his first appearance, the bold answer which he gives in reply to the King's inquiry into the cause of his sadness, all this won me over to him completely. But later, when the scene with the ghost came, when his soul was stirred to its depths, when he drew his sword and bravely followed the spectre whilst his hair stood on end with horror, I could perceive more plainly than ever that the man had absolute control over his features, and that he was completely absorbed in the impressions of the situation. . . . I do not hesitate to call Garrick the greatest and most excellent actor of the century.[19]

It was the opinion of Hannah More, who had the privilege to see Garrick's final Hamlet performance, that posterity would "never be able to form the slightest idea of his perfections." [20] She may well have been right, but the attempt, I believe, will not prove unprofitable, as we now turn to a composite reconstruction of *Hamlet* at Drury Lane during Garrick's management.

III

ACT I. Hamlet has enjoyed a long and persistent playing tradition. But it is also a play which offers ample opportunity for legitimately adding business and action to the skeletal frame of the stage directions found in the text.[21] The ghost scenes are typical instances. From Elizabethan times the appearance of the ghost had been regularly associated with traps, and the eighteenth century honored the tradition. In *The Prompter*, June 13, 1735, Aaron Hill suggested a way to conceal this awkward arrangement to greater advantage.

There never rises a *Ghost*, but, instead of exciting our *Horror*, The Poor Shade is sure to be laugh'd at, from the Awkwardness of these Peoples Invention.—Had they only the Wit, in Place of *shewing* us their TRAP, to conceal it, by contriving to *elevate*, at the same Time, a proper Length of that Part of the *Stage*, that is between the Ghost, and the *Audience*. No *Hole* being seen, for his Rising, he would *seem* to ascend, *through the Floor*, and bring with him, in Consequence, the *Alarm* he was sent to occasion.

For the second coming of the ghost in this scene, it has been suggested that on the Elizabethan stage two traps were required if sense was to be made of the lines

Bernardo.   'Tis here!
Horatio.   'Tis here!
Marcellus. 'Tis here! [22]

and although the tradition was later picked up in the nineteenth century, Garrick neatly solved the problem by cutting the sequence of lines from his acting version.

The costume of the ghost is interesting. He almost always appeared in armor, usually simulated, but sometimes real. When Garrick was playing the ghost during his first season at Goodman's Fields, so goes a popular story, "The stage, which rose very rapidly from the lamps, made it somewhat difficult for a performer to walk properly on it—and unfortunately it was the custom at that time for all Ghosts to appear in a complete suit—not of gilt leather—but of real armour." On one particular evening (December 9 or January 15, 1741/42, if the story does apply to Garrick) the armor had been "borrowed from the Tower and was somewhat of the stiffest—the moment therefore he was put up the trap-door—unable to keep his balance, he rolled down the stage to the lamps," of course, much to the delight of those in the pit.[23] In earlier years Barton Booth, in addition to placing a plume of feathers in his helmet, had covered the soles of his shoes with felt, allowing him to slide noiselessly over the stage like a true incorporeal being. How in a clanking suit of real armor he could have accomplished the "noiseless tread" so admired by Davies and Cooke must have been a wonder to behold.[24] A more practical suit of canvas or satin seems to have adorned the ghost at Garrick's Drury Lane. An amusing parody of stage-coronations which appeared in *Imperial Magazine*, October 1761, speaks of "the *canvas* suit of armour, usually worn by the ghost in *Hamlet*." When Lichtenberg (p. 11) saw Bransby play the ghost in 1775, "He looked, in truth, very fine, clad from head to foot in armour, for which a suit of steel-blue satin did duty; even his face is hidden, except for his pallid nose and a little to either side of it."

In the normal sequence of scenes in the Bell edition—the version Garrick acted most of his career—scene 2 brings us the next morning to the hall of state where after Hamlet's interview with his uncle and mother he remains behind for the "solid flesh" soliloquy. Horatio, Bernardo, and Marcellus then come to tell Hamlet of the strange nocturnal events occurring on the platform. After arranging to rendezvous later in the evening "twixt eleven and twelve," they all leave the stage; and Laertes, Ophelia, and Polonius appear immediately—without a scene change—for the farewells. Then the scene changes back to the platform. In Garrick's alteration for 1772, however, the Folger promptbook provides a different arrangement, which is perhaps an improvement. Here, after Hamlet and his friends depart, Garrick has in his own hand written an end to the act and has begun the second act, apparently in a new setting, with the farewell scene. The passage of time has been made clearer, I believe, by this alteration. It is now evening, Laertes has had time to prepare for his departure, and Polonius has been provided with a new line,

> . . . it's very late, ye moon is up
> And in full scanty lights ye go to ye vessell.

Garrick has thereby bridged the time gap effectively from the morning court scene to the second ghost scene which follows immediately, as I.3 in the Bell text, and II.1 in the 1772 alteration.

There are many accounts of Garrick's first encounter with the ghost. "As no Writer in any Age *penned* a Ghost like Shakespeare," reports the *St. James's Chronicle*, February 20-22, 1772, "so, in our Time, no Actor ever *saw* a Ghost like Garrick." Superior by far is the description by Lichtenberg, from which it is evident that beyond the perfecting of his own part, Garrick had directed the entire scene with an astute awareness of dramatic picturization and focus. For all its careful plotting and calculated postures, it must have been a supreme dramatic moment.

> Hamlet appears in a black dress, the only one in the whole court. . . . Horatio and Marcellus, in uniform, are with him and they are awaiting the ghost; Hamlet has folded his arms under his cloak and pulled his hat down over his eyes; it is a cold night and just twelve o'clock; the theatre is darkened, and the whole audience of some thousands are as quiet, and their faces as motionless, as though they were painted on the walls of the theatre; even from the farthest end of the playhouse one could hear a pin drop. Suddenly, as Hamlet moves toward the back of the stage slightly to the left and turns his back on the audience, Horatio starts, and saying, "Look my lord, it comes," points to the right, where the ghost has already appeared and stands motionless, before anyone is aware of him.

Garrick's movement to the left and away from the audience seems to have been designed to draw attention away from the rising of the ghost.

At these words Garrick turns sharply and at the same moment stag-
gers back two or three paces with his knees giving way under him;
his hat falls to the ground and both his arms, especially the left,
are stretched out nearly to their full length, with the hands as high
as his head, the right arm more bent and the hand lower, and the
fingers apart; his mouth is open: thus he stands rooted to the spot,
with legs apart, but no loss of dignity, supported by his friends,
who are better acquainted with the apparition and fear lest he
should collapse. His whole demeanour is so expressive of terror
that it made my flesh creep even before he began to speak. The
almost terror-struck silence of the audience, which preceded this
appearance and filled one with a sense of insecurity, probably did
much to enhance this effect. At last he speaks, not at the beginning,
but at the end of a breath, with a trembling voice: "Angels and
ministers of grace defend us!" words which supply anything this
scene may lack and make it one of the greatest and most terrible
which will ever be played on any stage.[25]

Fielding's Partridge was so terrified by the whole ghost business, especially Garrick's reaction, that his knees were set to
knocking—"if that little man there upon the stage is not frightened, I never saw any man frightened in my life." Perhaps Garrick did overplay his famous starting at the ghost. Johnson
characteristically jibed that such a reaction would in turn surely
frighten the spectre.[26] Nor was the *Theatrical Examiner* (1757,
p. 85) overly impressed: "The start at the ghost . . . may be picturesque, but it is grossly absurd to see a man fling himself into
so exact an attitude, which is impossible for him to remain steady
in, without two supporters." Other critics, as well, suggested that
it was unnecessary for Hamlet to collapse into the arms of Horatio and Marcellus. In his early performances at Dublin Garrick
held the posture of horror for so long that many thought he
needed the assistance of the prompter, and in 1772 the press was
still asking, "why will not the Actor speak—*Angels and Ministers!*
&c. upon the immediate Enterance of the Ghost?" [27]

Credit for the almost ludicrous effect must go to his hair-
dresser and wig-maker, an ingenious fellow named Perkins.[28] In
Garrick's Looking Glass (pp. 11-12) Samuel Pratt offers a hint
how the contraption was triggered:

> One minute makes a start, at most,
> But, if on entrance of a ghost,
> You stamp but loud enough, and fix,
> Instead of one, you may take six:
> 'Twere well, indeed, when it's come,
> With dext'rous dash of hand or thumb,
> You caus'd the hair, to stand an [*sic*] end.

Other actors of Hamlet, even though their hair did not rise in so miraculous a fashion, traditionally contrived to lose their hats at the sight of the ghost. One night—when the spectators were still allowed on stage for benefits at Drury Lane—Holland unburdened himself of his headpiece only to have some obliging fellow place it back on his head for him. "Holland unconcern'd play'd with it so," reports Cross, "& went off wth it (great Prudence)."

Benjamin Wilson's "Garrick as Hamlet," engraved by McArdell, depicts the famed encounter with the ghost (plate 12). Garrick stands horrified in his black French suit before a background of castle battlements in precisely the posture described by Lichtenberg. And, to be sure, his hair does seem to stand on end.

The ghost beckoned to the terrified Garrick, and Lichtenberg continuing the superb account (pp. 10-11) wishes we could see him,

> With eyes fixed on the ghost, though he is speaking to his companions, freeing himself from their restraining hands, as they warn him not to follow and hold him back. But at length, when they have tried his patience too far, he turns his face towards them, tears himself with great violence from their grasp, and draws his sword on them with a swiftness that makes one shudder, saying: "By Heaven! I'll make a ghost of him that lets me." That is enough for them. Then he stands with his sword upon guard against the spectre, saying: "Go on, I'll follow thee," and the ghost goes off the stage. Hamlet still remains motionless, his sword held out so as to make him keep his distance, and at length, when the spectator can no longer see the ghost, he begins slowly to follow him, now standing still and then going on, with sword still upon guard, eyes fixed on the ghost, hair disordered, and out of breath, until he too is lost to sight. You can well imagine what loud applause accompanies this exit. It begins as soon as the ghost goes off the stage and lasts until Hamlet also disappears.

In following the ghost in this manner, sword upon guard, Garrick had departed from the earlier convention of bravado and violence in which actors like Wilks had flourished and thrust at the ghost as if to chase it away.[29] Perhaps Garrick's sword trembled a bit, as he himself staggered out. Samuel Pratt has the manager advise his actors in *Garrick's Looking Glass* (p. 12):

> When Hamlet's phantom you pursue
> . . .
> Take care to stagger as you go:

Then as it waves you, not to vex it,
Let the sword tremble in your exit.

Ostensibly the ghost is leading his son to another part of the ramparts for his secret and dire disclosure of what is rotten in Denmark. In the Bell text the problem of having the ghost and Hamlet leave to go elsewhere and yet still be seen by the audience is handled thus: "Ex. Ghost and Hamlet; Hor. and Mar. retiring on the opposite side. Enter Ghost and Hamlet." There is, of course, no change of setting, and despite Hamlet's query, "Where wilt thou lead me?" it is evident that they are back where they started. Garrick re-entered as he had departed, sword on guard. In those early Dublin performances when the ghost announced, "I am thy Father's spirit," Garrick made a very respectable bow and sheathed his weapon.[30] Evidently he later did away with the bow, but in 1774 at Drury Lane, Gentleman William Smith, a copyist of Garrick, forgot himself and made "a very genteel bow" to his father, which prompted one wag in the pit to whisper, "This is Monsieur Hamlet." [31] During the subsequent interview the ghost traditionally was played almost motionless, with very little action. However, Bransby, who owned the part at Drury Lane from 1758 to the end of Garrick's reign, and who was described by the *Theatrical Review* (1772, II, 17) as "the shadow of a shade," was more animate. He sawed the air with the truncheon which was customarily carried everywhere by ghosts.[32]

The disappearance of the ghost is simply marked by "Exit" in the Bell text, although it is almost certain a stage-trap was employed, since the ghost must later be heard crying out from below the stage. When the ghost departed Garrick remained "rooted to the spot like one distraught." Not until Kemble did the convention begin of kneeling as the ghost descended.[33] The only occasion on which Garrick ever displeased Lichtenberg's sense of propriety was in the writing on the tablets. "He uttered the physiognomical observations, which he also notes down on his tablets: that one may smile and smile and be a villain, with an expression and a tone of petty mockery, almost as if he wished to describe a man who smiled perpetually, and yet was a villain." However, when Lichtenberg saw *Hamlet* for the second time he was "gratified and charmed to hear him declaim the same words in a manner entirely in accord with my own sentiments, namely, in the purposeful tone of one bent in immediate action" (pp. 30-31).

Act II. There is little to report of staging and business in Act II. In this act the character of Polonius is asserted. Critical opinion has long been divided on the true nature of this character, but the eighteenth-century public and actors had no doubts. He was a fool and a knave, always played by a low comedian. In *The Prompter,* May 27, 1735, Aaron Hill protested that Polonius was by Shakespeare's intentions a man of excellent understanding and great knowledge, but to an audience of the time he presented the "Image of an Old Buffoon," whose eyes were "turn'd *obliquely,*" whose face was dressed in "a foolish Leer," whose words were "*intermittently drawl'd* out, with a very strong Emphasis . . . tho' neither the *Words,* nor the *Sense,* have any *Comic Vein* in them." In his scenes with Ophelia and Hamlet, according to Hill, Polonius represented "the Figure and Manner of an Ideot."

Garrick strove to curtail the traditional farcical interpretation in 1754-55 when he prevailed upon Henry Woodward to take on the role for the first time and to play it more seriously, showing "dotage encroaching upon wisdom." Dressed in a grave habit of rich scarlet and gold, a costume different from convention, Woodward made the attempt at a new Polonius on his benefit night, March 20, 1755. The unconventional characterization appeared to the audience "flat and insipid," and after one more try in the next season on April 20, 1756, Woodward refused to play the role again. The manager's efforts, however, evidently accomplished some eventual good. Robert Baddeley, who played Polonius at Drury Lane from 1763 to the end of the management, was reported to be "just and natural," and avoided making the character nauseously ridiculous.[34]

Only a brief word may be offered on Rosencraus (as he is called in the Bell text) and Guildenstern. In 1772 the *St. James's Chronicle,* March 3-5, praised James Aickin and John Fawcett for being "as they ought to be, two very pliant courtly young Men"—and added, "Good Cloaths, tolerable Persons, and well-powdered Wigs (which is not always the Case) are the requisite Qualifications for these two young well-bred Gentlemen."

Act III. The third act of *Hamlet* is packed full with important events and theatrical moments such as the "to be, or not to be" soliloquy, the "Get thee to a nunnery" sequence, the speech to the players, the play scene itself, the king at prayer, and the closet scene. Curiously, the Bell text does not indicate a single change of setting during the entire act, although it is evident that a different setting was required at least for the closet scene.

There is no hint whether or not Garrick had anticipated Professor Dover Wilson by overhearing the plotting between Polonius and Claudius. The text reads, "Exeunt King and Pol." and then "Enter Hamlet." Where Ophelia goes is not clear either; she is not included in the exit directions, but she reappears without an entrance direction after the "To be, or not to be" soliloquy. Garrick appeared for the soliloquy in mourning black, now already feigning madness—as Lichtenberg describes him,

> with his thick hair dishevelled and a lock hanging over one shoulder; one of his black stockings has slipped down so as to show his white socks, and a loop of his red garter is hanging down beyond the middle of his calf.[35]

The slack stocking was *Hamlet* tradition of long standing, which may be seen in the famous frontispiece to Rowe's 1709 edition.[36] Another engraving, this one of a head and shoulder sketch, shows Garrick as Hamlet, with thick dishevelled hair and the one lock hanging over his shoulder just as Lichtenberg relates.[37]

> Thus he comes on the stage [Lichtenberg continues], sunk in contemplation, his chin resting on his right hand, and his right elbow on his left, and gazes solemnly downwards. And then, removing his right hand from his chin, but, if I remember right, still supporting it with his left hand, he speaks the words "To be or not to be" etc, softly, though, on account of the absolute silence (not because of some particular talent of the man's, as they say even in some of the newspapers), they are audible everywhere.

The Play Scene. From the *Theatrical Review*, May 1763, we learn that it had been customary to stage the mock play for the entertainment of the real audience in front of the house rather than for the royal party upon the stage. Hamlet's actor-friends performed "The Mouse-Trap" with their backs to the king and queen, who were located on the dais upstage. Hamlet and Ophelia were found down-front, an arrangement which prompted the *Theatrical Review* to question why these two were usually placed so far away from the rest of the court when rather they should have been positioned so that the prince had a full opportunity to observe his uncle's reactions. Francis Hayman, the scenographer-artist-book illustrator who was so useful in our discussion of *King Lear*, rendered at least three versions of the play scene. One is a very impressive oil painting, which perhaps is a version of the same subject Hayman treated for the Prince's Pavilion at Vauxhall Gardens shortly before 1745.[38] Here the king wearing the richest of eighteenth-century court finery rises from his throne which is set on a dais in the back-center of the composition. Polonius hovers behind the throne and the queen is on the other side. The players are enacting the murder on what would be the down-right-center section of the stage, if the painting has any theatrical validity. They face the audience. Hamlet is conspicuously absent from the rendition.

In another Hayman oil study of the scene, at the Folger Library and reproduced and discussed by Dr. William M. Merchant in a recent article,[39] the artist employs the same general composition with the notable exception that Hamlet, Ophelia, and Horatio are now found in the lower left corner of the canvas. Both paintings reflect the tradition of playing noted in the *Theatrical Review*.

Yet another Hayman illustration of this scene—this time for the 1744 Hanmer edition of Shakespeare (also reproduced and discussed by Dr. Merchant)—entirely reverses the arrangement. This time the murder is enacted up-center-stage, and the court is found in the fore-stage area, the king stage-right, and Hamlet and Ophelia stage-left. This frontispiece from Hanmer must have been created at about the same time that Hayman was preparing the Vauxhall paintings, and one can find some remote relationships, yet it does not reflect the Georgian stage tradition of placing "the Presence" in the dominating position, up-center-stage.

There is still another eighteenth-century engraving of "The Mouse-Trap"—not by Hayman—which is especially significant. It was printed in the *Universal Museum*, March 1769, and represents the production at Drury Lane.[40] Plate 15 is the murder being performed up-center, before a backscene which may well have contained a practical flight of stairs for Claudius' hurried exit.[41] In the forward stage-left area, and facing up to watch the play, are the king and queen. Down-right-center sits Ophelia with her fan in hand and Hamlet at her feet, his eyes intent upon the king. According to a 1759 pamphlet, *Reasons Why David Garrick, Esq. Should not Appear on the Stage* (p. 25), Garrick completely dominated the stage by playfully peering through Ophelia's fan. Not to be outdone herself, Mrs. Cibber, Drury Lane's best Ophelia, on one occasion while sitting upon the stage with Garrick at her feet, "rose up several times, and made as many courtesies, and these very low ones, to some ladies in the boxes" (*Theatrical Review*, May 1763). Even if we disregard the several Hayman illustrations as having no theatrical reference— which seems unlikely—we are still confronted with this illustration from the *Universal Museum* depicting the play scene in a manner which contradicts the complaint in the *Theatrical Review* that it "has ever been usual for the Actors of it, to perform with their backs to the King and Queen."

How was the scene staged by Garrick? One thing seems certain: Hamlet and Ophelia were in an advantageous position down-stage. A convenient solution to the placement of everyone else might be to situate the players of "The Mouse-Trap" down-stage, facing the audience, at least until 1763, the year the *Theatrical Review* made its complaint. It is not impossible that Garrick, whose sensitive ear was always tuned to the slightest criticism, then took his cue from the periodical and reversed the arrangement, thereby effecting a stage composition similar to that indicated in 1769 by the *Universal Museum.*

In any event, the Mouse-Trap having been sprung, the king cries for lights and makes a hasty retreat, followed by everyone in the court except Hamlet and Horatio. On his uttering of

> For some must watch, while some must sleep;
> Thus runs the world away.

Garrick always vigorously twirled a white handkerchief as he paced jubilantly about the stage. This was an habitual piece of business which Davies deplored Garrick never varied, thereby giving the impression of a lesson learned by rote rather than an effort of genuine feeling.[42]

In the Bell edition Hamlet is then summoned to his mother's chamber. Meanwhile the king orders Rosencrantz and Guildenstern to hustle away their charge to England. When these two gentlemen exit, Polonius appears to advise his lord of his plan to hide in the arras. The king is then left alone to his prayers. Hamlet's coming upon the king at prayer is omitted here, "as being unnecessary, and next, as tending to vitiate and degrade his character, much."[43] Although Davies states that Garrick had rejected the "horrid soliloquy" as an action "not only shocking, but highly improbable," the lines are found *in toto* in the Folger promptbook of the 1772 alteration.[44] They are, however, missing from Garrick's 1763 text. As for the king's prayer itself, the *St. James's Chronicle,* March 3-5, 1772, terms it "one of the most pathetic and highly finished repentant Struggles . . . which ever fell from the Pen of Genius!" and judges Thomas Jefferson, the player of Claudius at Drury Lane, most pleasing—"The Actor's

Merit in the above Soliloquy of Repentance is felt, and justly applauded."

The Closet Scene. There is no indication of the manner in which Garrick staged the killing of Polonius, but much of the remaining action in the closet scene was rooted in tradition that dated back at least to Betterton and the familiar engraving in the 1709 Rowe edition. In that engraving the ghost stands stage left, in armor, his beaker up, with a truncheon in his hand. The queen sits on a chair center, and looks in amazement at her son, who stands stage right, with mouth agape, hands and legs spread apart, the stocking on his right foot sagging. An overturned chair lies in the foreground downstage. Two large half-length portraits hang on the back wall, a detail which apparently bears little theatrical reference.

It was a matter of some critical dispute in the eighteenth century whether or not the two pictures—"The counterfeit presentment of two brothers"—should be hanging in the queen's chamber as they do in the Rowe edition engraving (and in the frontispiece to the 1734 Tonson edition), or if they should be miniatures taken from Hamlet's pocket. Apparently no one had yet thought of having Gertrude wear around her neck the miniature of Claudius, and Hamlet that of his father around his. The *St. James's Chronicle*, February 20-22, 1772, advises that stage tradition handed down from the author's own time had always dictated that the pictures be "in little." Thomas Davies corroborates by stating that "It has ever been the constant practice of the stage . . . for Hamlet, to produce from his pocket, two pictures in little, of his father and uncle, not much bigger than two large coins or medallions." At the same time, however, Davies, who wonders how "the graceful attitude of a man could be given in a miniature," suggests that since more elaborate decorations were now possible on the stage, the practice was no longer necessary, and two full-length portraits hung in different panels of the setting would be more appropriate.[45]

When the ghost entered "cas'd in canvass," in true theatrical tradition Garrick rose up from his seat, with an action described by Hugh Kelly as "The start—the heave—the stagger—and the stare,"[46] and contrived to kick over his chair. Drury Lane's carpenter had given special attention to Garrick's chair by tapering the feet and placing them well under the seat so that it fell at the slightest urging. Davies thought the chair-kicking a "poor stage-trick," but evidently Garrick did not always employ it.

"Happy as this [business] was," according to John Hill, "he had the moderation not to repeat it constantly." [47]

Francis Hayman did a rendition of the closet scene (plate 16). The illustration ostensibly has much theatrical validity and echoes in many details of composition the 1709 engraving for the Rowe edition. Here again the ghost is in armor, beaker up, truncheon in hand. The queen, however, is now out of her chair and expresses some particular concern for Hamlet's anxiety. Hamlet stands stage right in a posture quite similar to Garrick's familiar trade-mark, one hand struck out before him and the other brought up close to his body as if to ward off the spectre. The chair is here again turned over, but the portraits are missing from the wall.

Most Gertrudes took care never to look in the direction of the ghost even when bid to do so by Hamlet. Mrs. Pritchard, however, when Hamlet said, "Do you see nothing, there?" rather turned her head slowly round, "and with a certain *Glare* in her Eyes, which looked everywhere, and saw nothing, said *Nothing at all, yet all that's here I see!* which gave an Expression and Horror to the Whole not to be described." [48] It is not clear how the ghost departed, or for that matter, how he entered. The Bell text merely reads, "Enter Ghost" and "Exit Ghost." Hamlet's line, "Look where he goes, even now, out at the portal," suggests that a trap may not have been employed for the ghost's exit, despite Partridge's thinking he saw him "sink into the earth." The ghost need not even have used a door; he simply may have walked between the parallel wings. If live characters were allowed to do so, then certainly spectres were even more entitled to the privilege. Indeed, Dramaticus in *Gentleman's Magazine* (May 1789) considered it more appropriate for ghosts and aerial spirits to dissolve into plastered walls and wainscot panels than to disappear "through the gaping mouths of noisy trap-doors, as if spectres resided always in the bowels of the earth."

Act IV. The only event of import which may be recorded in any detail in Act IV is Ophelia's mad scene. Traditionally Ophelia was dressed in modified disorder and carried a handful of straw at her appearance here. In earlier years Mrs. Booth had portrayed her as a typically innocent, unhappy maid. But Mrs. Cibber, who played the role regularly at Drury Lane until her death in 1766, was, according to Davies, the first actress to interpret the part adequately. [49] In 1772 the *St. James's Chronicle* (March 3-5) reminisced on her performance:

> The Propriety of her Deportment, her Expression of Grief mixed with Terror at the Behaviour of Hamlet, and the Whole completed by a Harmony and Pathos in her Scenes of Madness, is only to be conceived by those who have seen her.

In her opening scenes perhaps she did speak "too tragically, and with a Sort of Stage Cant; but as the Part proceeded, the Actress grew warm, and when once she was seized with a Passeon, Whining and Monotony sunk before it."

Lichtenberg, to be sure, would have left us more details of Mrs. Cibber's performance than did the *St. James's Chronicle,* if only he had seen her act the role. He was, however, duly impressed with Mrs. Maria Smith, Drury Lane's Ophelia during the final four years of Garrick's management. In October of 1775 the astute reporter described Mrs. Smith as "a young woman and a good singer," whose

> long flaxen hair hung partly down her back, and partly over her shoulders; in her left hand she held a bunch of loose straw, and her whole demeanour in her madness was as gentle as the passion which caused it. The songs, which she sang charmingly, were fraught with such plaintive and tender melancholy that I fancied that I could still hear them far into the night, when I was alone. . . . I wish that Voltaire might have been here and heard Mrs. Smith's interpretation of Shakespeare.[50]

Act V. Like the witches in *Macbeth,* the grave-diggers were traditionally played as mere gallery stuff—some of the "rubbish" which Garrick had hoped to clear away by his 1772 alteration. It was the opinion of many, however, that the grave-diggers could have been played to critical approval if the buffoonery were considerably reduced. Walpole, citing the episode as an "admirable scene of nature," blamed Garrick for salaaming to French criticism by eliminating the scene altogether, when "if he had really been an intelligent manager," he would have made his alterations in the actors not in the play. The grave-diggers had always been represented by the lowest comedians—who incidentally usually rated large type billing on *Hamlet* playbills—and it was Walpole's contention that the roles should be distributed to those actors "who could best represent low nature seriously."[51] Instead the roles were personated with excessive grimace and gesticulation. Indeed, in the season before Garrick banished the scene, it was reported that Francis Waldron lisped the role of the second grave-digger at Drury Lane.[52]

As they dug the grave in a forward stage-trap, the comics

customarily discovered a number of skulls and bones, a business which prompted Partridge to express surprise at the profusion of human relics strewn about the stage. Real skulls evidently served the scene, often offending the more sensitive spectator. In 1755, Paul Hiffernan (*The Tuner*, No. 5, p. 18) objected to real skulls when a "wooden Substitution might be easily made by a Carpenter." And on September 22, 1783, the *Gazetteer and New Daily Advertiser* reported the discovery during some repairs to Drury Lane of "a human scull underneath the stage," the mystery of which was unravelled by an ancient scene-painter who identified it as Yorick's, "being lost many years since Mr. Garrick's time." As Professor Sprague has so neatly noted, the omission of the funeral scene from Garrick's later *Hamlet* productions explains how so important a property could have been misplaced. In a production of *Hamlet* which the German visitor Karl Gottlob Küttner saw in Manchester, 1783, the grave-trap was on the apron and could not be hidden by the curtain when the scene ended. (Another notice of a curtain dropping in the middle of an act.) A stage hand appeared and swept the skulls and bones back into the hole, replaced the cover, put down the carpet which was required for the carnage of the next scene, and then, his task finished, returned backstage. Küttner also saw one farcical grave-digger peel off a dozen waistcoats one after the other, to the delight of the gallery.[53] Although the waistcoat business was common to provincial productions at the time, there is no record of it at Garrick's theatre. In fact, Thomas King, one of Garrick's best actors and assistant director, stated that he had never "as a member of the Theatre Royal in London and Dublin" seen the grave-digger eat bread and cheese or sink to the degradation of the multiple waistcoats.[54]

Into this scene comes Hamlet to palaver with the grave-diggers. An early critic of Garrick's 1742 Dublin performances found him too solemn in his conversation here—"does not that droll character he talks with require a behaviour something more light and *degagé?*" A subsequent letter indicates that Garrick took heed and was "something easier" with the grave-digger thereafter.[55] Garrick was still wearing the black French suit in the graveyard which he had worn throughout the first four acts. Thomas Wilks discovered an impropriety here, since in such a familiar habit the grave-diggers should easily have recognized him immediately.[56]

While Hamlet reflects upon the fate common to Yorick, Alexander, and all mankind, the "Scene draws, and discovers the King, Queen, Laertes, and Priest, with a Corse." Garrick seems to have given Ophelia a simple funeral, very much unlike the gaudy affair with which Juliet was interred.[57] The small funeral party must come forward from their upstage positions to the grave-trap in which Ophelia is placed. The occasion provided another clap-trap opportunity for Garrick at the leaping into the grave. By the close of his career he evidently had not fully overcome that tendency for over-acting which several critics had noticed in his first few years on the stage. In some "Dramatic Strictures on the Performance of Hamlet," a critic in *St. James's Chronicle*, February 20-22, 1772, lamented that after delivering the advice to the players "with good Accent, and good Discretion," Garrick should then in a rant at Ophelia's grave contradict himself for the sake of applause.

After Hamlet's portent to the king and queen that "the dog will have his day," the funeral party, including Hamlet and Horatio, retires from the stage. In Garrick's acting version some eighty lines of the next scene in which Hamlet renders an account of his escape at sea are eliminated, and rather than shifting the locale at this point, the action continues in the graveyard. As soon as the stage is clear Hamlet and Horatio re-enter immediately, as Hamlet speaks,

> So much for this.
> Do you remember all the circumstance?

thereby giving the impression that the whole story of his escape and return to Denmark has been related to Horatio off-stage. I am inclined to agree with Francis Gentleman, who in an editorial annotation suggests that "retaining a dozen or fifteen" of the original lines "would make the plot more clear." Osric now appears in the graveyard to inform Hamlet of the proposed fencing match, which in this cutting has, indeed, been concocted rather quickly. Hamlet accepts the challenge and he, Horatio, and Osric leave the stage. Now the "Scene draws, and discovers King, Queen, Laertes, Gentlemen, and Guards. Re-enter Hamlet and Horatio." The reason for Garrick's continuing the previous scene in the graveyard now becomes evident. The grave-diggers dug their grave in the forward section of the stage and the shutters had drawn to reveal the funeral procession. One of two things then happened after the funeral: either the shutters closed again prior to the return of Hamlet and Horatio for the interview with

Osric, and then opened again awhile later to discover the setting for the final scene; or another set of shutters parted for this final discovery. In either event, since the action of the last scene obviously required a full-stage treatment, it is almost certain that only part of the stage—probably only the apron—was employed for the funeral.

There are no details on record for Garrick's staging of the fencing match and the subsequent killings. The Bell text provides the conventional direction, "Laertes wounds Hamlet; then in the scuffling they change rapiers, and Hamlet wounds Laertes." The Queen dies as she warns her son of the poisoned drink, and after hearing about the treachery of the envenomed rapier from Laertes, Hamlet "Stabs the King," who dies immediately, followed in turn by Laertes, and finally by the sweet Prince. When Garrick did away with the fencing match and altered the ending so blatantly in 1772, he was bowing not only to the force of French criticism, as so many commentators have observed, but also to the opinion of a number of his English colleagues. Francis Gentleman, for example, in his comments in the Bell text found the last scene as written by Shakespeare to be "very reprehensible." The *London Chronicle,* February 15-17, 1757, reflected the tenor of a considerable body of contemporary criticism which objected to the innocent dying with the guilty—a play that opens so nobly should have a grander close—"and the World is left to judge which is worst, the Fencing of the Actors, or the Folly of the Poet in introducing it."

In his 1772 alteration, Garrick of course retained the catastrophe, but he alleviated the general carnage by omitting the deaths of Gertrude and Laertes. In this new arrangement Claudius also fought with Hamlet for a moment before being slain. Claudius "defends himself, and is killed in the reencounter." Previously, the king used "to be stuck like a pig on the stage." [58] In this matter Garrick evidently heeded the advice of George Steevens, another supporter of the new ending, who wrote to him in 1771, "As you intend to stab the usurper, I beg, for your own sake, you will take care that this circumstance is not on his part awkwardly represented. . . . A stab given to an unarmed or a defenceless man has seldom a very happy effect." [59]

In both versions of the play, the Bell text and the 1772 alteration, Fortinbras fails to appear at the conclusion, and Horatio orders the bodies to be taken up for the final exit.

IV

On May 30, 1776, *Hamlet* was performed for the 152nd and last time during Garrick's career at Drury Lane. "Pit & Boxes were put together," according to Hopkins' entry for that night, and "most of the Tickets were sold for a Guinea a piece, a few under half a guinea & the whole quantity sold in about Two Hours." All the proceeds went to the Drury Lane Theatrical Fund for retired and infirm actors, which Garrick had been instrumental in establishing in 1766 and had generously supported thereafter. The following day John Eliot wrote to Garrick, "You astonished me last night. In your life you were never greater: I think never so great." Hannah More also saw this final *Hamlet* and wrote to the Reverend Dr. Stonehouse, "I would not wrong him and my-self so much, as to tell you what I think of it; it is sufficient that you have seen him: I pity those who have not." [60]

X

The Provok'd Wife

GARRICK'S REMARKABLE TALENTS as a director and actor were not limited to the staging of tragedy. The statistical breakdown of Drury Lane's repertory, 1747-1776, to the contrary, indicates that he produced 113 different comedies compared to 77 different tragedies. The performances of comedies (3,131) at Drury Lane far outnumber the performances of tragedies (1,899). No single comedy (1747-1776) attained the 116 performances given *Hamlet* or the 142 given *Romeo and Juliet,* but the comedies, *The Suspicious Husband* (126), *The Stratagem* (100), *Much Ado About Nothing* (105), *The Conscious Lovers* (96), *The Provok'd Wife* (95), and *The Clandestine Marriage* (87) all were played more frequently than either *King Lear* (83) or *Macbeth* (77).[1]

Garrick himself was equally at home in either genre. His Abel Drugger marked him the greatest comedian of his day, as his Lear ranked him the greatest tragedian. His Bayes was a capital bit of burlesque, his Archer and Ranger, light, elegant, dashing heroes, his Drugger a rich, broad portrayal of unutterable humor. To comedy he brought a body and limbs of surprising flexibility and elasticity, wonderfully marked features, remarkably expressive eyes,[2] and a mind as quick as his genius. Added to these impressive advantages was a keen sense of the comic. Lichtenberg's account of the scene between Garrick and Weston in *The Stratagem* has already been quoted as an example of the director's gift for focusing with utmost lucidity upon the truly comic aspects of a situation. The *London Chronicle's* (March 5-8, 1757) praise of Garrick's Abel Drugger will suggest as well his delicate sense of moderation in matters comic.

> . . . how admirably does he exhibit the minutest Circumstances, with the exactest Precision, without Buffoonry, or Grimace:—There is no Twisting of Features, no Squinting but all is as correct as if a real Tobacco Boy were before us. It is really surprising how he . . . can present us such a Face of Inanity.

Garrick's judicious restraint as Drugger was found by Lichtenberg to be indescribable.[3] Hannah More, who saw him play both Hamlet and Drugger in the last weeks of his career, exalted, "Had I not seen him in both, I should have thought it as possible for Milton to have written 'Hudibras,' and Butler 'Paradise Lost,' as for one man to have played *Hamlet* and *Drugger* with such excellence."[4] The *London Chronicle*, March 5-8, 1757, reflects the tenor of critical accolades for the manager's two-sided acting genius: "The Actor who can amazingly reach the Sublime in a Lear, or Hamlet, and then exhibit the most ridiculous Appearances, must be possessed of such two-fold and opposite Powers, as hardly ever before concentered in one Man, and are not likely to form such a Tragic-comic Genius again."

The glorious achievement of Shakespearean tragedy at Drury Lane coincided with a definite increase in appreciation of the Bard in critical and literary circles, and it was only natural that most of the comment of the period which concerns theatrical production should center upon the performances being offered by Shakespeare's High Priest. Comedy, on the other hand, then as now was a rather mercurial and transitory thing, which is more easily appreciated when seen than when talked about. For all the popularity enjoyed by comedy at Drury Lane, the type of information this book hopes to convey will be found sorely lacking in the available sources. Garrick the director, therefore, is better illuminated by a detailed consideration of the tragedies. One comedy, however, *The Provok'd Wife*, by dint of the extant promptbook, will serve the purpose of rounding out this study of Garrick's production methods. The picture that will emerge of Garrick's preparation of the script, his careful casting, his attention to the details of the production, and the staging methods will not differ appreciably from this same director's approach to tragedy. The theatrical ingredients—with the exception of the

nature of the script itself—were essentially the same in each instance.

II

The Provok'd Wife was a play ideally suited to Garrick's genius
for comic and satiric interpretation of character. It had first been
acted at Lincoln's-Inn-Fields in May, 1697, and then became
standard theatrical fare until Garrick played Sir John Brute for
the last time on April 30, 1776. It is to be regretted that the play
has not at all been popular since the retirement of Garrick, for it
is an eminently actable comedy. Its lush roles were perhaps
originally written for Betterton, Mrs. Barry, and Mrs. Bracegirdle,
each of whom had a great reputation as Sir John, Lady Brute,
and Belinda, respectively. In 1726 Colley Cibber took over the
role of Lord Brute, evidently basing his interpretation on Betterton's. Quin, who first played the part on January 3, 1719, at
Lincoln's-Inn-Fields, became, however, the accomplished favorite
in the role for the next 23 years until Garrick appeared at Drury
Lane on November 16, 1744. Sir John Brute was one of Garrick's
most popular comedy creations, but it was not universally recognized as one of his best interpretations. Opinion was always
mixed on the features of his portrayal. Many critics denied that
he measured up to Quin. In *The Rosciad,* Churchill awarded the
palm to Quin (but managed to mar the compliment with a pun
on the character's name):

> In Brute he shone unequalled; all agree
> Garrick's not half so great a Brute as he.

Walpole, who never liked Garrick, thought him a poor Lothario,
ridiculous as Othello, and inferior to Quin as Brute, and—here
his judgment must become suspect—also inferior to Quin as Macbeth. A diplomat to the end, Tate Wilkinson believed that the
interpretations of Garrick and Quin were vastly different, but
both readings were correct in their own right.[5] It was the opinion
of the *London Chronicle,* October 14-17, 1758, that Garrick mis-
interpreted the role. Instead of making the character the
"Brute," the ill-natured surly swine portrayed by Quin, Garrick
had presented him as a very attractive favorite, a "joyous agreeable wicked dog." This critic, however, seems to have based his
opinion on moral criteria—"It is amazing to me that Mr. Garrick
will *attempt* the part of Sir John Brute, a part which he not only
apparently mistakes, but in which he is absolutely prejudicial

to the morals of his countrymen." Yet, only a year earlier in the same *London Chronicle,* March 3-5, 1757, a different critic had heartily endorsed Garrick's interpretation by asserting in the face of recent criticism that the actor did play the role as brilliantly as he played other comedy roles.

> . . . a large uncouth Figure, with a deep toned Voice, is by no means necessary; on the contrary, the Appearance of one, worn-out with excessive Debauchery is the more natural of the two. . . . Mr. Garrick is not morosely sullen, but peevishly fractious with his Wife. In his Manner, there is an Appearance of Acrimony, rather than downright Insensibility and Rudeness.[6]

Garrick added a further dimension to the part which had not been within the scope of Quin's powers. Quin never could have been the noble rake. Garrick played Brute as naturally as possible, and combined the boisterous rioter—which Quin could thunder so well—with the gentleman debauchee. Although some spectators still preferred Quin's coarse, drink-sodden boor, a greater number were taken by Garrick's more subtle and delightful rendering of the debauched rakish gentleman. Lichtenberg describes (pp. 17-18) how Garrick facilitated his interpretation by a clever use of costumes and properties:

> Sir John Brute is not merely a dissolute fellow, but Garrick makes him an old fop also, this being apparent from his costume. On top of a wig, which is more or less suitable for one of his years, he has perched a small, beribboned, modish hat so jauntily that it covers no more of his forehead than was already hidden by his wig. In his hand he holds one of those hooked oaken sticks, with which every young poltroon makes himself look like a devil of a fellow in the Park in the morning.
>
> Sir John makes use of this stick to emphasize his words with bluster, especially when only females are present, or in his passion to rain blows where no one is standing who might take them amiss.

Some of the criticism evoked by Garrick's production of *The Provok'd Wife* was leveled not so much at Garrick's acting as at his poor judgment in offering the play at all. The eighteenth-century manager had the additional responsibility of being an arbiter of taste and morals. Garrick had taken great pains to make his production palatable to the decorous sensitivity of many of his colleagues, but the play had always been fair game for the literary moralists, and may well have been the comedy which provoked Jeremy Collier's *Short View of the Immorality and Profaneness of the English Stage* in 1698. When matters of taste began to change at the turn of the century, Vanbrugh himself sometime between 1704 and 1725 made some revisions in the play, notably the conversion of Sir John's disguise when drunk, from the habit of a clergy to the dress of a woman of quality. But the play was even now anything but puerile.

Realizing that his audience would scarcely tolerate the licence of even this second version, when Garrick decided to produce the play in 1744 he altered it extensively to satisfy the change in *mores* which had happened during the first half of the century. His arrangement of the play was made on a 1743 12mo Dublin edition which was then used as the prompter's copy during Garrick's subsequent management. This playhouse document, now at the Folger Library, has been worked over twice, first in pencil and the second time in ink. Almost all the changes are omissions. The details of the omissions, which number seventy-seven in all and range from a word or two to several whole pages of printed text, are discussed at length by Professor Bergmann. As might be expected the revisions were executed mainly in the interests of good taste, and most of Garrick's cuttings concern lines dealing with sex, cuckoldry, or objectionable words.

Despite his serious effort to clean up the play Garrick could not hope to satisfy everyone. Francis Gentleman, for one, judged it "scandalously licentious" even in this new version, and expressed surprise that the manager had contributed to keeping alive so censurable a piece, whose "merits are, or ought to be totally sunk into its infamy." [7] In February 1762 the *Universal Museum* enumerated the fundamental moral objections:

> If a flow of licentious wit, ridiculing the marriage state, virtue, and honour; if vicious characters, drawn in a favourable light; if virtue and vice, villainy and honour, being jumbled promiscuously together, with no moral than can speak but in favour of licentiousness, can inform an excellent comedy, this piece has great Merit.[8]

The Provok'd Wife was first produced under Garrick-Lacy management November 10, 1747, supported by an especially expert cast: Heartfree by Delane, Rasor by Yates, Taylor by Shuter, Lady Fancyful by Mrs. Clive, Belinda by Mrs. Woffington, and Lady Brute by Mrs. Cibber. The few available reviews supply the usual vacuous remarks. Mrs. Clive, for example, although physically unfit for Lady Fancyful, was excellent, and Mrs. Cibber performed well enough, but it was generally believed she wanted spirit as Lady Brute—"but if she does," commented the

London Chronicle, October 14-17, 1758, "it is my opinion rather an advantage to it, which would otherwise appear too licentious." The *Universal Museum,* February 1762, complained that Mrs. Cibber's voice "whines and flaggs" and she indulges in a "perpetual and inexpressive motion of the head, first one way, and then the other." In later years the best actresses of the company performed in this comedy. Mrs. Barry and Miss Younge played Lady Brute, Miss Bellamy took over Lady Fancyful, and Belinda was ably filled by Miss Houghton.

The play received 95 performances at Drury Lane during the twenty-nine years of the management. Save two, Garrick played every performance as Lord Brute. On January 23, 1765, Thomas King tried the role once while Garrick was on the Continent, and on April 2, 1770, James Love was foolish enough to appear in the role at his own benefit. That night Hopkins entered in the *Diaries:* "Mr. Love Sr John Brute. a fat performance (and as Mr. L—says) he wanted breath to blow the Jokes out." As the sixth most frequently played comedy during our period at Drury Lane, *The Provok'd Wife* enjoyed an important and profitable stage history. The *Cross-Hopkins Diaries* record several incidents of parenthetical interest. During a performance on November 7, 1753, "a whore [was] taken out for noise," and in the afterpiece on February 18, 1751, a leading actress "ran away with some Gentleman," bringing a sudden end to the entertainment. *The Provok'd Wife* was also the play coupled with the ill-fated *Les Fêtes Chinoises* on November 13, 1755.

III

The Folger promptbook of *The Provok'd Wife* is a fully annotated playhouse copy, and as such represents an extremely valuable document for eighteenth-century theatrical history. Its special significance in revealing the fundamental staging techniques and procedures practiced at Drury Lane has already been discussed in a previous chapter.

The insights which its markings and symbols offer into an understanding of the groove system, the use of stock scenes, and the occasional employment of the curtain are as fascinating as they are unequivocal. To convey fully the richness of this promptbook would require a separate annotated edition of the entire text, but a detailed account of several scenes at this time will serve nicely to illuminate the director at work.

Scene 2 of Act I is an excellent example of Garrick's altering and arranging of his business in order to move the action along.[9] The setting represents Lady Fancyful's dressing room, a *"Pic & chr Toilet"* set in the area of the *"3 gr."* [10] Although the printed text reads, "Enter Lady Fancyful, Madamoiselle, and Cornet," the absence of an entrance direction and the presence of the symbol (w) indicates that the shutters of the previous scene (I.1) parted to discover the performers on stage. The opening dialogue concerns the preparation of Lady Fancyful's toilet, during which Cornet is ordered to leave the room—*"Exit Cornet PS."* The text calls for Cornet to re-enter with a letter containing a new song written by a secret admirer of Lady Fancyful. Pipe is called in to sing the song, and then another servant enters with a second letter from the same admirer who requests a meeting in St. James's Park within the hour. Here Garrick has eliminated the delivery of the first letter, the song is done away with, and Cornet enters with only a single letter requesting the meeting and then leaves immediately *(PS & Exit)*. As a result, a page of dialogue and two characters, Pipe and a servant, are removed.

Lady Fancyful is eager for the assignation, and by her line, "How do I know what designs he may have? He may intend to ravish me, for aught I know," doth seem to protest too much. Some naughty coaxing on the part of her French maid persuades her to prefer nature to reason, and off they run to St. James's Park. The original stage direction for Madamoiselle to turn "to her Lady, and helping her on with her Things," has been cut by Garrick in the promptbook, suggesting that the flow of action was here facilitated by having Lady Fancyful's toilet already completed by this moment. It is interesting to note that the published texts of Garrick's version continue to print the direction despite its elimination from the promptbook. The two women leave, Madamoiselle "Forcing her Lady off *PS*," and the act concludes. Although the warning *"Ring"* appears approximately one page before the end of the act, there is no curtain direction. The notation is undoubtedly a cue for the musicians to prepare.

The next moment of special interest occurs in III.1 where the curtain rises (it has fallen at the end of Act II, according to the promptbook) to discover "Sir John, Lady Brute, and Belinda rising from the Table." The setting is *"Pal. 4h gr.,"* a stock scene which serves throughout as the living room. Sir John settles down in his chair to enjoy his pipe, while the ladies call for Lovewell to fetch their needlework. The prattle of Lady Brute and Belinda so disturbs Sir John that "He rises in a Fury, throws his Pipe at 'em, and drives 'em out, *PS*." The frontispiece to the edition of the play published by Rivington in 1776 *(New English Theatre)* depicts this precise moment. We find Garrick in the dress of a very fine gentleman rising from his chair, his feet in ballet-like position, his arm drawn back with pipe poised to be thrown. The figure of Garrick seems to be a good likeness, but the two women, who look like identical twins, could hardly bear any resemblance to any of the several actresses who played these roles during Garrick's management. As illustrated, the open door apparently is located upstage-right. This detail would seem to be a bit of artistic license on two counts. First, there is no suggestion in the promptbook that any but a proscenium door was here employed. When other doors are to be used the promptbook is very explicit. Secondly, the promptbook stipulates that the women are to be driven out the *PS* door. This direction together with the illustration might seriously challenge my arbitrary placement of PS at stage-left were it not for the fact that in another engraving of another scene from this same play (soon to be discussed) the exit—clearly marked *PS* in the promptbook—is shown stage-left. (Indeed, any attempt to establish PS by a collation of engravings and prompt directions leads only to chaos. For every instance in which PS is established at stage-left, there is another which just as conclusively establishes it on the other side. I can only hope that theatrical tradition is serving us well.)

A revealing bit of stagecraft is witnessed in Garrick's arrangement of the subsequent action of Act III, a sequence of staging which only could be gathered from the promptbook. After Lord Brute drives the women out, he is visited by a series of characters, all of whom eventually depart, leaving the stage empty. Then "Re-enter Lady Brute, sola *PS*," soon followed by Constant, her former lover, to whom she has been driven again by the repeated and insufferable abuses of her husband. In the printed editions this assignation transpires in the drawing room as simply the extension of this very long first scene of the act. At this point in the promptbook, however, Garrick had added a scene change which is not indicated by any printed text—"(w)*ch chr 1 gr.*"— and this intrigue is now carried out in another chamber significently found at the first groove. The reason for this arrangement soon becomes evident. The following scene is the drinking bout among Brute and his friends in the tavern: the direction reads, "Scene opens: Lord Rake, Sir John, &c. at a Table drinking," with

the prompt appendage, "(w) *Tav Ch 3d gr.*" Without the interpolated scene change it would have been necessary to shift from
one full-stage setting *("Pal 4th gr.")* directly to another full-stage
setting in the tavern. Such a transition obviously would have
consumed some time, for the drawing room furniture and properties must be removed and those necessary to the tavern must
be placed. Garrick solved his problem by inserting the hitherto
unrecorded change from the drawing room to Lady Brute's chamber. The shutters closed in the first groove to cover the previous
"*Pal.*" setting and Lady Brute and Constant played their brief
meeting on the apron. When this dialogue was concluded the
shutters parted again to reveal the tavern scene, full-stage. The
flow of action was allowed to proceed unimpeded.

The episodes connected with the drunken orgy and Brute's
female disguise were the highlights of any production of *The
Provok'd Wife* at Drury Lane. Fitzgerald offers the following
composite impression of the tavern scene which he culled from
various commentators:

> . . . it was a perfect triumph of roaring spirit and intoxication. It
> increased every instant. There was infinite variety in his rioting,
> which had an electric effect, and kept the house in a roar. His
> marked features—the eyebrows, and his eyes—never ceased to
> play. . . . He never forgot himself a moment, and as the drunkenness
> increased, the mouth opened more and more.[11]

The orgy ends with Sir John "reeling" out *PS* followed by the
rest of the merry-makers.

The setting shifts back to Lady Brute's chamber for a dialogue between her and Belinda, most of which Garrick has cut in
the promptbook to a bare dozen or so lines, allowing just time
enough to clear the tavern and prepare for the famous assault
upon the watch by Sir John. The cuttings in this transitional scene
are not noted in the later printed versions of the text.

The course of the drunken frolic brings the revelers to Covent
Garden, which is represented by "*Street 2 gr.*" It is late evening,
"*Lamps down,*" according to the promptbook. Sir John and his
companions enter *PS*, soon followed by "a Taylor, with a Bundle
under his Arm. *PS.*" They accost the tailor, and when it is discovered that the bundle contains a short cloak and wrapping
gown for Lady Brute, Sir John insists upon putting it on.

> *Sir John.*   . . . The Robe of my Wife—with Reverence let me ap-
> proach it. The dear Angel is always taking Care of

me in Danger, and has sent me this Suit of Armour
to protect me in this Day of Battle; on they go.

All.   O brave Knight!

Lord Rake. Live *Don* Quixote the Second.

The Constable and the Watch enter *PS* to investigate the street disturbance. Sir John, now fancying himself "Bonduca, Queen of the Welchmen," determines to "destroy your Roman Legion in an Instant," and snatching a watchman's staff he attacks the constabulary. The 1743 Dublin text on which the promptbook is fashioned provides the simple printed direction, "Fights." The added prompter's notation, *"off & reenter PS.,"* suggests that when Sir John began to get the worst of the battle he ran off, was pursued by the Watch, and then brought back to the stage. The direction provided in Garrick's published text (1st edition 1761) implies that at some later date perhaps the manager revised the business somewhat. Here we find, "Snatches a Watchman's Staff, strikes at the Watch, and falls down, his Party drove off."

A familiar painting by Zoffany, exhibited at the Society of Artists in 1765 as "Mr. Garrick's Drunken Scene in *The Provok'd Wife*," depicts this moment in the action. The painting, engraved in mezzotint by John Finlayson in 1768, shows besides Garrick, Henry Vaughan, Hullet, Thomas Clough, William Parsons, Thomas Phillips, and Watkins, in the characters of the Watchmen. To what extent the picture reflects in detail what was actually seen on the stage is difficult to say, but it must be acknowledged that its pictorial composition is excellent.

Zoffany also did an earlier painting of the solo central figure of Garrick in the group, which was most likely a preliminary study of the larger picture. Garrick modeled for it at Zoffany's studio in the Piazza, Covent Garden. In this solo figure painting Garrick is depicted

> in a yellow satin brocaded dress with a white lining, a green lace shawl and a lace cap with pink ribbons. From inside the raised skirt appears his right leg, and the knee of his black breeches with red ribbons, white stocking and black buckled shoe.[12]

Garrick's impersonation of Lady Brute was reported to have been superb: "You would swear he had often attended the Toilet, and there gleaned up the many various Airs of the Fair Sex: He is perfectly versed in the Exercise of the Fan, the Lips, the Adjustment of the Tucker, and even the minutest Conduct of the

Finger," recorded the *London Chronicle,* March 3-5, 1757. For his performances of Sir John in the last season, 1775-76, Garrick dressed the character in a ridiculous head-dress inspired by the raging female fashion of wearing pieces so tall that their owners could not fit into a coach or sedan-chair unless it was especially equipped with a cupola. Once erected after three arduous hours of setting, these head-pieces stood for days, in some instances acquiring mice as tenants.[13] On the night of October 31, 1775, when Garrick first introduced the head-piece, Hopkins entered in the *Diaries,*

> Mr G. never play'd better & when he was in Woms Cloths he had a head drest with Feathers Fruit etc. as extravagn as possible to Burlesque the present Mode of dressing—it had a monstrous Effect.

A clipping in the Folger Library describes this extraordinary cap as ornamented with a plume of feathers, multi-colored ribbons, oranges and lemons, and a profusion of flowers, all so ridiculous that the audience "gave repeated bursts of applause with such peals of laughter, that the roof of the theatre seemed to be in danger." Something akin to this head-dress, but not quite so grand as described, is seen on Garrick in the frontispiece to the play in Volume II of Bell's *British Theatre* (1776).

To return to the attack upon the Watch—once Sir John is overpowered by them he is trudged off to the Justice of the Peace, out *"OP."* At this point the promptbook reveals that Garrick concluded the third act—*"Act ends"*—although all editions print this scene as the one which opens Act IV. The promptbook arrangement is wiser theatrically, for it closes the act at the crescendo of its hilarity.

The next scene of special interest stage-wise is that which takes place in Spring Garden (IV.3 in the promptbook, IV.4 in the printed editions). In the previous action Lady Brute and Belinda have sent Constant and Heartfree an engaging note to invite these enterprising gallants to be at Spring Garden about eight in the evening where they will find "nothing there but Women, so you need no other Arms than what you usually carry about you." Since the letter is unsigned, Constant and Heartfree have no idea of its senders, but being play-fellows they set out for the rendezvous. The promptbook allows us to follow the action quite clearly.

The setting in Spring Garden provided by the promptbook is a *"Wood 4t gr."* The rather delightful sequence of comic events commences with Constant and Heartfree entering *"OP,"* and crossing the stage.

> *Constant.*   So, I think we are about the Time appointed:
>   Let us walk up this Way.

and they leave at the *"PS"* door.

> As they go off, Enter Lady Fancyful and Madamoiselle mask'd and dogging 'em. *OP*

Lady Fancyful fears some intrigue.

> *Lady F.*   Thus far I have dogged 'em without being discover'd. . . . How my poor Heart is torn and wrackt with Fear and Jealousy! Yet let it be any Thing but that Flirt Belinda, and I'll try to bear it.
>   [Ex. after Constant and Heartfree.

The dogging continues with

> Re-enter Constant and Heartfree. Lady Fancyful and Madamoiselle still following at a Distance.   *PS*

Constant still sees no females and begins to suspect they have been bantered, when

> Enter Lady Brute and Belinda, mask'd, and poorly dress'd.   *PS*

Lady Fancyful and Madamoiselle, still unseen by any of the other characters, determine to "slip into this close Arbour, where we may hear all they say," and they exit at the upper door, opposite promptside (*"U.D.O.P."*), probably behind a tree-wing.

The gallants do not recognize Lady Brute and Belinda. But the assignation begins promisingly enough, only to have Sir John enter (*"PS"*) unexpectedly, still drunk and still clad in female attire. Not recognizing his wife or Belinda either, Sir John mistakes them for two whores, and determined to share with his friends he "seizes both the Women." Heartfree, who from the first has experienced misgivings about this whole affair, takes this opportunity to run off across the stage, *"OP."* Meanwhile, Lady Brute breaks away from her husband, "runs to Constant twitching off her Mask, and clapping it on again," in desperation to let him know her real identity. Heartfree, in the meanwhile, re-enters and Belinda, in equal panic, "runs to him, and shows her Face, *OP.*" Heartfree saves the day with some fast talking, and Sir John reels off *"PS."* It has been a narrow escape for all.

Despite their near discovery, the women are eager to have their frolic. The couples pair off: "Lady Brute and Constant talk apart," while Belinda and Heartfree leave the stage, "*PS*," to take a turn in the garden. Now alone on stage with Lady Brute, Constant pushes the seduction with determination, kissing first her hand and then her neck, and finally he forces her upstage towards the arbor where Lady Fancyful and Madamoiselle are hiding. These two eavesdroppers "bolt out upon them, and run over the Stage," according to the promptbook in a diagonal cross from up-right to down-left—"*Enter, UDOP. Exit PS.*" Lady Brute is frightened out of her wits, as well she might be, and when Belinda and Heartfree return ("*PS*") from their stroll in the garden, she cries out, "Let's be gone, for Heaven's Sake . . . away, away, away." She exits, "running *PS*," evidently followed by everyone else, as the scene concludes.

Sir John's return home from his debauch was ranked Garrick's greatest moment in the play. The action of the scene (IV.5 in the promptbook, V.2 in the printed version) transpires in "Sir John's House. *Pal. Ch: on.*" Constant, Heartfree, Lady Brute, and Belinda enter "*PS*." As they prepare to sit down at cards, a servant rushes on *(PS)* to announce that Lord Brute has just staggered into the house. Constant and Heartfree scramble into the closet—the "*OP*" door—and Lady Brute's only hope is to wheedle her husband off to bed as soon as possible. Sir John enters, "all bloody and dirty," at the PS door. Lichtenberg (p. 18) describes this moment, which convinced him that if he had not seen Garrick in anything else, this one scene should certainly have persuaded him that he was "a most remarkable man."

> At the beginning his wig is quite straight, so that his face is full and round. Then he comes home excessively drunk, and looks like the moon a few days before its last quarter, almost half his face being covered by his wig; the part that is still visible is, indeed, somewhat bloody and shining with perspiration, but has so extremely amiable an air as to compensate for the loss of the other part. His waistcoat is open from top to bottom, his stockings full of wrinkles, with the garters hanging down, and, moreover—which is vastly strange—two kinds of garters; one would hardly be surprised, indeed, if he had picked up odd shoes. In this lamentable condition he enters the room where his wife is . . . he does not, however, move away from the doorpost, against which he leans as closely as if he wanted to rub his back. Then he again breaks into coarse talk, and suddenly becomes so wise and merry in his cups that the whole audience bursts into a tumult of applause.

Upon his wife's entreaty to go to bed, Brute instead sits "*down in his Chair*"—a direction entered by the prompter and not found in the printed version. Deciding to have some tea, Brute goes to the closet, "bursts open the Door with his Foot," to discover Constant and Heartfree who cross the stage in hasty retreat, out "*PS.*" Sir John rants abusively for a moment, returns to his chair, and "falls fast asleep snoring." At this point in Garrick's acting, Lichtenberg was filled with amazement.

> The way in which, with shut eyes, swimming head, and pallid cheeks, he quarrels with his wife, and uttering a sound where 'r' and & 'l' are blended, now appears to abuse her, and then to enunciate in thick tones moral precepts, to which he himself forms the most horrible contradiction; his manner, also, of moving his lips, so that one cannot tell whether he is chewing, tasting, or speaking; all this, in truth, as far exceeded my expectations as anything I have seen of this man.[14]

Lady Brute summons a servant, Rasor, to remove his master, then "Making a low Curtsey" to the unsavory drunken thing in the chair, she and Belinda leave the room, "*PS.*" Rasor appears—also "*PS*"—

> *Rasor.*   Come Sir, your Head's too full of Fumes at present, to make room for your Jealousy; but I reckon we shall have rare Work with you, when your Pate's empty. Come to your Kennel, you cuckoldy, drunken Sot, you.
> [Carries him out on his Back.

The frontispiece of the 1753 edition of *The Provok'd Wife* intends to depict this point in the action (plate 17). Any definite connection with Garrick's production must be considered suspect, however, for the 1753 edition, although announced "As it is Acted at . . . *Drury-Lane*," prints the Vanbrugh text, not Garrick's alteration, and the cast listing includes the Restoration performers. Nevertheless, the print has been commonly associated with Garrick, and copies of it will be found clipped and bound into several different Garrick scrapbooks at the Folger Library, with the added caption, "Garrick in Sir John Brute." Since the frontispiece appears for the first time in 1753, being found in no previous edition, some connection with Garrick is certainly possible and logical. It will be noted in this print that Rasor does carry Brute, chair and all, through a door which appears to be located PS as the promptbook specifies. Perhaps this detail has only some accidental significance, however, for Lady Brute and Belinda are also depicted in the illustration, whereas the promptbook clearly marks their departure before the entrance of Rasor.

Garrick chose this point to terminate the fourth act (*"Act ends"*). (The printed version, however, continues to print this scene as V.2.) The change revealed by the promptbook indicates Garrick's practice of strengthening act conclusions whenever possible.

IV

The last performance of *The Provok'd Wife* at Drury Lane occurred on April 30, 1776, as part of Garrick's final round of appearances. This night Hopkins recorded one of Garrick's most gracious, and perhaps most fitting gestures. During the drinking scene in the tavern, Colonel Bully's song (Vernon) was encored, whereupon Garrick stepped forward, stopped the play and said, "Come Col. give us that Song again for two very good Reasons, the first because your Friends desire it—and Secondly because I believe I shall never be in such good Company again." He might well have added that neither would the play itself. Although it was offered from time to time during the rest of the century, it may be said with justice, and much remorse, that *The Provok'd Wife* retired along with Garrick.

XI

"Slipping the Theatrical Shell"

DAVID GARRICK RETIRED from the stage in a blaze of glory no less brilliant than that which had illuminated his entire career. The reason most commonly whispered around London for his decision to make the final exit was that he could no longer control "the ungovernable and refractory tempers" of his actresses.[1] Closer to the truth was the fact that Garrick was tiring.

In earlier days at Goodman's Fields and at Drury Lane as well, Garrick had boasted that he possessed the stamina of "a little Hercules."[2] By the third decade of his career it was becoming evident that fatigue and the ceaseless burden of management were grinding away at his much-vaunted endurance. His Grand Tour in 1763-1765 afforded two seasons of respite from the theatrical campaigns. It was while in Rome that his thoughts first turned to the possibility of retiring, to luxuriating in the comforts which his tension-packed career allowed him to afford but not enjoy. He wrote to the Duke of Devonshire, "I have lost all relish for the Stage both as Manager and Actor."[3]

Nevertheless, he returned to Drury Lane for the season 1765-66, to the plaudits he seemed not able to resist. Thoughts of retiring were subdued momentarily and did not seriously stir again until 1772-73. On January 10, 1773 he informed Sir William Young of his intention to play Lear and Macbeth with new scenes, and "then exit Roscius."[4] At the opening of the next season the

London Chronicle (September 28-30, 1773) announced the manager of Drury Lane would retire after the winter. Garrick confirmed his determination to "retreat from the Theatre" in a letter to Lady Hertford.[5] But there were rather sudden complications. On January 25, 1774, his partner, James Lacy, died. He could not retire now and leave his theatre in so unsettled a state. And Willoughby Lacy, son of the man who had been his partner for twenty-seven years, was going to be a real problem. Almost immediately after the funeral there was a dispute over the part Willoughby was to play in the management, and within several days Garrick already was involved with the young man's lawyers.[6] Willoughby Lacy was to create more trouble for Garrick in the next two years than his father had been able to stir up in the previous twenty-seven.

Tired, beset by managerial conflicts, Garrick also had to face up to the fact that, alas, his own magnificent histrionic powers were fast fading. Observers, friendly and otherwise, were marking with increasing frequency his waning genius. It was reported he no longer played tragedy "with the same fire and spirit that he did fifteen or sixteen years ago,"[7] and his voice was less "musically clear."[8] According to the *Morning Chronicle*, January 17, 1772, half his beauties were lost "beyond the seventh or eighth row of the pit," and on December 28, 1775, the *St. James's Chronicle* sadly acknowledged the "melancholy truth" that Mr. Garrick had lost his "Voice and Articulation."[9] Although the faithful Hopkins continued to note Garrick's excellences in the *Diaries,* no one knew better than the manager himself that the time had come. On November 29, 1775, Hopkins wrote that "Mr. G. [was] never better" in *Hamlet,* but Garrick confided to his friend, Thomas Rackett:

> I play'd Hamlet . . . & after the play y^r father & mother went home with us to take part of my chicken—the moment I got into my great chair, I was as lifeless as the Brawns you have sent me . . . dead—dead—dead—however, I recover'd the next day and play'd Archer on ye Friday.[10]

On January 18, 1776, Garrick announced to his friend and financial advisor, James Clutterbuck: "I have at last Slipt my theatrical Shell." Though he felt he had never "play'd better" in all his life, Davy was resolved not to remain upon the stage in his advancing years, "to be pitied instead of applauded."[11]

He had sold his share of the Patent of Drury Lane for £35,000 to a syndicate consisting of James Ford, a physician, Simon Ewart, a wealthy brandy merchant (who withdrew almost immediately), and Thomas Linley, father-in-law of Richard Brinsley Sheridan, who was to be active in the management.

Although Garrick's decision to retire had been prompted in part by a combination of declining talents, increasing personnel problems, and a decreasing interest in the theatre itself, the stage really lost him because he was a very sick man. The kidney stones which had plagued him all during his career and finally killed him on January 20, 1779, were raging most violently in these last years of management. In a letter, December 19, 1775, in which he offered Colman the first opportunity to buy his share of the patent, he confided, "My disorder increases and distresses me very much." [12] No longer could he do justice to many of the more vigorous roles, such as Richard III, which in earlier years he had played with such fire. ("I can play Richard: but I dread the fight and the fall. I am afterwards in agonies." [13]) The pain was now too constant and too severe to ignore.

It had been thirty-five years ago that little Davy had first rung up the curtain of his career at the little outlaw theatre in Goodman's Fields. For the last twenty-nine years he had been joint-patentee and artistic director of the finest repertory theatre in all Europe. Garrick's influence as an actor and producer-director was felt in all facets of theatrical endeavor. He had become a significant figure, especially, in the literary as well as the theatrical production of Shakespeare's plays. Frequently called upon to clarify obscure passages or lines in the plays he could almost always oblige, bringing to bear his intuitive genius as an actor. He possessed one of the finest dramatic libraries of the time. This library, which contributed so much to the editions by Steevens, Johnson, and Capell, consisted of some 2,600 items, ranging across matters classical, theological, philosophical, literary, and artistic. His magnificent collection of old plays, including Shakespearean Folios and Quartos, he willed to the British Museum.

As Dr. Stone has pointed out, during the period of Garrick's triumphs dramatic criticism turned to the analysis of character, with new emphasis given to the significance of these characters as they were portrayed by him. In his *Lectures on the Truly Eminent English Poets* (1795), written twenty years after Garrick's retirement, Percival Stockdale offered just tribute to the manager's contribution to scholarship:

> Let the researches which have thrown light upon the works of Shakespeare have their just value. . . . But all the various genius

of our inimitable Bard was thrown into complete action and display by Garrick. All that commentators have done have contributed very little to the renown of Shakespeare, but he would have been very inadequately known, felt, and celebrated if Garrick had not lived.[14]

As an actor, Garrick's influence and reputation extended through France, Germany, Italy, and even to the very borders of the civilized western world, Russia.[15] But it was as director of Drury Lane that Garrick best served the art of the theatre. In the selection of plays Garrick constantly hoped to maintain some semblance of the high standards he had set for himself and his theatre at the outset of his management. At the same time he was wise enough to serve public wants. His perception rendered him expert in judging theatrical effect, and the dramatists whom he supported profited by his taste and wisdom.[16] During his directorship the stature and techniques of the theatre arts—scenery, costumes, lighting, and stage procedures—significantly matured. In the last half of his management especially, new plays, and many old ones, were newly decorated and costumed with surprising regularity. Garrick maintained as strong a company as possible, and although he was the mainstay, he cast his personnel to advantage, rehearsed them conscientiously for a respectable period of time, for the most part, and demanded their adherence to his instructions and regulations. In return for their efforts Garrick offered his performers more security in their profession than they had ever previously enjoyed. His expert managing and financing brought a new order into the government of the stage, a discipline whose intrinsic value was not fully understood until after his retirement. For chaos then reigned again at Drury Lane under Willoughby Lacy and the Sheridans. The once prosperous playhouse sank into artistic and financial despair so deep that the new managers were incapable of meeting their mortgage obligations to Garrick.[17]

His final round of performances in late May and early June of 1776 captured the imagination and stirred the emotions of all London, much of Britain, and some of the rest of the world. News of the Declaration did not reach the British people until August, although news from America was disturbing. Yet, the newspaper accounts of June, 1776, indicate that events at Drury Lane Theatre somewhat eclipsed the more consequential happenings across the sea in Britian's Colonies. Some refused to believe the retirement would be final. Wagers were entered in the betting books at White's that he would act again.[18] But Hannah More, who in the last three weeks had seen him take leave of his great roles, realized she was assisting "at the funeral obsequies of the different poets." [19]

The mobs packed so tightly into the pit they could not sit down, and at the command performance of *Richard III* before the play could begin it was necessary to open the pit door to release some of the pressure of the bulging crowd.[20] The final performance was *The Wonder* on June 10, 1776, with Garrick playing Don Felix. Hopkins entered into the *Diaries* that Garrick had generously given the profits of the night to the Theatrical Fund, and "after the play he went forward & addressed the Audience in so pathetic a Manner as drew Tears from the Audience & himself & took his leave of them for Ever."

In eloquent tribute the audience would not suffer the afterpiece to be played, nor could the actors, so affected, have performed it. All sensed, to be sure, that the curtain was being rung down on a magnificent epoch of theatrical history.

Notes

CHAPTER I: GARRICK'S ROUNDS

1. Denis Diderot, *The Paradox of Acting*, trans. Walter H. Pollock (New York, 1957), pp. 32-33.
2. "Theatrical Duplicity or a Genuine Narrative of the Conduct of *David Garrick* Esqʳᵉ to *Joseph Reed* on his Tragedy of *Dido*," MS in Folger Shakespeare Library.
3. Thomas Davies, *Memoirs of the Life of David Garrick* (London, 1808), I, 44.
4. *Pineapples of Finest Flavour, or a Selection of Sundry Unpublished Letters of the English Roscius*, ed. David M. Little (Cambridge, Mass., 1930), pp. 25-26.
5. Letter in Folger Shakespeare Library.
6. See K. A. Burnim, "Garrick's Quarrel with Lacy: A Significant Letter," *Yale Library Gazette*, XXXIII (July 1958), 29-34.
7. See *The Private Correspondence of David Garrick*, ed. James Boaden (London, 1831-32), I, 50.
8. MS in Forster Collection, Victoria and Albert Museum, cited by Dougald MacMillan, *Drury Lane Calendar* (Oxford, 1938), p. xi.
9. MS in Harvard Theatre Collection.
10. A general analysis of Drury Lane Theatre financing as revealed by the "Account Books" will appear in George Winchester Stone, Jr., *The London Stage, Part 4*, soon to be published by the Southern Illinois University Press. The "Account Books," which list payments for expenses, are available for only eight seasons: 1747-48; 1749-50; 1766-67; 1771-72; 1772-73; 1773-74; 1774-75; 1775-76. They should not be confused with the *Cross-Hopkins Diaries;* see below, footnote No. 22.
11. Letter in Forster Collection, Victoria and Albert Museum, quoted by MacMillan, *Drury Lane Calendar*, pp. xviii-xix. The letter also advises that Garrick had introduced a new regulation in the collection of box admissions, which required everyone to pay when first entering the box rather than at the end of the first act. The new ruling eliminated "the continual disturbance that was in the

boxes of opening & shutting doors, & frisking in & out." Some years later, after 1762, at the suggestion of an unidentified correspondent, Garrick introduced the modern ticket numbering scheme (see *Private Correspondence*, I, 150).

12. *London Morning Post*, September 25, 1786.

13. Letter dated September 1, 1752, in Folger Library.

14. "Theatrical Duplicity," pp. 36-37.

15. *Some Unpublished Correspondence of David Garrick*, ed. George P. Baker (Boston, 1907), p. 119.

16. See *Private Correspondence*, I, 205-207, 223-24.

17. Letter No. 459, in edition of Garrick's correspondence, now being prepared by George M. Kahrl for publication by the Harvard University Press.

18. MacMillan, pp. xx-xxi, Stone, *London Stage*, and James J. Lynch, *Box, Pit, and Gallery* (Berkeley, 1953), p. 14.

19. Letter dated September 10, 1757, Kahrl, No. 209.

20. *Theatrical Monitor*, December 19, 1767. Upon its founding in November, 1734, the *London Daily Post* became the official organ for advertising by London theatres. The name of the paper was changed on March 10, 1744, to the *General Advertiser*, and on December 1, 1752, to the *Public Advertiser*. A complete record of these advertisements for the Garrick period is on microfilm at the Folger Library.

21. *Memoirs of His Own Life* (London, 1790), IV, 201.

22. The diaries consist of 13 MS volumes, now at the Folger Library, in which Richard Cross and William Hopkins listed the plays for each evening of the season, the estimated house revenue, and many notices of unusual events during the performances. They are hereafter referred to as *Cross-Hopkins Diaries*. For an account of an earlier diary kept by Richard Cross before Garrick became manager of Plays, see *Course of Plays, 1740-2: An Early Diary of Richard Cross, Prompter to the Theatres*, ed. Harry Pedicord (John Rylands Library, 1958).

23. *Private Correspondence*, II, 108; also II, 24-32, 105-108.

24. *The Theatrical Public in the Time of Garrick* (New York, 1954), pp. 16-17.

25. Clippings in "Garrick Scrapbooks," Folger Library.

26. "The Increase in Popularity of Shakespeare's Plays in the Eighteenth Century," *Shakespeare Quarterly*, VII (Spring 1956), 191.

27. *The Diary of Sylas Neville, 1767-1788*, ed. Basil Cozens-Hardy (Oxford, 1950), p. 59.

28. *Dr Campbell's Diary of a Visit to England in 1775*, ed. James L. Clifford (Cambridge, Eng., 1947), p. 47.

29. Stone, *London Stage*, Part 4. The statistical breakdown covers the seasons 1741-42, the year of Garrick's debut, through 1775-76, the year of his retirement, and includes statistics for six years before his management. It is possible that these figures will be revised slightly before publication by Dr. Stone. In several instances, the figures vary somewhat from Harry Pedicord's analysis, *Theatrical Public*.

30. Figures from Stone, *London Stage*.

31. *London Morning Post*, September 25, 1786. All of Garrick's plans did not materialize that season. *All's Well* and *Merope* were in the repertory. *Coriolanus* was not performed until November 11, 1754, without Garrick. *The Chances* was not played until November 7, 1754, and *Sosia* appeared finally on December 15, 1756.

32. For a full description of the struggle and chicane between the two at this time, see Howard Dunbar, *The Dramatic Career of Arthur Murphy* (New York, 1946), pp. 51-77.

33. *Cross-Hopkins Diaries*: December 29, 1758—"Mr Oram (our Painter) dy'd—a Worthy honest Man;" December 28—"Mrs. Macklin dy'd;" January 8—"Mr Taswell dy'd—an excellent actor, the best in that way since Johnson."

34. *The Theatrical Review: For the Year 1757, and Beginning of 1758* (London, 1759), p. 5. See also *Theatrical Monitor*, November 7, 14 and December 5 and 16, 1767; *The Herald*, January 26 and March 5, 1758; *London Museum*, January 1770; and *Some Reflections on the Management of a Theatre* (London, 1770), pp. 14-18.

35. *An Enquiry into the Present State of Polite Learning in Europe* (London, 1759), pp. 172-73.

36. *Drury Lane Calendar*, p. xxvii.

37. *Private Correspondence*, I, 227. See also similar letters to Dr. Franklin, I, 463, and to Joshua Reynolds, I, 658.

38. Kahrl, No. 909.

39. *Pineapples of Finest Flavour*, p. 47.

40. *Pineapples*, p. 47. Although Garrick produced some 35 "sentimental plays," it is the conclusion of Pedicord (p. 124) that his "own sympathies were not with the ventures and he hoped to wean his audiences from the type." While Garrick could rejoice that John Hoadly "wept at yᵉ West Indian" (Baker, *Some Unpublished Correspondence*, p. 45), conversely he could advise Charles Jenner to write a comedy "calculated to make an Audience Laugh than cry—the Comedie Larmoyant is getting too much ground upon Us, & if those who can write the better Species of yᵉ Comic drama don't make a Stand for yᵉ Genuine Comedy & vis comica the Stage in a few years, will be (as Hamlet says) like Niobe all tears" (*Pineapples*, pp. 60-61).

41. Kahrl, No. 644.

42. *Private Correspondence*, I, 238-39. Tradition has made such a distinction between the audiences of the two houses, mainly because of Garrick's reputation as a Shakespearean and Rich's genius as a Harlequin. In this respect the distinction is valid, but the remainder of the repertories at both houses appear similar. In fact, there apparently was an agreement between the managers that once a new play had been in the repertory of the introducing house for two seasons, it then became common property. (See *New Monthly Magazine*, XII [December 1819], 535. Pedicord's *Theatrical Public* establishes that the audiences at both theatres were entitled to the claim of being heterogeneous, demonstrating, however, through social and economic classifications, that the eigtheenth-century theatre was "essentially a theatre of the upper-middle class" (p. 43).

43. Baker, *Some Unpublished Correspondence*, p. 78.

44. See especially the review of *The Institution of the Garter* in *Theatrical Review*, October 28, 1771, I, 121-36.

45. *David Garrick, Dramatist* (New York, 1938), p. 156.

46. Note in Garrick MS collection at Folger Library.

47. *David Garrick*, I, 249.

48. Letter dated April 15, 1768, cited by Theodore Martin, *Monographs: Garrick* (New York, 1906), p. 60. Yet in 1775 Walpole presented Garrick with a gift inscribed, "Horace Walpole to his esteemed friend David Garrick."

49. Letter to Fanny Burney from Mrs. Gast, April 27, 1784; *The Early Diary of Frances Burney*, ed. Annie R. Ellis (London, 1889), II, 327.

50. Jesse Foote, *The Life of Arthur Murphy* (London, 1811), pp. 163-64.

51. "The printed play obviously represents what Murphy thought the tragedy should be, and the manuscript represents Murphy's concept as modified during rehearsals by Colman and members of the cast. Analyzed from this point of view some of the changes in the acting version are inexcusable." (Dunbar, p. 238).

52. See *Macaroni and Theatrical Magazine*, February, 1773; *London Chronicle*, February 23-25, 1773; *Monthly Review*, March, 1773; and *Town and Country Magazine*, March, 1773. Dunbar (p. 243) notes that "Criticisms in the newspapers are sufficiently conflicting to suggest the possibility that politics, the-

atrical rather than national, affected the opinions of the reviewers. Indeed there can be no question that the feud between Garrick and Murphy influenced the reactions of several critics to *Alzuma*."

53. Dunbar, pp. 234-35.
54. W. Mason, *Memoirs of the Life and Writings of William Whitehead* (London, 1786), pp. 63-64.
55. "David Garrick: Producer. A Study of Garrick's Alterations of Non-Shakespearean Plays," unpubl. diss. (George Washington University, 1953).
56. See especially Bergmann's discussion of *The Chances, op. cit.*, p. 174; and Richard Cumberland, *Memoirs* (London, 1807), I, 292-93.
57. Thomas Campbell, *Diary* (entry April 8, 1775), p. 77.
58. In a letter to Joseph Baretti, June 10, 1761, cited by Eugene R. Page, *George Colman the Elder* (New York, 1935), p. 55.

CHAPTER II: SETTLING THE PARTS

1. "Theatrical Duplicity," p. 14.
2. *David Garrick*, I, 149.
3. John Adolphus, *Memoirs of John Bannister, Comedian* (London, 1839), I, 18.
4. Letter dated July 17, 1747, *Private Correspondence*, I, 53-54. Pritchard served as Drury Lane's treasurer until his death in 1763, and was succeeded by Benjamin Victor.
5. *David Garrick*, I, 149.
6. George Anne Bellamy, *An Apology for the Life of George Anne Bellamy*, 3rd ed. (London, 1785), IV, 145-47.
7. Nicholas Nipclose, *The Theatres. A Poetical Dissection* (London, 1772), p. 56. The authorship of this poem had been generally and wrongly attributed to Garrick; the remarks in it concerning George Garrick would seem to deny the case. The ascription to Francis Gentleman by Joseph Reed in "Theatrical Duplicity" seems more appropriate. See also Bernard Barrow, "Low-Comedy Acting Style on the London Stage 1730-1780," unpubl. diss. (Yale, 1957), I, 51-53.
8. *Private Correspondence*, I, 41, 45, 92.
9. *An Epistle from Theophilus Cibber to David Garrick* (London, 1759), pp. 21-27. See also *Private Correspondence*, I, 228, 566; II, 77.
10. Undated holograph letter ("Hampton Sunday") in Folger Library. The letter seems to have been written in February 1767, when on the twelfth Garrick gave a command performance of this play. His last appearance as Oakly prior to this had been May 26, 1763.
11. Holograph letter in Folger Library, CS907MS, p. 21.
12. *Cross-Hopkins Diaries*. Other entries include: May 16, 1759—"We borrow'd Mrs Barrington for D: Zeal [*Fair Quaker of Deal*]; May 27, 1759—"We borrow'd Smith from Cov. Garden to do Osmyn [*Mourning Bride*] Mr Mossop's Father being dead." MacMillan lists the part of Maria as "omitted" from *Barnwell* on May 17, 1759, but the *Diary* for that day reads: "We borrow'd Mrs Baker for Maria."
13. Elizabeth Steele, *The Memoirs of Sophia Baddeley* (London, 1787), I, 7-8. In autobiography, Charlotte Charke advises that early in her career she was selected "from the rest of the company as stock-reader to the theatre in case of disasters." *A Narrative of the Life of Mrs. Charlotte Charke* (London, 1827), p. 38.
14. *Old Theatre Ways* (London, 1935), pp. 53-62.
15. *David Garrick*, I, 314.
16. *Oxford Magazine*, VIII (March 1772), 97-110, and *Theatrical Review* (1771-72), I, 112-13.

17. Davies, *David Garrick*, I, 182.

18. *Theatrical Review* (1771-72), I, 258-59.

19. *The Entertainer*, November 12, 1754, p. 66.

20. *Court Miscellany*, IV (March 1768), 40.

21. *Morning Post and Daily Advertiser*, January 15, 1776.

22. *Theatrical Monitor*, October 24, 1767; and *Imperial Magazine; or Complete Monthly Intelligencer*, II (February 1761), 88. Theatrical criticism was seldom consistent and it was frequently motivated more by personal bias than a desire to report with integrity. Garrick himself owned stock in two or three news-papers and he attempted to be on friendly terms with the editors and pub-lishers of most of the others. His correspondence reveals that he sometimes engaged in undercover activities and agreements with editors. Garrick's widow told Edmund Kean that David always composed his own criticisms in many papers, and although such a statement must be somewhat of an exaggeration, it is clear that "Garrick watched very closely over the nurture of his reputation by the press" (Charles Harold Gray, *Theatrical Criticism in London to 1795* [New York, 1931], p. 201). *The Theatrical Monitor* (November 14, 1767), for one, complained of "this collusion of managers with news writers." See also David Williams, *A Letter to David, Esq. on his Conduct and Talents as Manager and Performer* (London, 1770), and William Kenrick, *A Letter to David Garrick*, 2nd ed. (London, 1772).

The level of much of the periodical writing may be visualized in a ludicrous error committed by Arthur Murphy writing under the pseudonym of Charles Ranger in *Gray's Inn Journal*. In desperation for something to fill out No. 39 on June 22, 1754, Murphy—apparently at the suggestion of Samuel Foote—trans-lated an essay from an old number of *Le Journal Litteraire*, which itself turned out to be a translation of Johnson's *Rambler* No. 190. George Anne Bellamy tells the story about John Hill (who wrote 19 articles on the theatre in the *London Advertiser and Literary Gazette* between 1751 and 1753) which suggests the prevalent practice of absentee reviewing. Hill had praised Bellamy in a recent review of *Romeo and Juliet* when: "he one evening swam into the Green-Room, during the representation of that play, and when I was called to go to the balcony, the scene on which he had been most exuberant in his eulogiums, he greatly astonished me by saying, 'I must go and see it, for I hear it is the finest piece of acting in the whole performance.' I could not resist turning back to him to ask if he had not wrote a critique upon it? To which he replied, with a becoming *non chalence*, that he had written it from what he had heard at the Bedford, and never till that evening had an opportunity of seeing it." (*Apology for the Life of George Anne Bellamy*, IV, 184).

23. *The Theatrical Review; or, New Companion to the Play-House*, 2 vols. (Lon-don, 1772); these reviews originally appeared in separate issues of *The Public Ledger* during that season and were then reprinted in these two volumes. For a discussion of their authorship see Gray, *Theatrical Criticism*, pp. 193-97.

24. See also reviews of *Douglas* (I, 146), *The Suspicious Husband* (I, 222), *Timon* (L, 258), *The Fair Penitent* (I, 177), and *The Recruiting Officer* (I, 158).

25. *The Actor* (London, 1750), pp. 72-82.

26. (1772), I, 24. See, however, this same reviewer's approbation of minor roles in reviews on I, 151; I, 188; I, 189; and I, 258.

27. Stone, *London Stage*.

28. *Memoirs of an Unfortunate Son of Thespis* (Edinburgh, 1818), p. 40.

29. Clipping in "Garrick Scrapbook," Folger Library. See also Davies, *David Gar-ick*, II, 476.

30. Bellamy, II, 127.

31. *David Garrick*, I, 187-88 and 233.

32. This run of *The Chances* had more than its share of trouble. Cross relates that

for the performance on November 16, 1754, "We staid 'till ten Minutes after six when ye Audience made a great noise to begin, & when the Curtain went up, pelted the Actors & wou'd not suffer 'em to go on 'till Mr Garrick told 'em, we began by the green room Clock & that we had not much exceeded the time— one above call'd out it was half an hour after six but we proceeded without farther Interruption."

33. George Anne Bellamy, *op. cit.*, II, 190-91.

34. Holograph letter in Folger Library. The letter is marked "Thursday 19th" but has no year date. The catalog assignment to "ca. 1770" is clearly wrong, for Mrs. Cibber died in 1766. Garrick does not refer to the play by name—merely the "New Play"—but my assignment of the date and play seems conclusive from the circumstances. Cross entered in the *Diary* April 28, 1756, that "Mrs Cibber went sick to bath in Passion Week, & plays no more this Season." *The Maiden Whim*, which is the only new play Garrick would have been concerned with at the time, opened on Saturday, April 24, and Garrick's letter was written two days earlier. Mrs. Cibber had been replaced by Miss Minor, and the farce had only that one performance (See MacMillan, *Drury Lane Calendar*, p. 50).

35. Arthur Murphy, *The Life of David Garrick* (London, 1801), I, 339, and Davies, *David Garrick*, I, 258.

36. *Private Correspondence*, I, 292-302, 347; and Dunbar, p. 193.

37. Cited by MacMillan, p. xxv.

38. *Brief Remarks on the Original and Present State of the Drama* (London, 1758), pp. 12-13.

39. *Theatrical Monitor*, October 24, 1767.

40. *The Life of David Garrick* (London, 1899), pp. 440-50.

41. *The Professional Life of Mr. Dibdin* (London, 1803), I, 74; see also Nicholas Nipclose, *The Theatres*, p. 31.

42. *David Garrick*, I, 253.

43. Reed, "Theatrical Duplicity," p. 14.

CHAPTER III: PLOT AND PRACTICE

1. *The Professional Life of Mr. Dibdin*, I, 98.

2. "Theatrical Duplicity," p. 40.

3. *Private Correspondence*, I, 503.

4. Charles Beecher Hogan, "An Eighteenth-Century Prompter's Notes," *Theatre Notebook*, (January-March, 1956), 37-44; see also Allardyce Nicoll, *A History of Late Eighteenth-Century Drama*, 1750-1800 (Cambridge, Eng., 1927), pp. 40-41.

5. Davies, *Dramatic Miscellanies*, II, 179.

6. *Apology for the Life of George Anne Bellamy*, I, 52-53.

7. William Cooke, *The Elements of Dramatic Criticism . . . Concluding with Some General Instructions for Succeeding in the Art of Acting* (London, 1775), pp. 195-96.

8. Charles Macklin is generally credited with making the first attempts at organized and purposeful rehearsals; see William Cooke, *Memoirs of Charles Macklin* (London, 1804), p. 404, and John Hill, *The Actor* (1755 ed.), pp. 239-40. For a discussion of the "regular and masterly Manner of governing their Rehearsals" which had been devised by the managerial triumvirate of Cibber, Wilks, and Booth see Benjamin Victor, *History of the Theatres of London and Dublin* (London, 1761), II, 4-5, and Colley Cibber, *An Apology for the Life of Colley Cibber*, 3rd ed. (London, 1750), pp. 441-42.

9. *Court Magazine*, I (October 1761), 76-77.

10. "Theatrical Duplicity," pp. 51-52. During the rehearsals of *Dido* Garrick passed most of his time in ill-health at Bath.

11. Wilkinson, *Memoirs*, I, 145; also IV, 156.

12. *Life of Bellamy*, II, 113.

13. Stone, *London Stage, Part 4*, and Davies, *David Garrick*, I, 148.

14. *Private Correspondence*, I, 163-64. It was Davies' contention that Garrick had been unnecessarily disquieted by the mistakes in *The Coronation* committed by the very pretty Mrs. Davies, and although pardon had been begged, "neither *attrition* nor *contrition* would do." Garrick turned a cold and unremitting shoulder, persecuted them at rehearsals, and refused even to return a courteous greeting on the street (*Private Correspondence*, I, 164-65). Davies, however, had acquired a reputation for an "habitual want of readiness." See Fitzgerald, *Life of Garrick*, pp. 382-83.

15. Holograph letter in Folger Library. See also *Private Correspondence*, I, 615-55, for an exchange of letters between Aickin and Garrick.

16. *Private Correspondence*, II, 78.

17. Holograph letter, Folger Library, Garrick case III, folder 2, 1291.

18. G. P. Baker, *Some Unpublished Correspondence*, pp. 79-80.

19. *Theatrical Review* (1771-72), I, 49; also I, 3. For similar notices see *Cross-Hopkins Diaries*, November 4, 1771, and March 18, 1775. In *The Present State of the Stage in Great-Britain and Ireland* (London, 1753), Richard Cross was complimented for often coming to the rescue of indolent actors with "treacherous memory" (p. 35).

20. Respectively, *Westminster Magazine*, October, 1774; *The Entertainer*, November 17, 1754; *Gray's Inn Journal*, January 26, 1754; "Theatrical Duplicity," p. 49; Dunbar, pp. 189-92; and *Private Correspondence*, I, 321.

21. *Private Correspondence*, I, 503.

22. *Gibbon's Journal*, ed. D. M. Low (London, 1929), p. 185.

23. G. W. Stone, Jr., "Garrick's Handling of Shakespeare's Plays and his Influence Upon the Changed Attitude of Shakespearean Criticism During the Eighteenth Century," 2 vols. unpubl. diss. (Harvard, 1938), II, 315.

24. Foote, *Murphy*, p. 150.

25. *Dramatic Miscellanies*, II, 41-44.

26. Robert Gale Noyes, *Ben Jonson on the English Stage 1660-1776* (Cambridge, Mass., 1935), p. 253.

27. Kahrl, No. 280.

28. See also *Cross-Hopkins Diaries*, February 5 and 9, 1754, December 5, 1760.

29. See above, p. 32.

30. *Gibbon's Journal*, for November 26, 1762, pp. 185-86.

31. *Private Correspondence*, II, 36; also II, 19-24 and 34.

32. *Dramatic Miscellanies*, II, 43; see also Murphy, *Life of Garrick*, I, 336-37, and *Private Correspondence*, I, 321.

33. Helfrich Peter Sturz, *Vermischte Schriften* (Starnberg am See, 1946), p. 61.

34. "David Garrick at Rehearsal. Written by himself. From an Original Letter in the Possession of the Publisher," in a nineteenth century pamphlet, *Behind the Curtain*, attached to Vol. II of an extra-illustrated *Life of Garrick*, by Davies, now at Folger Library.

35. Holograph letter to unidentified nobleman, Folger MS V. b. 30.

36. *Dramatic Miscellanies*, II, 44.

37. Percival Stockdale, *The Memoirs of the Life, and Writings of Percival Stockdale* (London, 1809), II, 160. For a comparison of Garrick and Woodward in the role of Marplot see *London Chronicle*, December 19-21, 1758.

38. Garrick's MS autograph notebook in Harvard Theatre Collection.

39. David Williams, *A Letter to David Garrick*, p. 67; also *Court Magazine*, I (October 1761), 76-77.

40. "Memoirs of John Palmer, Esq.," *General Magazine and Impartial Review*, II (January 1788), 9-16. For other notices of actors being tutored see *Fortnight's*

Register, November 6-20, 1762; *London Chronicle,* October 3-5, 1758; *Town and Country Magazine,* III (May 1771), 264; Adolphus, *Bannister,* p. 24; Nipclose, *Theatres,* pp. 41-46; and *St. James's Chronicle,* October 8-10, 1772.

41. See also *London Chronicle,* February 15-17, 1757; [Hugh Kelly], *Thespis* (London, 1766), pp. 10-11; Charles Churchill, *The Rosciad,* 2nd. ed. (London, 1761), ll. 229-38; *Westminster Magazine,* November, 1778, p. 563; *A Letter to Mr. Garrick on the Opening of the Theatre,* pp. 13-16; and *Some Reflections on the Management of a Theatre,* p. 7.

42. Bergmann, p. 63.

43. In 1767 John Brownsmith published a handbook for the benefit of those who wanted their carriages at a proper time, entitled *The Dramatic Timepiece . . . being the Calculation of the Length of Time Every Act Takes in the Performing in All the Plays at the Theatre-Royal.* Few of the plays listed required more than two and one half hours to play: for example, *Venice Preserv'd,* 2 hr. 9 min.; *Fair Penitent,* 1 hr. 59 min.; *Zara,* 1 hr. 46 min.; *King Lear,* 2 hr. 34 min.

44. See Barrow, *op. cit.,* and Arthur C. Sprague, *Shakespeare and the Actors. The Stage Business in his Plays* (Cambridge, Mass., 1944), for reviews in detail of the traditional manner in which many scenes or stock types of business were almost invariably presented.

45. Robert Baker, *Remarks on the English Language,* 2nd ed. (London, 1779), p. xviii.

46. Nipclose, *Theatres,* p. 46.

47. *Theatrical Examiner,* p. 32; see also *Theatrical Monitor,* October 24, 1767, and *London Chronicle,* February 13-15, 1759.

48. See *London Evening Post,* February 10-13, 1770; *Universal Museum,* I (January 1762), 46; *London Chronicle,* December 31, 1768; and Bergmann, *op. cit.*

49. *Lichtenberg's Visits to England,* ed. Margaret Mare and W. H. Quarrell (Oxford, 1938), pp. 25-27.

50. Cited by Frank Hedgecock, *David Garrick and his French Friends* (London, 1912), p. 344.

51. Cumberland, *Memoirs,* I, 80. For excellent accounts of the acting styles of the period see Bertram Joseph, *The Tragic Actor* (London, 1959), pp. 67-172, and Alan Downer, "Nature to Advantage Dressed," *PMLA,* LVIII (December 1943), 1002-37.

52. Jean Georges Noverre, *Letters on Dancing and Ballets,* trans. Cyril W. Beaumont (London, 1951), p. 83.

53. Letter to Sturz, cited by Hedgecock, p. 244.

54. Dibdin, *The Professional Life,* II, 102. See also Williams, *Letter to David Garrick,* p. 49, and Samuel J. Pratt, *Garrick's Looking Glass; or the Art of Rising on the Stage* (London, 1776), pp. 10-11.

55. Everard, p. 4.

56. Letter to Thomas Love, cited by Charles R. Williams, "David Garrick, Actor-Manager: Two Unpublished Letters," *Cornhill Magazine,* LXVI (March 1929), 291.

57. Letter dated London, October 18, 1750, to an unidentified friend, Folger Library.

58. Cited by Stone, "Garrick's Handling of Shakespeare's Plays," II, 349. "I dread a Stroler, they contract such insufferable Affectation that they disgust me—" letter to James Love, March 3, 1765, Kahrl, No. 370.

59. [Francis Gentleman], *The Dramatic Censor, or Critical Companion* (London, 1770), I, 55-56. See also *The Present State of the Stage in Great-Britain and Ireland,* p. 20, and *Theatrical Review* (London, 1763), pp. 106-7.

60. Undated holograph letter to unidentified nobleman, Folger MS V.b. 30.

61. *The Herald,* January 19, 1958. See also Thomas Fitzpatrick, *An Enquiry into the Real Merit of a Certain Popular Performer* (London, 1760), pp. 23-26; Pratt,

Garrick's Looking Glass, p. 9; John Hill, *The Actor*, p. 309; and *Court Magazine*, I, (December 1761), 171.

62. *The Rational Rosciad*, quoted. in *London Chronicle*, February 10-12, 1767. See also *Gentleman's Magazine*, XVII (1747), 71; *Theatrical Monitor*, October 24, 1767; Williams, *Letter to David Garrick*, pp. 33-36; and Macklin's description of Garrick found among his private papers and quoted in Fitzgerald, *Life of Garrick*, p. 278.

63. *The Herald*, January 19, 1758.

64. Pp. 6-7.

65. James T. Kirkman, *Memoirs of the Life of Charles Macklin* (London, 1799), II, 261-70.

66. James Boswell, *The Life of Samuel Johnson*, ed. Roger Ingpen (Boston, 1925), I, 1030-31.

67. Letter of January 23, 1776, *Private Correspondence*, II, 128. Exactly two years earlier Mrs. Clive had written him: "Wonderful Sir, Who have been for these thirty years contradicting an old established proverb—you cannot make brick without straw; but you have done what is infinitely more difficult, for you have made actors and actresses without genius; that is, you have made them pass for such, which, has answered your end, though it has given you infinite trouble" (*Private Correspondence*, I, 610).

CHAPTER IV: NEW DRESS'D AND FINE SCENES

1. Wren's drawing, reproduced from the original in All Souls College, Oxford, was first published in Hamilton Bell, "Three Plans by Sir Christopher Wren," *Architectural Record*, XXXIII (1913), 359ff. See also Allardyce Nicoll, *Development of the Theatre* (London, 1927), pp. 162-64, and W. J. Lawrence, *The Elizabethan Playhouse and Other Studies* (Stratford, Eng., 1912), pp. 159-89.

2. *Apology*, pp. 338-40.

3. Cumberland, *Memoirs*, I, 57.

4. Harvard Theatre Collection, fMS. Thr 12. For a detailed analysis of the document see Stone, *London Stage*.

5. *Private Correspondence*, I, 54, and *General Advertiser*, September 9, 1747.

6. Davies, *David Garrick*, I, 375-76; see also Wilkinson, *Memoirs*, IV, 108-16.

7. William Salt Library, Stratford; Kahrl, No. 315.

8. *Theatrical Public*, pp. 10-15. In 1760, before the major alterations, the *Royal Female Magazine* (April 1760) set the capacity on a benefit night of the largest of London's theatres (unidentified) at about 2,668 spectators. The periodical perhaps was referring to Covent Garden, which at the time of its erection in 1732 was "larger, by one part in three," than Drury Lane (Aaron Hill, cited by George C. D. Odell, *Shakespeare from Betterton to Irving* [New York, 1920], I, 219). Pedicord estimates that in 1759 Covent Garden held 2,500 people. When Edward Oxnard, a New England Royalist living in London during the American Revolution, visited Drury Lane on November 27, 1775 (after the Adam's alterations), he estimated that the two-shilling gallery (the second gallery) would hold near 500 and that in all 3,000 spectators were present ("Extracts from the Journal of Edward Oxnard," *New England Historical and Genealogical Register*, XXVI [1872],) 115.

9. For "Covent Garden Inventory" see Richard Southern, *Changeable Scenery* (London, 1952), pp. 191-211; for "Crowe Street Theatre Inventory," see James Boaden, *Memoirs of the Life of John Philip Kemble* (Philadelphia, 1825), pp. 595-602.

10. *Memoirs*, IV, 91-92.

11. *The Case of the Stage in Ireland . . . Wherein the Qualifications, Duty, and Importance of a Manager are Carefully Considered . . .* (Dublin, n. d.), pp. 35-37.

12. *The Actor*, p. 22.

13. *Life of Kemble*, p. xiv.

14. Clipping, Folger Library.

15. See E. Croft-Murray, *John De Voto, A Baroque Scene Painter*, the Society for Theatre Research Pamphlet Series (1952).

16. Book III, sec. 10, pp. 217ff.

17. *Changeable Scenery*, p. 96.

18. *Memoirs of Mrs. Siddons* (Philadelphia, 1893), pp. 403-4.

19. *Theatrical Disquisitions, or, a Review of the Late Riot at Drury Lane Theatre, on the 25th and 26th of January* (London, 1763). See also *Three Original Letters to a Friend in the Country on the Cause and Manner of the Late Riot at the Theatre-Royal in Drury-Lane* (London, 1763).

20. Aaron Hill, *Works*, II, 376.

21. *Letter to the Hon. Author of the New Farce, Called the Rout . . . Containing some Remarks upon the New-revived Play of Anthony and Cleopatra* (London, 1759), p. 39.

22. The production of *Les Fêtes Chinoises* had been in preparation for more than eighteen months before it was offered in November 1755 *(Gentleman's Magazine*, XLIX [1779], 226). Noverre had staged the sumptuous ballet and Boquet, the designer for the Paris Opera, had been commissioned for the new costumes and scenery. Nothing had been spared to insure its success: "The scenery was superb and the dresses magnificent. The procession was composed of ninety persons; the palanquin and the chariots were very rich . . . in a word, those Fêtes Chinoises, which achieved so brilliant a success at Paris, were nothing in comparison with those of London" *(Lettre écrite de Londre . . . au sujet des ballets du sieur Noverre* [written by someone who appears to have been a member of the *corps de ballet*], cited by Hedgecock, p. 131). In the anti-French rioting which greeted the production, Drury Lane was torn to shreds, yet Cross, whose *Diary* offers a blow-by-blow account of the week's bedlam, makes no mention of the scenery being damaged. Perhaps Garrick's "fertile judgement and economy" did finally bring the scenes to good use four years later in *The Orphan of China* (see Foote, *Murphy*, p. 151). Murphy himself in his account of the play merely states that "the manager prepared a magnificent set of Chinese scenes and the most becoming dresses" *(Life of Garrick*, I, 338). See also *Monthly Mirror*, XIII (January 1802), 48.

23. Playbill at Folger Library.

24. *Court Magazine*, I (December 1761), 172.

25. *St. James's Chronicle*, March 20-22, 1764.

26. Davies, *David Garrick*, II, 256.

27. *Town and Country Magazine*, I (February 1769), 97.

28. David Erskine Baker, *Biographia Dramatica, or a Companion to the Playhouse. A New Edition* (London, 1782), II, 227.

29. Undated holograph letter, cataloged "ca. 1770," at Folger Library, V.a. 8.

30. See respectively, *Town and Country Magazine*, November 1770, January 1772, March 1773, December 1774, and February 1776.

31. See respectively, *London Chronicle*, December 9, 1772, *Westminster Magazine*, February and October, 1774, *Cross-Hopkins Diaries*, February, 17, 1775, and *Private Correspondence*, II, 43.

32. *London Spy and Read's Weekly Journal*, October 24-31, 1761.

33. See Paul Sawyer, "Processions and Coronations on the London Stage, 1726-1761," *Theatre Notebook*, XIV (Autumn 1959), 7-12.

34. *Private Correspondence*, II, 499.

35. For the finest research on De Loutherbourg see Ralph G. Allen, "The Stage Spectacles of Philip James De Loutherbourg," unpubl. diss. (Yale, 1960).

36. These expenditures and subsequent totals for costume and lighting are provided by Dr. Stone from the forthcoming *London Stage*, and are included here with his kind permission.

37. In his offer of services, De Loutherbourg had requested an annual salary of £600. Angelo (I, 15) claims that he was paid only £500. Itemized payments to him in 1774-75 total much less, so perhaps the salary agreed upon was less or some payments were not included in the accounts.

38. See Lily B. Campbell, "A History of Costuming on the English Stage between 1660 and 1823," *University of Wisconsin Studies in Language and Literature*, No. 2 (1918), 187-223; and A. M. Nagler, *Sources of Theatrical History* (New York, 1952), pp. 382-98.

39. *Royal Female Magazine*, II (December 1760), 271.

40. Clipping dated October 13, 1775, Folger Library. Hugh Kelly, on the other hand, puffed that at Drury Lane every play was properly decorated and the actors were dressed with propriety according to their stations, whereas at the other house abuses in this respect were flagrant; see *Court Magazine*, I (October 1761), 76-77.

41. Holograph letter, Folger Library, Garrick Corr. Case II, folder 5, 1414-3.

42. Lichtenberg, pp. 21-23.

43. "On Dramatic Costume," *Gentleman's Magazine*, XCV (January 1825), 4.

44. MacMillan, p. xxix.

45. G. W. Stone, Jr., "The Authorship of *Tit for Tat*," *Theatre Notebook*, X (October-December 1955), 22-28.

46. *Private Correspondence*, I, 303, 623, 624.

47. In *Theatrical Review for 1771-1772*, the reviewer of *Measure for Measure* at Covent Garden writes: "When the *Duke* made his Entry in the fifth Act, the Guards attending are drest in *English* Regimentals. This is an oversight, not unworthy of notice in future." Had the costume situation so improved at both houses by 1771 that such improprieties could be termed "oversights" rather than the normal course of events?

48. *London Spy*, October 10, 1761.

49. For a detailed description of winglights in the nineteenth century see *The Cyclopaedia; or, Universal Dictionary of Arts, Sciences, and Literature*, ed. Abraham Rees (London, 1819), Vol. XII, under "Dramatic."

50. *Public Advertiser*, December 8, 1774.

51. Henry Angelo, *Reminiscences* (London, 1828), II, 326.

52. Angelo, I, 10-15. In gratitude for the elder Angelo's advice and assistance, Garrick presented him with a silver cup.

53. W. B. Boulton, *Thomas Gainsborough* (Chicago, 1907), pp. 128-29.

54. Kahrl, No. 834.

CHAPTER V: DRAW THE SCENE

1. *Theatrical Criticism in London*, p. 57.

2. I shall discuss, however, in the subsequent appropriate chapters many prints which, supported by evidence from promptbooks, correspondence, and reviews, will be found to be as valid as photographs or designs. Also see my article, "Eighteenth-Century Theatrical Illustrations in the Light of Contemporary Documents," *Theatre Notebook*, XIV (Winter 1959-60), 45-55.

3. See Edward A. Langhans, "Staging Practices in the Restoration Theatres 1660-1682," unpubl. diss. (Yale, 1955).

4. James Cawdell, *The Miscellaneous Poems of J. Cawdell, Comedian* (Sunderland, 1785). The print represents Cawdell delivering "An Eulogium Written and

Delivered by the Author in Character of a Delegate from the Poor of Suther-
land, at a Charity Play," presented February 9, 1784. This print is incorrectly
identified as "Garrick" by the *Catalogue of Dramatic Portraits in the Theatre
Collection of the Harvard College Library* (Cambridge, Mass., 1931), II, 94,
entry 140.

5. Evidently fires on altars really burned. For a production of *Merope,* May 19,
1753, Cross entered in the *Diary:* "The lamp at yᵉ Altar boil'd over & Frank
heath was burnt in yᵉ loins in getting it out." Frank Heath and his wife were
wardrobe master and mistress at Drury Lane, and probably Heath was appearing as one of the Soldiers or crowd in this final scene of *Merope.*

6. Certain symbols appear with some consistency in the promptbooks: the circle
with a *w* inside (w) usually indicates to the prompter that a scene change is
coming up; a plain circle or one with a dot inside (.) usually indicates that
no scene change is to occur and the scene is to continue. In the promptbook
of *The Chances,* for example, the first act opens with "(.) chamber," meaning
no change since the chamber is already set at the beginning of the play. This
is followed in turn in the other scenes with: "(w) Town," "(.) Town," and "(w)
Chamber"—signifying in order: remove the first setting of the chamber to reveal the town scene, maintain the town scene, and remove the town scene to
return to the chamber. Unfortunately the symbols cannot always be trusted
for consistency. In the promptbooks of *MND* and *Alfred* the only symbol appearing throughout is the plain circle, yet from other notations in these prompts
it is evident that scene changes must occur. I suspect that although each prompter employed similar symbols, the shorthand did not always mean the same
thing to all prompters, and that most markings of this nature were designed
mainly to call the prompter's attention to the page.

7. See Richard Southern, *Changeable Scenery,* pp. 163-76, and 193-96.

8. Oxnard, p. 9.

9. *Theatrical Review* (1772), II, 160.

10. The rest of the account, which also may be found in *Drury Lane Journal,* February 13, 1752, continues: "Then Harlequin appears disconsolate and prostrate
upon a couch in an elegant apartment: Lightening flashes: and four Devils, in
flame-colour'd stockings, mount through trap-doors, surround him with double-
tongued forks, and the whole stage with the scenery and all upon it, rise up
gradually, and is carried altogether into the air."

11. *DNB,* IX, 238. Carver's name does not appear for payment in any of the Drury
Lane "Account Books."

12. Boaden, *Kemble,* p. 601.

13. *Late Eighteenth Century Drama,* p. 31.

14. Montague Summers, *The Restoration Theatre* (New York, 1934), p. 164. See also
Southern, *Changeable Scenery,* pp. 163-76.

15. Pierre J. Grosley, *A Tour to London,* trans. Thomas Nugent (London, 1772),
I, 178.

16. Everard, p. 50.

17. Barton-Tichnor Collection, Boston Public Library.

18. See Allardyce Nicoll, *Late Eighteenth Century Drama,* p. 30, and *History of
Early Eighteenth Century Drama* (Cambridge, Eng., 1929), p. 29n, and *Development of the Theatre,* p. 174.

19. William A. Armstrong, "Madame Vestris: A Centenary Appreciation," *Theatre
Notebook,* XI (October-December, 1956), 18.

20. *Works of the Late Aaron Hill,* II, 376-77.

21. *Changeable Scenery,* p. 344.

22. *Rules and Examples of Perspective Proper for Painters and Architects,* Book I
(London, 1707).

23. For a further discussion of this point, and the possibility that Hill helped in-

troduce the *scena per angolo* into England, see my article, "Some Notes on Aaron Hill and Stage Scenery," *Theatre Notebook*, XII (Autumn 1957), 29-33.

24. Russell Thomas, p. 68.

25. From his reconstructions of Restoration productions, Richard Southern concludes that "it appears that practical doors, or at least practical openings, were in use from the very beginning, though employed only now and then . . . the proscenium door was to remain the principal way of access to the scenes" (*Changeable Scenery*, p. 146).

26. This interesting MS is attached to a copy of James Kirkman's *Memoirs of the Life of Charles Macklin* in the Harvard Theatre Collection, and has been published by Denis Donoghue, "Macklin's Shylock and Macbeth," *Studies: an Irish Quarterly Review*, XLII (Winter 1954), 427-28.

27. *Memoirs*, IV, 91-92. Italics mine.

28. In 1782, Richard Daly, the manager of Dublin's Smock Alley Theatre, attended a performance at Covent Garden of *The Castle of Andalusia* with the play's author, John O'Keeffe. Since Daly had already staged this play in Dublin, he passed the whole performance comparing his work with Covent Garden's. At one point in the play he turned to the author and exclaimed, "Why, O'Keeffe, instead of P.S. I make my fellow come on O.P.; and why does that Alphonso go off at the side door? I make my fellows go off at the centre-door." See O'Keeffe, *Recollections* (London, 1826), II, 44.

29. Built-up set-pieces were used as early as 1716 in Aaron Hill's *The Fatal Vision;* see my article, "Aaron Hill and Stage Scenery," pp. 29-30.

30. See Gerald Miller, *English Inn Signs* (London, 1951), p. 151.

31. MS at Harvard Theatre Collection, TS 116.255.3.

32. *The Letters of Horace Walpole*, ed. Paget Toynbee (Oxford, 1904), VII, 429.

33. Folger Library, Garrick case II.

CHAPTER VI: *Macbeth*

1. The ranking of *Macbeth* as the third most frequently played tragedy in the Drury Lane repertory, 1741-76, with 105 performances, is by Stone, *London Stage*. Pedicord (p. 201) lists 77 performances during Garrick's management, 1747-76, ranking it as the sixth most frequently played tragedy.

2. John Downes, *Roscius Anglicanus* [1708], ed. Montague Summers (London, n. d.), p. 33.

3. G. W. Stone, Jr., "Garrick's Handling of *Macbeth*," *Studies in Philology*, XXXVIII (October 1941), 615.

4. *Dramatic Miscellanies*, II, 73.

5. *Ibid.*, II, 119.

6. "Garrick's Handling of *Macbeth*," p. 615.

7. "Till within these twenty-five years," Davies writes in 1785, "our Tamerlanes and Catos had as much hair on their heads as our judges on the bench" *(Dram. Misc.*, I, 84). For a hilarious account of an accident involving these tragical flows, Barry, and Ryan in the final scene of *Macbeth*, see *Drury Lane Journal*, March 19, 1752.

8. In *Dram. Misc.*, II, 82, Davies gives the following criticism of Quin's Macbeth: "Quin's figure and countenance . . . spoke much in his favour; but he was deficient in animated utterance, and wanted flexibility of tone. He could neither assume the strong agitation of mind before the murder of the king, nor the remorse and anguish in consequence of it:—much less could he put on that mixture of despair, rage, and frenzy, that make the last scenes of Macbeth. During the whole representation he scarce deviated from a dull, heavy, monotony."

9. See also *Private Correspondence*, I, 19-20, for a criticism of Garrick's readings from an observer who saw *Macbeth* during its first run in 1744.

10. See especially a review of her acting in the role in *Universal Museum*, I (January 1762), 45-46.

11. See Hogan, *Shakespeare in the Theatre*, I, 292-300, and II, 363-81. The "Account Book" for 1749-50 lists payment "to 28 Extra" for *Macbeth*, probably employed in the battle scene.

12. This promptbook once belonged to the actor-manager Henry Irving, who received it from a Mr. C. Roeder. In the presentation letter accompanying the copy Roeder wrote to Irving: "As a past admirer, I beg leave to offer you from my Shakespearean Library a valuable, and I may say unique copy of *Macbeth*, as performed at the Theatre Royal, Drury Lane, London, in the course of *1773*, when Garrick acted as Macbeth. You will see that this copy was the stage-manager's own copy."

13. Hogan, *Shakespeare in the Theatre*, II, 363-81.

14. *Notes by Horace Walpole on Several Characters of Shakespeare*, ed. W. S. Lewis (Farmington, Conn., 1940), pp. 7-8. See also *St. James's Chronicle*, January 19-21, 1768. The only woman to appear as a witch during the century was Miss Ann Pitt, who played one regularly at Covent Garden between 1769 and 1776; see Hogan, *Shakespeare*, II, 376-81.

15. Robert Wyndham Ketton-Cremer, *Early Life and Diaries of William Windham* (London, 1930), p. 30.

16. Traditionally, prompt-side (P.S.) in the English theatre has been located on the actor's left hand, stage-left (see W. J. Lawrence, *Old Theatre Ways*, p. 26). My investigations into promptbooks, illustrations, and other pertinent sources have not succeeded in confirming or refuting the supposition that such was the arrangement at Drury Lane during Garrick's management. In my reconstructions I have arbitrarily decided to follow tradition and place P.S. at stage-left.

17. See A. C. Sprague, *Shakespeare and the Actors*, p. 228. Macklin made his entrance with his army over a practical bridge; see Nagler, *Sources*, p. 398.

18. In the nineteenth century the first entrance position would have been behind the first wing from the front, designated as the prompt wing. Therefore the wing behind the prompt wing would be "1st Wing" and the entrance behind it termed the "2nd Entrance" and so on down the line of wings. See the diagram printed in Southern, *Changeable Scenery*, p. 343. The term "Prompt wing," however, has never come to my attention as existing as an eighteenth-century expression, and I have arbitrarily assumed that the actual first wing on stage was the *1st wing*, and the *1st Entrance* was located behind it. In any event, an entrance designated as effected at a wing position was located upstage of the wing itself.

19. Donoghue, p. 427.

20. *Dram. Misc.*, II, 88.

21. Murphy, *Life of Garrick*, II, 15; and Collé's *Journal* for July 1751, cited by Hedgecock, p. 109.

22. Murphy, *Life of Garrick*, I, 82.

23. John Hill, *The Actor*, p. 266.

24. *Dram. Misc.*, II, 93-94.

25. *Dramatic Censor*, I, 90.

26. Davies, *Dram. Misc.*, II, 99.

27. Cooke, *Memoirs of Macklin*, p. 27.

28. See *St. James's Chronicle*, October 28-30, 1773.

29. "Tit for Tat," p. 25; also *St. James's Chronicle*, October 28-30, 1773.

30. Davies, *Dram. Misc.*, III, 55.

31. *The Actor, a Poetical Epistle* (London, 1764), p. 16.

32. *Drury Lane Journal*, March 19, 1752.

33. Davies, *Dram. Misc.*, II, 105-6.
34. Sprague, *Shakespeare and the Actors*, p. 260.
35. *St. James's Chronicle*, May 15-18, 1773.
36. Among the stock painted pieces listed in Rich's "Covent Garden Inventory" is "Macbeth's cave."
37. October 30, 1773. The critic is comparing Garrick's with Macklin's production. This same account of Garrick entering the cave, however, had appeared four years earlier, *verbatim*, in *The Public Intelligencer*, 1769, cited by Hedgecock, p. 405n.
38. Donoghue, p. 424.
39. See above, p. 81.
40. Davies, *David Garrick*, II, 189.
41. The phenomenon of the tragic carpet persisted throughout the eighteenth century and dictated to a great degree the staging of death scenes. The impropriety of the convention was criticized by many observers of the period, among whom was Pierre Grosley a visitor from France in 1765 who recorded that "Scenes of battery and carnage are generally preceded by laying a large thick carpet upon the Stage, to represent the field of battle, and which is afterwards carried off with the dead bodies" *(Tour to London, I, 179)*. See also Goldsmith's comments in *The Bee*, October 6, 1759; and *Public Advertiser*, October 9, 1766. John O'Keeffe relates a rather convulsive account of an actor in a Dublin performance of *The Grecian Daughter* in 1773 who was so "possessed with full inspiration from the Tragic Muse," that by his twisting and writhing about during his death scene he "wrapped himself up in this tragic table-cloth . . . that nothing could be seen of him but the tip of his nose, red with fury" *(Recollections*, cited by W. J. Lawrence, "The Tragic Carpet," *New Statesman and Nation*, I, new series [April 18, 1931], 284).
42. According to the Bell text the scene changes from Dunsinane to some unspecified locale for the battle, but the promptbook omits the shift.
43. *Letters on Dancing*, pp. 84-85. The insertion of a dying speech was judged by most critics as a most suitable alteration: "nothing could be more suitable or striking, than to make him mention, with dying breath, his guilt, delusion, the witches, and those horrid visions of future punishment, which must ever appall and torture the last moments of such accumulated crimes" *(Dramatic Censor, I, 103)*.
44. *Private Correspondence*, II, 126. Charles Macklin is usually credited with the first attempt at Scottish historical costume in *Macbeth*, October 23, 1773, at Covent Garden.
45. Letter in Folger Library; there is no year date but it is manifestly 1775.

CHAPTER VII: *Romeo and Juliet*

1. *Roscius Anglicanus*, p. 22, and Pepys, *Diary*, entry for March 1, 1762.
2. See Hogan, *Shakespeare in the Theatre*, I, 404, and Odell, I, 51-53.
3. Theophilus Cibber, *Romeo and Juliet, A Tragedy, Revis'd and Alter'd from Shakespeare . . . To Which is Added, a Serio-Comic Apology* (London, 1748), p. 79.
4. *Morning Post*, August 26, 1786, in which this letter from Garrick to Somerset Draper, dated September 16, 1744, is first published.
5. *Romeo and Juliet. With Alterations, and an additional scene; by D. Garrick* (London, 1766).
6. Hogan, *Shakespeare*, I, 405.
7. Letter published in *Public Advertiser*, August 31, 1786.
8. Cited by W. Cooke, *Memoirs of Macklin*, p. 160.

9. Holograph letter, Folger Library.

10. Kahrl, No. 114.

11. Kirkman, *Life of Macklin*, I, 326.

12. In Michael Kelly, *Reminiscences*, II, 10-12, cited by Matthews, *Actors and Actresses*, I, 234.

13. *Life of Garrick*, I, 194.

14. See John Doran, *Annals of the English Stage*, ed. R. H. Stoddard (London, 1890), I, 366. For further parallels see *Ladies Magazine*, II (November 17- December 1, 1750), 26-28; and William Kenrick, *The Kapelion, or Poetical Ordinary* (London, 1750), pp. 127-35.

15. Holograph letter of Violette Marie Garrick, dated "London Octr 6 *1750*," to a friend; in Folger Library. Mrs. Garrick apparently shared some of her husband's keen theatrical intuition; according to Dr. Burney, she was "an excellent appreciator of the fine arts; and attended all the last rehearsals of new, or of revived plays to give her opinion of effects, dresses, and machinery" *(Early Diary of Frances Burney*, p. 112).

16. *Gentlemen's Magazine*, XX (October 1750), 437.

17. *Life of Garrick*, I, 193.

18. In editorial comment to the Bell text, Francis Gentleman writes that Mercutio "by critics and actors of late, . . . has been depicted a vacant, swaggering blade."

19. Cited by Sprague, *Shakespeare and the Actors*, p. 302.

20. *A Letter to Miss Nossiter Occasioned by her First Appearance on the Stage* (London, 1753), p. 8. This pamphlet is attributed to MacNamara Morgan by Dr. Stone.

21. The illustration has recently been printed with the cited identification in Raymond Mander and Joe Mitchenson, *A Picture History of the British Theatre* (London, 1957), pl. 115. No source is offered for the assignment. In 1927, Allardyce Nicoll (*Development of the Theatre*, p. 176) printed the picture with the simple caption, "Romeo and Juliet in the Eighteenth Century."

22. *Dramatic Censor*, I, 180.

23. Cited by Sprague, *Shakespeare and the Actors*, p. 308.

24. *Diary of a Journey to England in the Years 1761-1762*, trans. Countess Kielmansegge (London, 1902), pp. 221-22.

25. *Tagebuch seiner Reise nach England*, cited by John A. Kelly, *German Visitors*, p. 25.

26. In *The Fairy Prince*, Covent Garden, November 12, 1771, "After an Overture, the Curtain rises, and discovers a wild Country; the whole Scene dark, 'till at one corner, the *Moon* rising, a *Satyr* is seen (by her Light) to come forth" *(Theatrical Review*, I, 179).

27. *Gentlemen's Magazine*, XXIII (November 1752), 530; also *Ladies Magazine*, IV (February 1753), 60.

28. *Two Dissertations on the Stage* (London, 1756?), pt. I, p. 69.

29. *The Actor*, p. 283.

30. Luigi Riccoboni, *General History of the Stage*, 2nd ed. (London, 1754), pp. xiv-xv; and Boaden, *Life of Mrs. Siddons*, p. 397.

31. The essential manner of staging the tomb scene had not changed by 1826 when James Boaden complained that Juliet should not be discovered on the ground level of the monument. "Our stage Romeo," he writes in the *Life of Mrs. Siddons* (p. 396), "batters a couple of doors fiercely with the crow in his grasp, which very unnaturally fly open outwards; and there, in all her supposed maiden strewments, lies Juliet, above ground, ingeniously obvious to the audience." Labelling this arrangement as grossly absurd, Boaden suggests that it would be better "if Romeo descended into the monument and bore Juliet in his arms to revisit the glimpses of the moon; a far more natural arrangement, and in which Herculean labour he might receive invisible assistance from an ascending

trap within the monument." Boaden admits, however, that the start when Juliet is discovered is a "fine thing."

32. *Monthly Mirror*, XIV (November 1802), 337.
33. *Life of Garrick*, I, 152.

CHAPTER VIII: *King Lear*

1. Letter of May 17, 1776, cited by Christian Gaehde, *David Garrick als Shakespeare-Darsteller* (Berlin, 1904), p. 139.
2. *London Journal 1762-1763*, ed. Frederick A. Pottle (New York, 1950), pp. 256-57.
3. *The Early Diary*, I, 191.
4. *Private Correspondence*, I, 539.
5. *Private Correspondence*, I, 539; and *James Beattie's London Diary 1773* (Aberdeen, 1946), p. 41.
6. Davies, *Dram. Misc.*, II, 261; and Lynch, p. 76.
7. *The Spectator*, No. 40, April 16, 1711.
8. Cooke, *Memoirs of Macklin*, pp. 104-7.
9. Stone, *London Stage;* and Pedicord, p. 198.
10. *Cross-Hopkins Diaries*, October 28, 1756.
11. Davies, *Dram. Misc.*, II, 263. In Colman's version at Covent Garden in 1763, the love scenes were omitted and the final catastrophe asserted. The audience would have none of it, and when Colman finally printed his version, the happy ending was restored. See Odell, I, 381, and Victor, *History of the Theatres*, III, 119-20.
12. For a discussion of the textual restorations made by Garrick, see G. W. Stone, "Garrick's Production of *King Lear:* a Study in the Temper of the Eighteenth-Century Mind," *Studies in Philology*, XLV (January 1948), 89-103.
13. John Hill, *The Actor* (1755), p. 151.
14. Holograph letter to Tighe, Folger Library. See also Arthur Murphy's discussion of Garrick's interpretation of the madness, *Gray's Inn Journal*, Nos. 16 and 17, January 12 and 19, 1754.
15. Davies, *Dram. Misc.*, II, 280. The scurrilous *Theatrical Monitor* (October 24, 1767), claimed that Garrick never understood, "therefore never could speak, King Lear's curse on Goneril."
16. *Private Correspondence*, I, 157-59. For a more detailed discussion of Garrick's acting in the role see Sprague, *Shakespearean Players and Performances*, pp. 21-40, and *Shakespeare and the Actors*, pp. 281-97; also Joseph Pittard, *Observations on Mr. Garrick's Acting* (London, 1758), an account short on details but which conveys the excitement of the stunning performance.
17. *Theatrical Review* (1772), I, 218.
18. *Dramatic Censor*, I, 373; and *Theatrical Review* (1772), I, 218.
19. John Hill, cited by Gray, *Theatrical Criticism*, p. 113.
20. *General View of the Stage*, pp. 234-35.
21. Pittard, pp. 14-18.
22. Davies, *David Garrick*, I, 48-49. Garrick reputedly gained insight into the expression of madness from an old neighbor, who while playing with his daughter dropped her from a second story window, dashing her to pieces, and then pitifully and insanely relived the same action daily.
23. See W. M. Merchant, "Francis Hayman's Illustrations of Shakespeare," *Shakespeare Quarterly*, IX (Spring 1958), 142-47.
24. Holograph letter, Folger Library. The rest of the letter is of some importance, at it corroborates many of the details of Garrick's quarrel with Lacy in the summer of 1745 (above, p. 3). For the balance of this long letter and the details of the dating, see my article, "The Significance of Garrick's Letters to Hayman," *Shakespeare Quarterly*, IX (Spring 1958).

25. Kirkman, *Memoirs of Macklin*, II, 257.
26. The theatrical validity of another of Hayman's illustrations, for the Jennens edition of *Othello*, is similarly established in a second letter from Garrick to the artist a year later. On August 18, 1746, Garrick wrote to Hayman about the final scene of *Othello*: "The Scene wch in my Opinion will make the best Picture, is that point of Time . . . when Emilia discovers to Othello his Error about the Handkerchief. . . . The back ground you know must be Desdemona murder'd in her bed; the Characters upon the Stage are Othello, Montano, Gratiano & Iago: Othello (ye Principal) upon ye right hand (I believe) must be Thunder-struck into Horror, his Whole figure extended, wth his Eyes turn'd up to Heav'n & his Frame sinking, as it were at Emilia's Discovery. I shall better make you conceive my Notion of this Attitude & Expression when I see you; Emilia must appear in the utmost Vehemence, with a Mixture of Sorrow on Account of her Mistress, & I believe should be in ye middle; Iago on ye left hand should express the greatest perturbation of mind, & should Shrinke up his Body, at ye opening of his Villany, with his Eyes looking askance (as Milton terms it) on Othello, & gnawing his Lip in Anger at his Wife. . . . The other less capital Characters must be affected according to ye Circumstances of the Scene . . ." (Holograph letter, Folger Library). As plate 11 will show, Hayman executed his plate for this scene with keen regard for Garrick's counsel. For further discussion see my article, "The Significance of Garrick's Letters to Hayman."
27. *Thespis*, p. 7.
28. In *Monthly Mirror*, XIII (February 1802), 123.
29. *Dram. Misc.*, II, 213.
30. See Hogan, *Shakespeare in the Theatre*, II, 345-50.
31. *Cross-Hopkins Diaries*, May 13, 1776.

CHAPTER IX: *Hamlet*

1. See Paul Conklin, *A History of Hamlet Criticism 1601-1821* (London, 1957), p. 30.
2. Stone, *London Stage*. Pedicord (p. 198) lists 116 performances at Drury Lane, 1747-76.
3. See Hazelton Spencer, "*Hamlet* Under the Restoration," *PMLA*, XXXVIII (December 1923), 770-77; and Hogan, *Shakespeare*, I, 105.
4. G. W. Stone, "Garrick's Long Lost Alteration of *Hamlet*," *PMLA*, XLIX (September 1934), 896; and Hogan, *Shakespeare*, II, 188.
5. Hedgecock, p. 77; and Frank A. Marshall, ed. *Henry Irving Shakespeare* (London, 1890), VIII, 12.
6. "Garrick's Long Lost Alteration of *Hamlet*," p. 900.
7. *Memoirs of Kemble*, I, 64-66.
8. *Private Correspondence*, II, 126.
9. *Westminster Magazine*, I (January 1773), 34.
10. *Macaroni and Theatrical Magazine*, December 1772, p. 119. See also *London Chronicle*, December 17-19, 1772, and *St. James's Chronicle*, December 19-22, 1772.
11. *Biographia Dramatica* (1812 ed.), II, 144.
12. Conklin, p. 30.
13. After his first performance in Dublin, August, 1742, a well-wisher wrote him: "Till you came upon the stage to let us know that the music would not attend you, I never thought of it; and as it was formerly said of Milton's poetry, that it was so sublime and grand in itself, that it needed not the embellishment of rhyme, so can I say of you in the part of Hamlet, that the satisfaction I

received from thence was so great, that music could not have added any thing to make it more complete than it was" (*Private Correspondence*, I, 14).

14. Wilkes, *General View of the Stage*, pp. 249-50.

15. Among them, Holland, Mossop, Fleetwood, Powell, Lewis, Cautherley, and Smith. For the influence of Garrick's interpretation on the literary criticism of the play see Conklin, pp. 44-62.

16. Oxnard, p. 115.

17. *Bemerkungen eines Reisenden durch Deutschland, Frankreich, England, und Holland* (Altenburg, 1775), III, 218-19.

18. *Recollections*, p. 349. When Garrick first played Hamlet he wore built-up shoes to make himself taller, but by 1750, according to John Hill, the world had "so entirely overlooked the deficiency of stature in Mr. Garrick that he now leaves off the coark soals which used to give him half an inch in height" (*The Actor*, p. 66). It is therefore interesting that Taylor should mention the use of the shoes as late as 1775-76.

19. Friedrich Justinian Freiherr von Günderode (*gennant von* Kellner), *Beschreibung einer Reise aus Teutschland durch einen Theil von Frankreich, England, und Holland* (Breslau, 1783), cited by John Kelly, *German Visitors*, p. 61.

20. *Private Correspondence*, II, 148.

21. For a comprehensive account of stage business in *Hamlet* during its three and a half century history, see Sprague, *Shakespeare and the Actors*, pp. 127-84.

22. W. J. Lawrence, *Pre-Restoration Stage Studies* (Cambridge, Mass., 1927), p. 107.

23. *Gazetteer and New Daily Advertiser*, November 11, 1784.

24. Davies, *Dram. Misc.*, III, 32, Cooke, *Macklin*, p. 376.

25. Lichtenberg, p. 9.

26. James Boswell, *Journal of a Tour to the Hebrides*, ed. Frederick A. Pottle and Charles H. Bennett (New York, 1936), p. 22.

27. *Private Correspondence*, I, 12-14, 25; and *St. James's Chronicle*, February 20-22, 1772.

28. See Frederick Reynolds, *Life and Times* (London, 1826), I, 88. A mechanical wig which did the same trick in a Dutch performance is described in *The Gazetteer*, October 8, 1791.

29. Davies, *David Garrick*, I, 56.

30. *Private Correspondence*, I, 13.

31. *St. James's Chronicle*, October 4-6, 1774.

32. *St. James's Chronicle*, June 4-7, 1768.

33. Sprague, *Shakespeare and the Actors*, p. 144.

34. Davies, *Dram. Misc.*, III, 42-44; *Theatrical Review* (1772), II, 17, and *St. James's Chronicle*, March 3-5, 1772. The *Dramatic Censor* (I, 57) judged Macklin to be by far the best Polonius of the age. Macklin played the role at Covent Garden in the seasons 1750-51, 1751-52, but never at Drury Lane.

35. Page 16.

36. "The players are afraid we should lose sight of Hamlet's pretended madness, if the black stockings, discovering a white one underneath, was not rolled half way down the leg" (*The Connoisseur*, September 19, 1754).

37. This anonymous engraving is reproduced in Hedgecock, p. 67.

38. Scholarly opinion on the relationship of this painting (plate 15) to the actual Vauxhall painting (which is apparently lost?) seems rather inconclusive. Mr. Boase, *op. cit.*, p. 90, acknowledges the assistance of Mr. E. K. Waterhouse in obtaining the photograph reproduced here as plate 15, but advises that as for the painting itself, "I have been unable to trace its whereabouts. If on the scale of the Vauxhall paintings, it may be one of the original pieces." Lawrence Gowing, "Hogarth, Hayman, and the Vauxhall Decorations," *Burlington Magazine*, XCV (January 1953), 16, doubts that its design could have "served for anything called, by Vauxhall standards, a large picture." The most recent

commentator, W. M. Merchant, *Shakespeare and the Artist* (Oxford, 1959), p. 46, seems satisfied that the photograph of the mysterious painting is a version of the one done by Hayman for Vauxhall.

39. "Francis Hayman's Illustrations of Shakespeare," *Shakespeare Quarterly*, IX (Spring 1958).

40. This engraving has been recently reprinted by Raymond Mander and Joe Mitchenson in *A Picture History of the British Stage* (London, 1957), plate 70, with the puzzling caption, "An engraving published 1730. Probably depicts Robert Wilks at Drury Lane." However, the reproduction offered here from the periodical clearly carries the inscription (which is cropped from the reproduction by Mander and Mitchenson) *"Engraved for ye Universal Museum."* This periodical seems not to have appeared until January 1762.

41. See above, p. 99, for an example of a similar scenic arrangement in the first act of Cumberland's *The Fashionable Lover*, 1772.

42. *Dram. Misc.*, III, 96-97.

43. Francis Gentleman's editorial note for this scene in the Bell text.

44. *Dram. Misc.*, III, 104.

45. *Dram. Misc.*, III, 109.

46. In the prologue to *The Romance of an Hour*, printed in *Town and Country Magazine*, December 1774.

47. *The Actor*, p. 276; and Genest, V, 437; Davies, *Dram. Misc.*, III, 111.

48. *St. James's Chronicle*, February 20-22, 1772; also *Dram. Censor.*, I, 56.

49. *Dram. Misc.*, III, 126. In the seasons that Mrs. Cibber was at Covent Garden between 1750 and 1754, Ophelia was played at Drury Lane by Mrs. Clive. On occasion other actresses appeared in the role but it was considered Mrs. Cibber's property.

50. Page 17. In reviewing Mrs. Smith's first appearance as Ophelia on December 18, 1772, *Macaroni and Theatrical Magazine* (December 1772) reported that her singing was enchanting, and the audience was "enraptured."

51. *Notes on Several Characters of Shakespeare*, pp. 5-7.

52. *Theatrical Review* (1772), II, 18.

53. *Beyträge zur Kenntnis vorzüglich des Innen von England und seiner Einwohnen*, cited by John A. Kelly, *German Visitors*, pp. 95-96.

54. Letter of October 12, 1796, cited by W. J. Lawrence, "The Folly of the Grave-Digger's Waistcoats," *The Stage*, June 5, 1924.

55. *Private Correspondence*, I, 11, and I, 21-22.

56. *General View*, p. 161.

57. An "Account Book" entry on January 3, 1750, records a payment of 15s. 6d. "To a Coffin for Ophelia."

58. Davies, *Dram. Misc.*, III, 146.

59. *Private Correspondence*, I, 452.

60. *Private Correspondence*, II, 148, 156.

CHAPTER X: *The Provok'd Wife*

1. Pedicord, p. 136 and Appendix C.

2. The acclaim for Garrick's remarkable eyes was unbounded. The *Theatrical Monitor*, October 24, 1767, marked that Garrick's soul was in his eyes. Frances Burney had never seen "such brilliant, piercing eyes as Mr. Garrick's . . . when I have chanced to meet them, I have not really been able to bear their lustre" (*Diary*, I, 113). See also Taylor, *Recollections*, II, 3, and Neville, *Diary*, p. 9.

3. Pages 3-4.

4. William Clark Russel, *Representative Actors* (London, 1875), p. 111.

5. See Joseph Knight, *David Garrick* (London, 1894), 179-80, for Wilkinson's comments and a summary of the differences between Garrick and Quin in this role.

6. Theatrical criticism in the *London Chronicle* beginning January 1, 1757, was written by an unidentified critic, perhaps Murphy or Johnson. The later reviews which began October 1758 are clearly by another critic. For a discussion of these reviews—"The really great step in the development of theatrical criticism in this decade"—see Gray, pp. 128-42.

7. *Dramatic Censor*, II, 469.

8. See also *Theatrical Review* (1772), I, 204, which remarked that "Mr. Garrick's fondness for this Character, gives occasion for drawing conclusions not greatly in his favour."

9. The play was performed in approximately 2 hours, 23 minutes, according to Brownsmith's *Dramatic Timepiece*.

10. Again for the sake of clarity I submit all printed directions in quotes without italics, and the prompter's annotations in italics, regardless of their original form.

11. *Life of Garrick*, p. 270.

12. Described from the original portrait in the possession of Somerset Maugham by Mander and Mitchenson, *Artist and the Theatre*, p. 48.

13. The fashion is illustrated in W. S. Lewis, *Three Tours Through London* (New Haven, 1941), p. 55. In his *Recollections* (I, 162), O'Keeffe reports a near tragedy to a spectator at the first performance of *Bon Ton* in Dublin, as Brereton spoke the prologue: "the feathers of a lady's headdress caught fire, from the chandelier hanging over the box; it was soon in a blaze, and her life hardly saved."

14. See also a similar account of this moment in *London Chronicle*, March 3-5, 1757.

CHAPTER XI: "SLIPPING THE THEATRICAL SHELL"

1. Davies, *David Garrick*, II, 344.

2. Letter to Peter Garrick, February 6, 1742, Kahrl, No. 22.

3. Letter, March 24, 1764, Kahrl, No. 345.

4. Forster Collection, Kahrl, No. 735.

5. *Ante* October 4, 1773, Kahrl, No. 805a and *Private Correspondence*, I, 574.

6. Letter to Richard Cox, February 1, 1774, Kahrl, No. 828.

7. *Theatrical Monitor*, November 7, 1767.

8. Nipclose, p. 43.

9. See also Campbell, *Diary*, p. 64; Williams, *Letter to Garrick*, pp. 60-62; and Bellamy, *Apology*, I, 19.

10. Cited by Stone, "Garrick's Handling of Shakespeare's Plays," I, 112.

11. *Pineapples*, pp. 74-75.

12. *Private Correspondence*, II, 118.

13. Kahrl, No. 1033.

14. See Stone, "David Garrick's Significance in the History of Shakespearean Criticism," *PMLA*, LXV (March 1950), 183-197.

15. See Harry Malnick, "David Garrick and the Russian Theatre," *Modern Language Review*, L (April 1955), 173-75.

16. This point is clearly made throughout Bergmann's dissertation.

17. *Private Correspondence*, II, 303 and 328.

18. Lewis, *Three Tours*, p. 62.

19. *Private Correspondence*, II, 148.

20. *Cross-Hopkins Diaries*, June 5, 1776.

A SELECTED BIBLIOGRAPHY

Adam, Robert and James. *The Works in Architecture of Robert & James Adam*. London, 1931.

Adolphus, John. *Memoirs of John Bannister, Comedian*. 2 vols. London, 1839.

Allen, Ralph G. "The Stage Spectacles of Philip James De Loutherbourg," unpubl. diss. (Yale, 1960).

Angelo, Henry. *Reminiscences*. 2 vols. London, 1828-30.

Armstrong, William A. "Madame Vestris: A Centenary Appreciation," *Theatre Notebook*, XI (October-December 1956), 11-18.

Avery, Emmett I. "The Finances of an Eighteenth-Century Theatre," *The Theatre Annual*, XIII (1955), 49-59.

———. "The Shakespeare Ladies Club," *Shakespeare Quarterly*, VII (Spring 1956), 153-158.

———. George Winchester Stone, Jr., and Arthur H. Scouten. "The London Stage, an Account of the Growth and Maturity of the Professional Theatres in London, 1700-1776," unpubl. MS at Folger Library.

Bagster-Collins, Jeremy F. *George Colman the Younger*. New York, 1946.

Baker, George Pierce. *Some Unpublished Correspondence of David Garrick*. Boston, 1907.

Barker, Richard H. *Mr. Cibber of Drury Lane*. New York, 1939.

Barrow, Bernard. "Low-Comedy Acting Styles on the London Stage 1730-1780," 2 vols. unpubl. diss. (Yale, 1957).

Barton, Margaret. *Garrick*. New York, 1949.

Beattie, James. *James Beattie's London Diary 1773*. Aberdeen, 1946.

Bell, Hamilton. "Three Plans by Sir Christopher Wren," *Architectural Record*, XXXIII (1913), 359.

Bellamy, George Anne. *An Apology for the Life of George Anne Bellamy*. 6 vols. 3rd ed. London, 1785.

Bellamy, Thomas. *The Life of Mr. William Parsons, Comedian*. London, 1795.

Bergmann, Frederick Louis. "David Garrick: Producer. A Study of Garrick's Alterations of Non-Shakespearean Plays," unpubl. diss. (George Washington University, 1953).

Bernard, John. *Retrospections of the Stage*. 2 vols. London, 1830.

Boase, T. S. "Illustrations of Shakespeare's Plays in the Seventeenth and Eighteenth Centuries," *Journal of the Warburg and Courtauld Institutes*, X (1947), 83-108.

Boswell, James. *Journal of a Tour to the Hebrides*, ed. Frederick A. Pottle and Charles H. Bennett. New York, 1936.

——. *London Journal 1762-1763*, ed. Frederick A. Pottle. New York, 1950.

Brewster, Dorothy. *Aaron Hill: Poet, Dramatist, Projector*. New York, 1913.

Brownsmith, John. *The Dramatic Timepiece: Or Perpetual Monitor. Being a Calculation of the Length of Time Every Act Takes in the Performing, in all the Acted Plays at the Theatres-Royal*. London, 1767.

——. *The Theatrical Alphabet. Containing a Catalogue of Several Hundred Parts . . . in Different Plays and Farces; with the Number of Lengths noted that each Part Contains*. London, 1767.

Burney, Frances. *The Early Diary of Frances Burney 1768-1778*, ed. Annie R. Ellis. 2 vols. London, 1889.

Burnim, Kalman A. "Garrick's Quarrel with Lacy," *Yale Library Gazette* (July, 1958), 29-34.

——. "The Significance of Garrick's Letters to Hayman," *Shakespeare Quarterly*, IX (Spring 1958), 149-152.

——. "Some Notes on Aaron Hill and Stage Scenery," *Theatre Notebook*, XII (Autumn 1957), 29-33.

Byrne, Muriel St. Clare. "The Stage Costuming of *Macbeth* in the Eighteenth Century," *Studies in English Theatre History*. London, 1952.

Campbell, Lily B. "A History of Costuming on the English Stage Between 1660 and 1823," *University of Wisconsin Studies in Language and Literature*, No. 2 (1918), 187-223.

Campbell, Thomas. *Dr Campbell's Diary of a Visit to England in 1775*, ed. James L. Clifford. Cambridge, England, 1947.

Case of the Stage in Ireland . . . Wherein the Qualifications, Duty, and Importance of a Manager are Carefully Considered and Explained. Dublin, n. d.

Cawdell, James. *The Miscellaneous Poems of James Cawdell, Comedian*. Sunderland, 1785.

Charke, Charlotte Cibber. *A Narrative of the Life of Mrs. Charlotte Charke. Written by Herself*. 2nd ed. London, 1755.

Chetwood, W. R. *A General History of the Stage*. London, 1749.

Churchill, Charles. *The Rosciad*. 2nd ed. London, 1761.

Cibber, Colley. *An Apology for the Life of Colley Cibber*. 3rd ed. London, 1750.

Cibber, Theophilus. *An Apology for the Life of Mr. T— C—, Comedian, Being a Proper Sequel to the Apology for the Life of Mr. Colley Cibber . . . Supposed to be Written by Himself*. London, 1740.

——. *An Epistle from Mr. Theophilus Cibber to David Garrick, Esq.* London, 1759.

——. *The Lives and Characters of the Most Eminent Actors and Actresses of Great Britain and Ireland, from Shakespear to the Present Time . . .* (Contains the *Life of Barton Booth*). London, 1753.

——. *Romeo and Juliet, a Tragedy, Revis'd and Alter'd from Shakespear . . . To Which is Added a Serio-Comic Apology for Part of the Life of Mr. Theophilus Cibber, Comedian*. London, 1748.

——. *Two Dissertations on the Theatres . . . Containing a General View of the Stage, from the Earliest Times, to the Present*. London, 1756.

A Collection of the Dresses of Different Nations, Ancient and Modern, Particularly Old English Dresses . . . To Which are Added the Habits of the Principal Characters on the English Stage. 2 vols. London, 1773.

Colman, George (the Younger). *Random Records.* 2 vols. London, 1830.

Congreve, Francis Aspry. *Authentic Memoirs of the Late Mr. Charles Macklin, Comedian.* London, 1798.

Conklin, Paul. *A History of Hamlet Criticism 1601-1821.* London, 1957.

Cooke, William. *The Elements of Dramatic Criticism . . . Concluding with Some General Instructions for Succeeding in the Art of Acting.* London, 1775.

———. *Memoirs of Charles Macklin.* London, 1804.

Croft-Murray, E. *John De Voto, a Baroque Scene Painter.* London, 1952. (The Society for Theatre Research Pamphlet Series, No. 2.)

Cross, Richard and William Hopkins. *Diary 1747-1776. Drury Lane.* 13 vols. MSS in Folger Library.

Cumberland, Richard. *Memoirs of Richard Cumberland.* 2 vols. London, 1807.

Curwen, Samuel. *Journal and Letters of the Late Samuel Curwen.* 3rd ed. New York, 1845.

Cyclopaedia; or, Universal Dictionary of Arts, Sciences, and Literature, ed. Abraham Rees. 39 vols. London, 1819.

Davies, Thomas. *Dramatic Miscellanies.* 3 vols. Dublin, 1784.

———. *Memoirs of the Life of David Garrick, Esq.* 2 vols. London, 1808.

———. *Memoirs of the Life of David Garrick, Esq.* 4 vols. extra-illustrated. London, 1780. (At Folger Library.)

The Devil Upon Crutches in England, or Night Scenes in London. By a Gentleman of Oxford. 2nd ed. London, 1756.

Dibdin, Charles. *The Professional Life of Mr. Dibdin.* 4 vols. London, 1803.

Dibdin, Charles (the Younger). *Professional & Literary Memoirs of Charles Dibdin the Younger,* ed. George Speaight. London, 1956.

Diderot, Denis. *The Paradox of Acting,* trans. Walter H. Pollock. New York, 1957.

Donoghue, Denis. "Macklin's Shylock and Macbeth," *Studies: An Irish Quarterly Review,* XLII (Winter 1954), 421-428.

Dow, Alexander, *Zingis.* London, 1769.

Downer, Alan S. "Nature to Advantage Dressed: Eighteenth-Century Acting," *PMLA,* LVIII (December 1943), 1002-37.

Downes, John. *Roscius Anglicanus* [London, 1708], ed. Montague Summers. London, n. d.

Dunbar, Howard. *The Dramatic Career of Arthur Murphy.* New York, 1946.

D—ry L-ne P-yh-se Broke Open. In a Letter to Mr. G—. London, 1748.

"Drury Lane Theatre *Account Books,*" for the seasons 1766-67, and 1771-72 through 1775-76. MSS at Folger Library.

"Drury Lane Theatre Treasurer's Book," for the season 1749-50. MS at Folger Library.

"Drury Lane Theatre Treasurer's Book," for the season 1747-48. Microfilm at Folger Library of privately owned MS.

"Drury Lane Theatre Financial Statement. 1747. 11 April." MS in Harvard Theatre Collection, in collection identified as "Drury Lane Theatre Letters and Documents."

"Drury Lane Theatre. Indenture Between Lacy & Garrick and Clutterbuck, 1753," MS in Harvard Theatre Collection.

"Drury Lane Theatre. Scrapbooks of Clippings," 12 vols. in Folger Library.

Emery, John Pike. *Arthur Murphy.* Philadelphia, 1946.

England, Martha Winburn. "Garrick's Stratford Jubilee: Reactions in France and Germany," *Shakespeare Survey,* IX (1956), 90-100.

Everard, Edward Cape. *Memoirs of an Unfortunate Son of Thespis.* Edinburgh, 1818.

Fitzgerald, Percy. *The Kembles.* 2 vols. London, 1871.

———. *The Life of David Garrick.* London, 1899.

———. *A New History of the English Stage.* 2 vols. London, 1882.

[Fitzpatrick, Thomas]. *An Enquiry into the Real Merit of a Certain Popular Performer* . . . London, 1760.

Foot, Jesse. *The Life of Arthur Murphy, Esq.* London, 1811.

[Foote, Samuel]. *An Examen of the New Comedy Call'd The Suspicious Husband . . . To Which is Added, a Word of Advice to Mr. G-rr-ck.* 3rd ed. Dublin, 1747.

———. *A Treatise on the Passions . . . With a Critical Enquiry into the Theatrical Merit of Mr. G-k, Mr. Q-n, and Mr. B-y.* London, n. d.

Forster, John. *The Life and Times of Oliver Goldsmith.* 6th ed. 2 vols. London, 1877.

Furness, Horace H. "Pay List of Drury Lane Theatre in 1765," *Notes and Queries,* XI, 6th series (June 13, 1885), 461-462.

Gaehde, Christian. *David Garrick als Shakespeare-Darsteller.* Berlin, 1904. (*Schriften der Deutschen Shakespeare-Gesellschaft.* Band II.)

GARRICK, DAVID.

———. "Autograph Notebook," MS in Harvard Theatre Collection.

———. *Cymon. A Dramatic Romance.* London, 1767.

———. "David Garrick at Rehearsal. Written by Himself. From an Original Letter in the Possession of the Publisher," *Behind the Curtain,* 19th-century pamphlet attached to Davies, *Memoirs of the Life of David Garrick,* extra-illustrated edition at Folger Library.

———. *The Diary of David Garrick. Being a Record of His Memorable Trip to Paris in 1751,* ed. Ryllis C. Alexander. New York, 1928.

———. *Dramatic Works of David Garrick.* 3 vols. London, 1768.

———. *An Essay on Acting: In Which Will be Consider'd the Mimical Behaviour of a Certain Faulty Actor . . . To Which Will be Added, a Short Criticism on his Acting Macbeth.* London, 1744.

———. *The Journal of David Garrick Describing his Visit to France and Italy in 1763,* ed. George Winchester Stone, Jr. New York, 1939.

———. *The Manuscript Diary of David Garrick's Trip to Paris in 1751,* ed. Elizabeth Stein. New York. 1922.

———. *Neck or Nothing.* Photostatic copy of playhouse MS, in Harvard Theatre Collection.

———. *A Peep Behind the Curtain: or, The New Rehearsal.* London, 1767.

Garrick, David. *Pineapples of Finest Flavour, or a Selection of Sundry Unpublished Letters of the English Roscius, David Garrick,* ed. David Mason Little. Cambridge, Mass., 1930.

———. *The Private Correspondence of David Garrick,* ed. James Boaden. 2 vols. London, 1831-32.

——. *Some Unpublished Correspondence of David Garrick,* ed. George Pierce Baker. Boston, 1907.

——. *The Songs, Choruses, and Serious Dialogues of the Masque Called The Institution of the Garter, or, Arthur's Round Table Restored.* London, 1771.

——. *Three Farces by David Garrick,* ed. Louise Brown Osborn. New Haven, 1925.

——. *Three Plays by David Garrick,* ed. Elizabeth Stein. New York, 1926.

"Garrick and his Contemporaries," Collection of Prints, Bills, and Clippings in Scrapbooks at Folger Library.

Mr. Garrick's Conduct, As Manager of the Theatre-Royal in Drury-Lane, Considered. In a Letter Addressed to Him. London, 1747.

Genest, John. *Some Account of the English Stage From the Restoration in 1660 to 1830.* 10 vols. Bath, 1832.

[Gentleman, Francis]. *The Dramatic Censor, or, Critical Companion.* 2 vols. London, 1770.

Gibbon, Edward. *Gibbon's Journal,* ed. D. M. Low. London, 1929.

Goldsmith, Oliver. *An Enquiry into the Present State of Polite Learning in Europe.* London, 1759.

Gray, Charles Harold. *Theatrical Criticism in London to 1795.* New York, 1931.

Grosley, Pierre J. *A Tour to London,* trans. Thomas Nugent. 2 vols. London, 1772.

Hall, Lillian A. *Catalogue of Dramatic Portraits in the Theatre Collection of the Harvard College Library.* 4 vols. Cambridge, Mass., 1931.

Hedgecock, Frank A. *David Garrick and His French Friends.* London, 1912.

Henderson, John. *Letters and Poems by the Late Mr. John Henderson, With Anecdotes of his Life,* ed. John Ireland. London, 1786.

Hiffernan, Paul. *Dramatic Genius.* 2nd ed. London, 1772.

Hill, Aaron. *The Works of the Late Aaron Hill.* 4 vols. London, 1753.

Hill, John. The Actor: *A Treatise on the Art of Playing.* London, 1750. 2nd edition with changes, 1755.

Hogan, Charles Beecher. *Shakespeare in the Theatre 1701-1800.* 2 vols. Oxford, 1952-57.

Jonson, Ben. *Every Man in his Humour . . . With Alterations and Additions. As It Is Perform'd at the Theatre-Royal in Drury-Lane.* London, 1752.

[Kelly, Hugh]. *The School for Wives.* 2nd ed. London, 1774.

——. *Thespis. Or, A Critical Examination Into the Merits of All the Principal Performers Belonging to Drury Lane Theatre.* London, 1766.

Kelly, John Alexander. *German Visitors to English Theatres in the Eighteenth Century.* Princeton, 1936.

Kenrick, William. *A Letter to David Garrick, Esq.* 2nd ed. London, 1772.

Ketton-Cremer, Robert Wyndham. *The Early Life and Diaries of William Windham.* London, 1930.

Kielmansegge, Count Frederick. *Diary of a Journey to England in the Years 1761-1762,* trans. Countess Kielmansegge. London, 1902.

Kilbourne, Frederick W. *Alterations and Adaptations of Shakespeare.* Boston, 1906.

Kirkman, James Thomas. *Memoirs of the Life of Charles Macklin.* 2 vols. London, 1799.

Knight, Joseph. *David Garrick*. London, 1894.

Langhans, Edward. "Staging Practices in the Restoration Theatres 1660-1682," unpubl. diss. (Yale, 1955).

Lawrence, William J. "The Folly of the Grave-Digger's Waistcoat," *The Stage*, June 5, 1924.

———. "The Pioneers of Modern English Stage-Mounting; Phillipe Jacques De Loutherbourg, R. A.," *Magazine of Art*, XVIII (1895), 172-177.

———. "Stage Scenery in the Eighteenth Century," *Magazine of Art*, XVIII (1895), 385-388.

———. "The Tragic Carpet," *The New Statesman and Nation*, I, new series, April 18, 1931.

A Letter to Miss Nossiter Occasioned by her First Appearance on the Stage. London, 1753.

A Letter to Mr. Garrick on His Having Purchased a Patent for Drury-Lane Play-House. London [1747].

A Letter to Mr. Garrick on the Opening of the Theatre, With Observations on the Conduct of Managers . . . London, 1758.

A Letter to Mr. G---k, Relative to His Treble Capacity of Manager, Actor, and Author; With Some Remarks on Lethe. London, 1749.

A Letter to the Hon. Author of the New Farce, Called The Rout . . . *Containing Some Remarks Upon the New Revived Play of Antony and Cleopatra*. London, 1759.

Lewes, Charles Lee. *Memoirs of Charles Lee Lewes, Containing Anecdotes, Historical and Bibliographical, of the English and Scottish Stages*. 4 vols. London, 1805.

Lewis, Wilmarth Sheldon. *Three Tours Through London in the Years 1748-1776-1797*. New Haven, 1941.

Lichtenberg, Georg Christlob. *Lichtenberg's Visits to England*, ed. Margaret Mare and W. H. Quarrell. Oxford, 1938.

Lloyd, Robert. *The Actor. Addressed to Bonnell Thornton, Esq*. London, 1764.

Lynch, James J. *Box, Pit, and Gallery*. Berkeley, 1953.

MacMillan, Dougald. *Catalogue of Larpent Plays in the Huntington Library*. Huntington Library, 1939.

———. "David Garrick, Manager," *Studies in Philology*, XLV (October 1948), 630-646.

———. *Drury Lane Calendar 1747-1776*. Oxford, 1938.

Malnick, B. "David Garrick and the Russian Theatre," *Modern Language Review*, L (April 1955), 173-175.

Malton, Thomas. *A Compleat Treatise on Perspective*. London, 1775.

Mander, Raymond and Joe Mitchenson. *The Artist and the Theatre*. London, 1955.

———, and ———. *A Picture History of the British Theatre*. London, 1957.

Mason, William. *Memoirs of the Life and Writings of William Whitehead*. London, 1786.

Matthews, Brander and Lawrence Hutton, ed. *Actors and Actresses of Great Britain and the United States*. 5 vols. New York, 1886.

"Memoirs of John Palmer, Esq.," *General Magazine and Impartial Review*, II (January 1788), 9-16; (February 1788), 59-64; (March 1788), 114-118.

Merchant, William M. "John Runciman's 'Lear in the Storm'," *Journal of the Warburg and Courtauld Institutes*, XVII (July-December 1954), 385-387.

——. *Shakespeare and the Artist*. Oxford, 1959.

——. "Visual Elements in Shakespeare Studies," *Shakespeare Jahrbuch*, 92: 280-290.

Messink, James. "The Pageant of Shakespear's Jubilee," MS in Folger Library.

Motter, T. H. Vail. "Garrick and the Private Theatricals," *ELH*, XI (March 1944), 63-75.

Murphy, Arthur. *The Apprentice*. London, 1756.

——. "Character of Garrick," *The Universal Magazine*, March 1801, pp. 163-167.

——. *The Desert Island*. London, 1760.

——. *The Grecian Daughter*. London, 1772.

——. *The Life of David Garrick*. 2 vols. London, 1801.

——. *The Orphan of China*. 2nd ed. London, 1759.

——. *Zenobia*. London, 1768.

Neville, Sylas. *The Diary of Sylas Neville, 1767-1788*, ed. Basil Cozens-Hardy. Oxford, 1950.

Nipclose, Nicholas [Francis Gentleman?]. *The Theatres. A Poetical Dissection*. London, 1772.

Noverre, Jean Georges. *Letters on Dancing and Ballet*, trans. Cyril W. Beaumont. London, 1951.

Noyes, Robert Gale. *Ben Jonson on the English Stage 1660-1776*. Cambridge, Mass., 1935.

Odell, George C. D. *Shakespeare from Betterton to Irving*. 2 vols. New York, 1920.

O'Keeffe, John. *Recollections*. 2 vols. London, 1826.

Oman, Carola. *David Garrick*. London, 1958.

Oxnard, Edward. "Extracts from the Journal of Edward Oxnard," *New England Historical & Genealogical Register*, XXVI (1872), 8-10, 115-121, 254-259.

Page, Eugene R. *George Colman the Elder*. New York, 1935.

Parry, Edward Abbott. *Charles Macklin*. London, 1891.

Parsons, Mrs. Clement. *Garrick and His Circle*. New York, 1906.

Pedicord, Harry William. *The Theatrical Public in the Time of Garrick*. New York, 1954.

Pittard, Joseph. *Observations on Mr. Garrick's Acting*. London, 1758.

[Powel, John]. "Tit for Tat," MS in Harvard Theatre Collection.

[Pratt, Samuel Jackson]. *Garrick's Looking-Glass: Or the Art of Rising on the Stage*. London, 1776.

The Present State of the Stage in Great-Britain and Ireland. London, 1753.

Reasons Why David Garrick, Esq. Should Not Appear on the Stage, in a Letter to John Rich, Esq. London, 1759.

Reed, Joseph. "Theatrical Duplicity or a Genuine Narrative of the Conduct of *David Garrick* Esqre to *Joseph Reed* on *His Tragedy of Dido*," MS in Folger Library.

Reflections Upon Theatrical Expression in Tragedy. London, 1755.

Reynolds, Frederick. *Life and Times of Frederick Reynolds.* 2 vols. London, 1826.

Rosenfeld, Sybil. "David Garrick and Private Theatricals," *Notes and Queries,* CLXXXI (October 25, 1941), 230.

——. "The Wardrobes of Lincoln's Inn Fields and Covent Garden," *Theatre Notebook,* V (October-December 1950), 15-19.

Russell, D. A. "Hamlet Costumes from Garrick to Gielgud," *Shakespeare Survey,* IX (1956), 54-59.

Scouten, Arthur H. "The Increase in Popularity of Shakespeare's Plays in the Eighteenth Century," *Shakespeare Quarterly,* VII (Spring 1957), 189-202.

Shakespeare, William. *Bell's Edition of Shakespeare's Plays, As They Are Now Performed at the Theatres Royal in London; Regulated From the Prompt Books of Each House.* 9 vols. London, 1773-74.

——. *Romeo and Juliet. With Alterations, and an Additional Scene; by D. Garrick. As it is Performed at the Theatre-Royal in Drury-Lane.* London, 1776.

[Shirley, William]. *Brief Remarks on the Original and Present State of the Drama.* London, 1758.

Some Reflections on the Management of a Theatre. London, 1770.

Southern, Richard. *Changeable Scenery. Its Origin and Development in the British Theatre.* London, 1952.

——. *The Georgian Playhouse.* London, 1948.

——. "Hogarth: Prints of Scenes," *Theatre Notebook,* VIII (October-December 1953), 19.

Sprague, Arthur Colby. *Shakespeare and the Actors. The Stage Business in His Plays.* Cambridge, Mass., 1944.

——. *Shakespearean Players and Performances.* Cambridge, Mass., 1953.

Steele, Elizabeth. *The Memoirs of Sophia Baddeley.* 6 vols. London, 1787.

Stein, Elizabeth. *David Garrick, Dramatist.* New York, 1938.

Stockdale, Percival. *The Memoirs of the Life and Writings of Percival Stockdale.* 2 vols. London, 1809.

Stone, George Winchester, Jr. "The Authorship of *Tit for Tat,*" *Theatre Notebook,* X (October-December 1955), 22-28.

——. "David Garrick's Significance in the History of Shakespearean Criticism," *PMLA,* LXV (March 1950), 183-97.

——. "Garrick and an Unknown Operatic Version of *Love's Labour's Lost,*" *Review of English Studies,* XV (July 1939), 323-328.

——. "Garrick's Handling of *Macbeth,*" *Studies in Philology,* XXXVIII (October 1941), 609-628.

——. "Garrick's Handling of Shakespeare's Plays and His Influence Upon the Changed Attitude of Shakespearean Criticism During the Eighteenth Century," 2 vols. unpubl. diss. (Harvard 1938).

——. "Garrick's Long Lost Alteration of *Hamlet,*" *PMLA,* XLIX (September 1934), 890-921.

——. "Garrick's Presentation of *Antony and Cleopatra,*" *Review of English Studies,* XIII (January 1937), 20-38.

——. "Garrick's Production of *King Lear:* A Study in the Temper of the Eighteenth-Century Mind," *Studies in Philology,* XLV (January 1948), 89-103.

———. "The God of his Idolatry," *Joseph Quincy Adams Memorial Studies*, ed. James G. MacManaway and others. Washington, 1948, pp. 115-128.

Stone, George Winchester, Jr. "*A Midsummer Night's Dream* in the Hands of Garrick and Colman," *PMLA*, LIV (June 1939), 467-482.

———. "Shakespeare's *Tempest* at Drury Lane During *Garrick's Management*," *Shakespeare Quarterly*, VII (Winter 1956), 1-7.

Sturz, Helfrich Peter. *Vermischte Schriften*. Starnberg am See, 1946.

Tate, Nahum. *The History of King Lear*. Corke, 1761.

The Theatrical Campaign, For MDCCLXVI and MDCCLXVII. London, 1767.

Theatrical Biography: Or, Memoirs of the Principal Performers of the Three Theatres Royal. 2 vols. London, 1772.

Theatrical Disquisitions, or, a Review of the Late Riot at Drury Lane Theatre, on the 25th and 26th of January. London, 1763.

Theatrical Examiner: An Enquiry into the Merits and Demerits of the Present English Performers in General . . . London, 1757.

Theatrical Monitor: or Green-Room Laid Open. London, 1767.

The Theatrical Review. London, 1763.

The Theatrical Review . . . Containing a Critical Account of Every Tragedy, Comedy, Opera, Farce, &c. Exhibited at the Theatres During the Last Season. 2 vols. London, 1772.

The Theatrical Review for the Year 1757, and Beginning of 1758 . . . London, 1758.

Thomas Russell. "Contemporary Taste in the Stage Decorations of London Theatres, 1770-1800," *Modern Philology*, XLII (November 1944), 65-78.

———. "Spectacle in the Theatres of London, 1767-1802," unpubl. diss. (Chicago 1942).

Thomson, Margaret Hunter. "The Theatrical Value of the English Eighteenth Century Satirical Print," unpubl. diss. (Yale 1944).

Three Original Letters to a Friend in the Country, On the Cause and Manner of the Late Riot at the Theatre-Royal in Drury-Lane . . . London, 1763.

Victor, Benjamin. *The History of the Theatres of London and Dublin From the Year 1730 to the Present Time*. 2 vols. London, 1761.

Vincke, Gisbert Freiherrn. "*Shakespeare und Garrick*," *Shakespeare Jahrbuch*, IX (1874), 1-21.

Walpole, Horace. *The Letters of Horace Walpole*, ed. Paget Toynbee. 16 vols. Oxford, 1904.

———. *Notes by Horace Walpole on Several Characters of Shakespeare*, ed. W. S. Lewis. Farmington, Conn., 1940.

Wecter, Dixon. "David Garrick and the Burkes," *Philological Quarterly*, XVIII (October 1939), 367-380.

Wells, Mitchell. "Spectacular Scenic Effects of the Eighteenth-Century Pantomime," *Philological Quarterly*, XVII (January 1938), 67-81.

Wilkinson, Tate. *Memoirs of His Own Life*. 4 vols. London, 1790.

Williams, Charles Riddell. "David Garrick, Actor-Manager: Two Unpublished Letters," *Cornhill Magazine*, LXVI (March 1929), 289-297.

Williams, David. *A Letter to David Garrick, Esq. on His Conduct and Talents as Manager and Performer*. London, 1770.

Wood, Frederick T. "Goodman's Fields Theatre," *Modern Language Review*, XXV (October 1930), 442-456.

———. "*The Merchant of Venice* in the Eighteenth Century," *English Studies*, XV (1933), 209-218.

Wyatt, Benjamin. *Observations on the Design for the Theatre Royal, Drury Lane*.

Index